REDACTED

BEFORE YOU START TO READ THIS BOOK, take this moment to think about making a donation to punctum books, an independent non-profit press,

@ https://punctumbooks.com/support/

If you're reading the e-book, you can click on the image below to go directly to our donations site. Any amount, no matter the size, is appreciated and will help us to keep our ship of fools afloat. Contributions from dedicated readers will also help us to keep our commons open and to cultivate new work that can't find a welcoming port elsewhere. Our adventure is not possible without your support.

Vive la Open Access.

Fig. 1. Detail from Hieronymus Bosch, *Ship of Fools* (1490–1500)

REDACTED: WRITING IN THE NEGATIVE SPACE OF THE STATE. Copyright © 2024 by the editors and authors. This work carries a Creative Commons BY-NC-SA 4.0 International license, which means that you are free to copy and redistribute the material in any medium or format, and you may also remix, transform and build upon the material, as long as you clearly attribute the work to the authors (but not in a way that suggests the authors or punctum books endorses you and your work), you do not use this work for commercial gain in any form whatsoever, and that for any remixing and transformation, you distribute your rebuild under the same license. http://creativecommons.org/licenses/by-nc-sa/4.0/

First published in 2024 by punctum books, Earth, Milky Way.
https://punctumbooks.com

ISBN-13: 978-1-68571-190-0 (print)
ISBN-13: 978-1-68571-191-7 (ePDF)

DOI: 10.53288/0466.1.00

LCCN: 2024943921
Library of Congress Cataloging Data is available from the Library of Congress

Editing: SAJ and Eileen A. Fradenburg Joy
Book design: Hatim Eujayl and Vincent W.J. van Gerven Oei
Cover design: Vincent W.J. van Gerven Oei
Cover image: *Snake and Raven,* by Doris Cross. Erasure poem from Doris Cross's series "Dictionary Columns," generated from the 1913 *Webster's Dictionary,* Secondary School Edition, c. 1965.

This publication was made possible by a generous grant from the Institute of East Asian Studies, University of California, Berkeley.

HIC SVNT MONSTRA

Redacted

Writing in
the Negative Space
of the State

Edited by
Lisa Min
Franck Billé, and
Charlene Makley

Contents

Introduction Lisa Min, Franck Billé, and Charlene Makley	17
Redaction: Sketch for a Self-Analysis Joshua Craze	27
Letters from the Depthless Deep Lisa Min	48
Disappearing the Cofounders: The Story of Imagine, a Language School in Xinjiang M▮▮▮ and Darren Byler	69
"What About This One with the Mice?" Shane Carter	87
Condensed Meanings: Redaction Dialogues on Ethnography in Occupied Tibet Charlene Makley and Donyol Dondrup	97
Redaction Inverted: Erasure Poetry and the Intent to Reveal Rachel Douglas-Jones	121
A Redacted Fairy Tale ChatGPT	141
Eco-Redaction as Method Umut Yıldırım	151
On Redactions: Fragmented Thoughts on FOIA Requests and Appeals David H. Price	167
Collaborations and Disclosures in Authoritarian Fields A▮▮ and N▮▮	179
Dear Kafka Annie Malcolm	189

Stealing and Redacting: Fieldwork among Transnational Thieves in Eastern Romania   197
Trine Mygind Korsby

Research through Passing in _____ and _____   209
Emily T. Yeh and A____ Marie Ranjbar

From Behind Black Bars: Productive Redactions and Mass Incarceration in Xinjiang Uyghur Autonomous Region, 2017–2022   221
Alessandro Rippa and Rune Steenberg

Things Not Revealed: A Redacted Ethnography of the CIA   237
Carole McGranahan

Where Are ~~Ohlone~~ Place Names?   245
Kären Wigen

█████ in the Field: Lies, Silences, Half-Truths   249
Franck Billé

Bibliography   263

Contributors   275

Index   281
Anjali Nath

List of Poems and Illustrations

Statue of Confederate Gen. Robert E. Lee	14
Top/Not Secret	24
Of Specters or Returns, by Jane Jin Kaisen	42
WeChat, August 2020	54
"Zong! #7," by M. NourbeSe Philip	84
Reaching Guantánamo (excerpt), by Solmaz Sharif	94
"A Note about 'Two Systems'" (excerpt), by Sarah Howe	136
██████████████████████████	148
Dictionary Columns, by Doris Cross	162
A Bureaucrat Erases a Building, by DALL-E	174
Rows of Bureaucrats Redacting Words on Pieces of Paper, by DALL-E	176
"Intermezzo II," by Tony C. Brown	186
"I Never Understood Wind," by Donald J. Trump	194
My Sensitivity, by Jill Magid	206
White Sands Missile Range; Alamogordo, New Mexico; Distance ~35 miles, by Trevor Paglen	218
Covid graph redacted	235
Palm, Fingers and Fingertips (Left Hand) 000395, by Jenny Holzer	258
Right Hand, DOD-044403, by Jenny Holzer	260

Acknowledgments

The spark that set off this project was a day-long conversation that took place in 2019 at a workshop at University of California, Berkeley. Although the central focus at the time was the violence of Xinjiang, we also discussed the challenges of working in politically charged contexts such as Tibet, North Korea, Russia, and Central Asia. Following this very productive workshop, the three of us got together to see if we might further explore redaction as an organizational theme to bring together such unruly and varied experiences in an edited collection. We thank the Institute of East Asian Studies and the Tang Center for Silk Road Studies at UC Berkeley for their generous support at this early stage, as well as throughout crucial junctures in the making of this book.

As the conversation grew, what quickly became evident was that the notion of authoritarianism was more of a barrier than a useful shorthand for describing political worlds. We could no longer employ this term to describe a phenomenon "over there," defined against the pristine shores of democracy here, because the political terrain of the United States and Europe was also shifting in new and troubling ways. If we were really going to look at redaction, we had to cross these kinds of neat divides, we had to reach for art, poetry, memes, and other ways of writing to convey, in the mode of redaction, things unsayable and unsaid. In this regard, we were greatly inspired by the pioneering work of Solmaz Sharif, Jenny Holzer, Joshua Craze, Jill Magid, and Doris Cross, who brought us into the aesthetic fold of redaction to more carefully consider form and its impact. We are grateful to them (and to the individuals curating their work) for allowing us to reprint some of the pieces that proved so generative for us. The images and poetic citations that intersperse this volume are therefore less illustrations of redactions than they are forms of thought in their own right.

Through the inside out of the pandemic, through deaths and births of loved ones, and through the horrors of political and natural disasters, this project held ground, creating for us a place to come back to when things stopped making sense again. We thank our brilliant contributors for their patience and willingness to think with us, for helping us tend to the wild tendrils of where a mind could go with redaction, and for each in their own way presenting redaction in the ethnographic intimacy of the field encounter. And our deep appreciation to those perhaps not directly discernible here but who intersected with the project at various points along the journey: Katherine Verdery, Madeleine Reeves, Alexei Yurchak, Yael Navaro, Natalya Ryzhova, Christian Sorace, Marissa Smith, Stuart McLean, Elizabeth Cullen Dunn, Anand Pandian, Gretchen Bakke, Annie Danis, Jessica Calvanico, and Katie Kinkopf. Every exchange, every conversation has truly been a joyfully collective endeavor.

Finally we thank the wonderful team at punctum books, without whom this book would not be here in this form today: SAJ, our meticulous copyeditor, and Eileen A. Fradenburg Joy and Vincent W.J. van Gerven Oei, our visionary editors, who saw what this project could be from the very beginning.

Statue of Confederate Gen. Robert E. Lee

"In the aftermath of the white supremacist terrorism at Charlottesville, all the monuments must fall. The murder of Heather Heyer was prompted by the proposed removal of a statue of Robert E. Lee. These statues are material nodes in the network of white supremacy. They are the visible form of the established order of racial hierarchy. No longer 'unseen,' they are active and violent in and of themselves."

— Nicholas Mirzoeff, "All The Monuments Must Fall #Charlottesville," August 14, 2017, http://www.nicholasmirzoeff.com/bio/all-the-monuments-must-fall-charlottesville.

"... for characterization of defacement can never confront its object head-on, if only because defacement catches us unawares and can only be known unexpectedly, complicit with the violence of daily life. The writer must confront the resistances. Why else do we write? The shortest way between two points, between violence and its analysis, is the long way round, tracing the edge sideways like the crab scuttling. This we also call the labor of the negative."

— Michael T. Taussig, *Defacement: Public Secrecy and the Labor of the Negative* (Stanford University Press, 1999), 2.

Photo by Mk17b, CC BY-SA 4.0 via Wikimedia Commons

Introduction

Lisa Min, Franck Billé, and Charlene Makley

> *The political is not topical or thematic, it is tactical and formal. It is not, as its strictest definition supposes, something relegated to legislative halls, but something enacted wherever power is at hand, power being at hand wherever there is a relation, including the relation between text and reader.*
> —Solmaz Sharif[1]

> *Hovering within and outside visibility, it commands its power by means of a revelation we can never fully know.*
> —Pamela M. Lee[2]

When it comes to the political, the act of blacking out, withholding information, marking an absence, sits in awkward tension with the myth of borderless access and frictionless communication. There has to be more; is there more to redaction that might be gleaned from this paradox? From the unease, the discomfort, that which we don't know what to do with yet, that which emerges from the tenuous space between transparency and opacity? These are the beginnings that open this collection.

Redaction is most readily identified as a technique of the state, one that aims to erase, sanitize, and proliferate the aura of power as sacred and elusive.[3] As a technique, it also attributes a sense of expertise, reason, and authenticity to the state as an all-knowing, thinking entity.[4] Redaction is

---

1 Solmaz Sharif, "The Near Transitive Properties of the Political and Poetical: Erasure," *Evening Will Come: A Monthly Journal of Poetics* 28 (2013), https://www.thevolta-org.zulaufdesign.com/ewc28-ssharif-p1.html.
2 Pamela M. Lee, "Open Secret: The Work of Art between Disclosure and Redaction," *Artforum*, May 2011, https://www.artforum.com/print/201105/open-secret-the-work-of-art-between-disclosure-and-redaction-28060.
3 David H. Price, *Threatening Anthropology: McCarthyism and the FBI's Surveillance of Activist Anthropologists* (Durham: Duke University Press, 2004); David H. Price, *Anthropological Intelligence: The Deployment and Neglect of American Anthropology in the Second World War* (Durham: Duke University Press, 2008); David H. Price, *Cold War Anthropology: The CIA, the Pentagon, and the Growth of Dual Use Anthropology* (Durham: Duke University Press, 2016); and Katherine Verdery, *My Life as a Spy: Investigations in a Secret Police File* (Durham: Duke University Press, 2018).
4 Conversely, botched redactions—as in the investigation of Paul Manafort, Trump's former campaign manager—are seen as indexical of state inadequacy,

generally understood as text-based censorship that conspicuously masks parts of printed discourse, conveying a sense of the secret, the impossible, the inaccessible, and the indefinitely unknowable. Redaction thus appears to hold a tacit relationship to truth, with black lines at once obscuring and signaling a deeper, underlying layer of discourse. When confronted with redaction, the task and challenge then would presumably be to uncover this truth beneath. This would be to follow the logic of "the transparency society."[5]

Looking back on the political developments of the last decade, we can say that more transparency, more information, and more communication have not led to more clarity of thought, more nuanced understandings of the political terrain, or more equitable and livable worlds. If anything, it seems to have had the opposite effect. This impulse toward transparency has led us astray, to something like what Byung-Chul Han calls the "postpolitical," where politics no longer have to "articulate political will or to produce new social coordinates," where politics exist without "*reference*."[6] For Han, transparency cannot detect "what lies outside the system. It confirms and optimizes only what already exists."[7] Transparency as "freedom of information," as "accumulation of information," ultimately does not and cannot yield truth because it "lacks direction"; it is so "smooth" that it ceaselessly "glides"; it is movement without "reference."[8]

As anthropologists writing in and about authoritarian environments such as China, Russia, or north Korea, we know that transparency will fail us.[9] However, official frameworks regulating the ethics of our research, such as Institutional Review Boards (IRBs), operate under the assumption that transparency offers protection for research subjects. Research protocols are reviewed, monitored, and designed to protect "the rights and welfare of human research subjects," but the political contexts and the way relationships work and are negotiated in such places are easily overlooked in the name of "informed consent."[10]

---

unprofessionalism, and ineptitude. See for instance: Herbert B. Dixon Jr., "Embarrassing Redaction Failures," *American Bar Association*, May 1, 2019, https://www.americanbar.org/groups/judicial/publications/judges_journal/2019/spring/embarrassing-redaction-failures/. For another instance involving *The New York Times*, see Tim Cushing, "New York Times Suffers Redaction Failure, Exposes Name of NSA Agent and Targeted Network in Uploaded PDF," *Techdirt*, January 28, 2014, https://www.techdirt.com/2014/01/28/new-york-times-suffers-redaction-failure-exposes-name-nsa-agent-targeted-network-uploaded-pdf/.

5   Byung-Chul Han, *The Transparency Society*, trans. Erik Butler (Stanford: Stanford University Press, 2015).
6   Ibid., 7.
7   Ibid.
8   Ibid., 1, 8.
9   We use "north Korea" with a lowercase n as a "marker" of the politics involved in naming this place. See Lisa Min, "North Korea So Far: Distance and Intimacy, Seen and Unseen" (PhD diss., University of California, Berkeley, 2020).
10 As stated in "Information Sheet: Institutional Review Boards Frequently

All good intentions unravel as soon as one lands in another political reality. In order to pursue fieldwork in these places we have had to learn other strategies, to become attuned to opacity and distance, to make room for the unsaid and unsayable; we have had to find ways to notice, to maintain relations, to remain suspended in ellipses, all while attempting to protect our interlocutors and save ourselves from ourselves, from our movements in a field strewn with discontinuities and gaps (see Billé, Korsby, Malcolm, and Yeh and Ranjbar in this collection). In our writing, we have become adept at forms of literary concealment to evade the punishing force of a political landscape that cannot be fully grasped (see M▮ and Byler, Makley and Donyol Dondrup, Min, Rippa and Steenberg, and A▮ and N▮ in this collection). We are trained to anonymize, edit names, create composite persona, blending traits and conversations from a number to interlocutors in order to mute all potentially revelatory markers, as if these redactions will protect us and everyone who has been in contact with us.[11] Here too, there is an assumption that redacting practices will conceal a preexisting layer of truth.

Deconstructing further our own disciplinary and institutional relationship to truth, the notion of redaction we mobilize speaks to the ambiguities and aporias of all ethnographic practice. Of course, no ethnographic account, whatever the medium or genre, can be a transparent representation of the truth. Thus everyone working ethnographically must negotiate forms of hybridity and erasure, on various levels beyond what we typically imagine as illiberal or authoritarian pressures. On one level, we patch and smooth out gaps, rewriting a more linear research program. On another, we face disciplinary conventions and assumptions that limit our choices of medium, form, and audience. What is key here is that there is something about the way we have pursued research and writing all along that needs to be reimagined.

Our sense is that working in such contexts requires more than a disavowal of "the state" as a discrete, locatable, self-aware entity. It instead calls for new forms of writing and multimodal interventions that can convey the ambivalent experiences of living in state-inflected worlds, where the coordinates of risk and danger to ourselves and our interlocutors are exceptionally opaque, and where the researcher is always already entangled and complicit (see Douglas-Jones in this collection). In the approaches we bring together here, redaction is not just the censorship of texts to be mitigated

---

Asked Questions: Guidance for Institutional Review Boards and Clinical Investigators," *U.S. Food and Drug Administration*, January 1998, https://www.fda.gov/regulatory-information/search-fda-guidance-documents/institutional-review-boards-frequently-asked-questions.

11 What has not been adequately considered are the ethics of "actual fieldwork relationships" and experiences. For a reflection on the use of pseudonyms in anthropology, see Erica Weiss and Carole McGranahan, "Rethinking Pseudonyms in Ethnography: An Introduction," *American Ethnological Society*, December 13, 2021, https://americanethnologist.org/online-content/collections/rethinking-pseudonyms-in-ethnography/rethinking-pseudonyms-in-ethnography-an-introduction/.

by liberal practices of transparency, but a more embodied politics of concealment and revelation, a dialogical process fraught with uncertainty and risk, but also shielded to some extent in the darkness afforded by its very illegibility (see Craze, Price, and Yıldırım in this collection). "The shortest way between two points, between violence and its analysis, is the long way round, tracing the edge sideways like the crab scuttling," as Michael Taussig says.[12]

In this light, redaction is not merely a technique of the state. It is an acute mode of expression that attempts to convey the multiple, unbounded, contradictory, androgynous, and dialogic self as it encounters this political terrain.[13] Though the story of redaction begins in erasure and obliteration, we follow the poet Solmaz Sharif's example and take on the task of the censor, writing through the horror and ambivalence of this position, to attempt an appropriation of erasure towards a different end, towards the poetic.[14]

Redacted brings together a collection of essays from anthropologists, geographers, writers, artists, and activists that explore redaction in politically charged contexts where conventional methods of fieldwork, writing, or activism break down. As shifts in the political landscapes of the United States and Europe increasingly demonstrate, illiberalism is not a phenomenon exclusive to the socialist and postsocialist world.[15] Scholars of "postsocialism" such as Dace Dzenovska and Larisa Kurtović offer an examination of the experience of "political liberalism of the post-Cold War period," which serves as a resource in making sense of the shifting political terrain of Western liberal democracies.[16] Redaction practices are therefore becoming vital in research and writing across a range of regions and topics previously considered "safe." Increasingly we are seeing human rights activists in the US and Europe facing jail terms and fines for rescuing migrants at sea,

---

12 Michael T. Taussig, *Defacement: Public Secrecy and the Labor of the Negative* (Stanford: Stanford University Press, 1999), 2.

13 "Androgynous" as per Marilyn Strathern, whereby redaction might be imagined as "a social microcosm *to the extent* that it takes a singular form." In other words, when singularity is inherently composite, what she calls the "one-is-many mode," it disentangles the state versus people relation from the simply hierarchical or oppositional. Marilyn Strathern, *The Gender of the Gift: Problems with Women and Problems with Society in Melanesia* (University of California Press, 1988), 14-15. See also Hoon Song's elaboration of Strathern's notion of androgyny, which "makes relationality an art of 'secrecy and exposure.'" Hoon Song, "Two Is Infinite, Gender Is Post-Social in Papua New Guinea," *Angelaki* 17, no. 2 (2012): 12.

14 Sharif, "The Near Transitive Properties of the Political and Poetical."

15 Dace Dzenovska and Larisa Kurtović, "Introduction: Lessons for Liberalism from the 'Illiberal East,'" *Society for Cultural Anthropology*, April 25, 2018, https://culanth.org/fieldsights/introduction-lessons-for-liberalism-from-the-illiberal-east. See also Natalie Koch, "'On the Cult of Personality and Its Consequences': American Nationalism and the Trump Cult," in *Spatializing Authoritarianism,* ed. Natalie Koch (Syracuse: Syracuse University Press, 2022), 194–221.

16 Dzenovska and Kurtović, "Lessons for Liberalism."

for leaving water for people crossing borders illegally, and for participating in protests. To protect themselves and their interlocutors, scholars are increasingly having to employ various redacting subterfuges.[17]

At the same time, across rapidly proliferating media platforms, the very notion of truth appears to have become unmoored. We seem to be living in an age of "post-truth."[18] New transnational nexuses of state- and corporate-controlled social media afford users vast possibilities for experiencing profound feelings of what Lee McIntyre, citing the comedian Stephen Colbert, called "truthiness."[19] When it comes to "truthiness," Colbert says, truth comes from "the gut."[20]

Social media has platformed new forms of authoritarian capitalism, which mediate experiences of truth as an algorithmic sociality primed for a political economy of attention, surveillance, and data-mining over any kind of liberal transparency. The automated spirals of such mediations fuel the pleasures and horrors of conspiracy as much as the social refuges of online communities. Meanwhile, Anne Applebaum speaks of "Autocracy Inc.," the ways in which oligarchs and state leaders around the world now collaborate to attack democratic systems from within and without, using social media and digital finance tools to find new common grounds in cynical forms of "neo-traditionalism" that weaponize the rageful combatants of culture wars.[21]

As the Covid pandemic broke, we saw how truth-seekers across the political spectrum trafficked in similar rumors and misinformation, frequently juxtaposing them with official advice. In the US, the Trump administration responded by proliferating rumors and undermining recommendations by the Centers for Disease Control and Prevention (CDC), creating a rift between what was understood as "official"—and by extension "true"—and what was "unofficial," and therefore subject to scrutiny and discretion. It seems that once the binary between the official and unofficial became jumbled, it only increased the need or desire to hold on even tighter to them. Following the 2022 White Paper protests in China, and the way Euro-American anti-maskers and anti-vaxxers came to identify with Chinese protesters' calls for freedom demonstrates how this impulse toward a binary rendering of politics can lead to profound misunderstanding. As Christian Sorace and Nicholas Loubere elucidate, the "false binary" between "freedom" and "biopolitical state intervention [...] risks misread-

---

17 Jason De León, *The Land of Open Graves: Living and Dying on the Migrant Trail* (Berkeley: University of California Press, 2015).
18 Marius Gudonis and Benjamin T. Jones, eds., *History in a Post-Truth World: Theory and Praxis* (New York: Routledge, 2021), and Lee McIntyre, *Post-Truth* (Cambridge: MIT Press, 2018).
19 McIntyre, *Post-Truth*, 5.
20 Stephen Colbert noted this at the 2006 White House Correspondents' Dinner. See "User Clip: Stephen Colbert on 'Truthiness,'" C-SPAN, April 29, 2006, https://www.c-span.org/video/?c4293026/user-clip-stephen-colbert-truthiness.
21 Anne Applebaum, "Autocracy Inc.," 19th Annual Seymour Martin Lipset Lecture, *National Endowment for Democracy*, December 1, 2022, https://www.ned.org/events/nineteenth-lipset-lecture-anne-applebaum-autocracy-inc/.

ing the Chinese protests by interpreting the protesters' rejection of the authoritarian biopolitics of the State's zero Covid policy as a tacit demand for the necro-politics of the United States."[22] In other words, it sees solidarity as a matter of state opposition, even if the terms of the opposition are composed of radically different values.

It is in this sense that we see a focus on multimodal redaction as a way to enter into this obscured domain of modern democratic polities, where power can run amok in the name of "the people."[23] In critically and poetically engaging with redaction, we seek ways to transcend longstanding frameworks of power, the reverberations of Cold War geopolitics that continue to divide the world into east versus west, authoritarianism versus democracy, and good versus evil through liberal and neoliberal imaginaries. Such tropes figure the political as a left-right spectrum, populism and nationalism versus global and transnational cosmopolitanism, but these familiar coordinates are being reconfigured in novel, recursive, and unrecognizable ways, the consequences of which are perplexing and ever evolving. The mixing of "real facts" with "fake facts" in such a context creates what Alexei Yurchak calls a "distorting effect," displacing political analysis onto a performative plane, where it becomes more important to reproduce the form of these binaries that shape the political realm, rather than attend to the truth value of what is being said.[24]

Working in this newly complex political landscape of "hypervisibility" and "hypercommunication" demands a reconsideration of the terms and subjects of surveillance, censorship, erasure, and subjectivity, including of the practitioner and the self: the anthropologist, writer, poet, artist, and activist.[25] It requires careful attunement to the ordinary and the everyday.[26]

---

22 Christian Sorace and Nicholas Loubere, "Biopolitical Binaries (or How Not to Read the Chinese Protests)," *Made in China Journal*, December 2, 2022, https://madeinchinajournal.com/2022/12/02/biopolitical-binaries-or-how-not-to-read-the-chinese-protests/.

23 Susan Buck-Morss, *Dreamworld and Catastrophe: The Passing of Mass Utopia in East and West* (Cambridge: MIT Press, 2002).

24 Alexei Yurchak, "Fake, Unreal, and Absurd," in *Fake: Anthropological Keywords*, eds. Jacob Copeman and Giovanni da Col (Chicago: HAU Books, 2018), 92. More specifically, on pages 94–96, Yurchak points to a reframing of the political terrain in terms of "patriots" versus "traitors" and "foreign agents," which can be observed in both the United States (in the instance of foreign "interference" during the election of Donald Trump) and Russia (in the division of Russia into "pro-Putin nationalists" and "anti-Putin liberals"). The danger of such renderings is the displacement of "real politics" onto the plane of the performative, where "[t]he main effect of this practice is not necessarily that the audiences are fooled into believing every imaginary story and fact, but rather that they learn that 'facts' may be read not for how true or false they are, but for how effective or ineffective, patriotic or unpatriotic, pro-Russian or pro-Western they are" (96).

25 Han, *The Transparency Society*, 12.

26 On the "everyday," see Kathleen Stewart, *Ordinary Affects* (Durham: Duke University Press, 2007). And for "attunement" see Kathleen Stewart, "Atmospheric Attunements," *Environment and Planning D: Society and Space* 29, no. 3 (2011):

It requires deep reflection on temporality and shifting notions of safety amid political precarity, an understanding that what was once publicly expressible may not be in the future, and vice versa. It calls for a confrontation with ways of doing and disseminating research, and for seeking novel forms that reflect this new political reality. As Hito Steyerl put it, "Now more than ever, real life is much stranger than any fiction one could imagine. So somehow the forms of reporting have to become crazier and stranger, too. Otherwise they are not going to be 'documentary' enough, they are not going to live up to what's happening."[27]

We thus take up redaction as a way of coming to terms with both power and complicity, desire and disavowal, since it is first and foremost a procedure of the state that we appropriate but also emulate. And so, redactions come to mark the negative space in which political power and the aesthetic experience of that power is as seductive as it is menacing, unruly as it is generative. In thinking and practicing redaction as both a poetic intervention and scholarly orientation, our aim is to inhabit the grain and texture of erasure, to be co-present with the violent and intimate touch of blacklined texts, absent present images, empty or emptied spaces, and voids.

We follow themes of refusal, excess, temporality, disembodiment and embodiment, non-communication and communications, presence, absence, rhythm, delight, and intimacy in order to think and write with and through power in the provocative mode of an "open secret," within "the spectral radiance of the unsaid."[28] The blank and blacked out pages dispersed throughout the volume are such reminders, our own redactions of this very political moment as we write in the spring of 2024, redactions both necessary and disciplined that mark not only the present but the future anterior of other such redactions to come.

What is it about redaction, its forms, affective potentials, and aesthetic qualities, that makes it so striking? How might redaction as an experimental practice open up new dialogic possibilities in conveying the stakes of political encounters, and more specifically, in the writing we produce from those politically charged spaces and potentially dangerous contexts? We invite readers to join us in this exploration of redaction through writings and multimodal experiments that take up redaction as an aesthetic intervention, as well as essays that reflect on these redacted forms of media in a political reality where distinctions between democracy and authoritarianism, liberalism and illiberalism, left and right are increasingly difficult to draw.

445–53.

27 Hito Steyerl and Laura Poitras, "Techniques of the Observer: Hito Steyerl and Laura Poitras in Conversation," *Artforum*, May 2015, https://www.artforum.com/print/201505/techniques-of-the-observer-hito-steyerl-and-laura-poitras-in-conversation-51563.

28 Taussig, *Defacement*.

"If anthropologies of social life under authoritarian regimes in Central Asia and beyond teach us anything, however, it is precisely that cynicism is no insulation from complicity; that publics can critique and yet conform; that ambivalence is the very hallmark of making a livable life in circumstances of political disillusion or disgust. The forms of the outside cultivated through critique are not immune to incorporation. The cunning of #Trumpistan might lie precisely in leading us to expect that Trump's America will be any different."

—Madeleine Reeves, "#Trumpistan: On the Cunning Familiarity of the Authoritarian Absurd," *Cultural Anthropology*, April 25, 2018, https://culanth.org/fieldsights/trumpistan-on-the-cunning-familiarity-of-the-authoritarian-absurd.

NOT SECRET

THIS IS A COVER SHEET

FOR CLASSIFIED INFORMATION

ALL INDIVIDUALS HANDLING THIS INFORMATION ARE REQUIRED TO PROTECT IT FROM UNAUTHORIZED DISCLOSURE IN THE INTEREST OF THE NATIONAL SECURITY OF THE UNITED STATES.

HANDLING, STORAGE, REPRODUCTION AND DISPOSITION OF THE ATTACHED DOCUMENT WILL BE IN ACCORDANCE WITH APPLICABLE EXECUTIVE ORDER(S), STATUTE(S) AND AGENCY IMPLEMENTING REGULATIONS.

(This cover sheet is unclassified.)

NOT SECRET

STANDARD FORM 703

Redaction
Sketch for a Self-Analysis

Joshua Craze

A drop of ink has fallen upon the paper and I have walled it round. Now every point of the area within the wall is either black or white; and no point is both black and white. That is plain. The black is, however, all in one spot or blot; it is within bounds. There is a line of demarcation between the black and the white. Now I ask about the points of this line, are they black or white?
—C.S. Peirce[1]

I've been looking at redacted documents for over a decade. The news cycle has spun past me many times. I'm still here. One friend — a journalist — tells me that I'm almost a historian, in a tone that suggests I'm actually a fossil: an object of inquiry, rather than an inquirer. Another — an art critic — reassures me that in a couple of years, I might be fashionable again, if only I were to work on something else. Both friends treat my recalcitrance as a character defect, and gently propose that I might like to find another obsession, one more suited to this era of pandemic and post-truth. "I know galleries," my friend entreats, "that would be interested in whatever you do *next*." The adverb is an invitation, a chasm. That's not how obsessions work, I tell them. You don't get to choose. Obsessions are the hostile actions of evil spirits. They besiege you. My friends fall silent when I tell them that, leaving me alone with my documents. I prefer it that way. In the ▇▇.

During these static days, locked down on the couch, I'm often trapped in the tyranny of the screen, my life's rhythms determined by the simultaneous depression of command and tab, which transports me between windows, teleporting me between worlds, until I realize hours have passed, and I haven't gone anywhere at all. There is only one window, and its contents don't really vary. Normally, I'm looking at redacted documents, and normally, I'm searching for sense. At some moment during this process — and I can't tell you when, exactly — I short-circuit. Only seconds earlier, I was all active, probing intellect, flicking rapidly between CIA documents as I tried to correlate the purported dates of Abu Zubaydah's rendition from Faisalabad and subsequent passage to ▇▇ ▇▇. Then, suddenly — I'm

---

[1] Charles S. Peirce, "The Logic of Quantity," cited in Daniel Heller-Roazen, *No One's Ways: An Essay on Infinite Naming* (New York: Zone Books, 2017), 113.

lost. Not distracted, not looking at email, just staring at the document in front of me, frozen. It's then that the words blur into the black, and I can no longer see the difference between absence and text. It's then that I struggle to account for all this lost time, sat inside, squinting into ▮▮ ▮▮. What have I been doing?

* * *

In the beginning, I was looking for words. It was the first decade of this benighted century, and a declaration of war against an abstract noun had resulted in a decidedly concrete campaign against nouns proper and absent. Who had been disappeared? Where were the black sites?[2] As I began my research into the war on terror, it was as if I were sat in front of a jigsaw of the map of the world and it was full of holes. I hoped to find the fugitive pieces hidden in redacted documents.

My own work as a journalist and researcher was only a minor and belated part of the effort to chronicle and contest the American war on terror.[3] By the time I began researching national security policy, Freedom of Information Act (FOIA) requests by activists, journalists, and lawyers had produced a public archive of hundreds of thousands of pages of government documents. Some of those pages were so redacted that they recalled the concrete poetry of the 1960s. Sometimes, I would stare at a page containing only a single phrase, like the lonely survivor of a government campaign to eliminate all the witnesses. Which, in a sense, is exactly what such phrases were.[4]

---

2 These American prisons were once so secret that then-President George W. Bush asked not to be told their locations, in case he accidentally blurted them out.

3 Amongst other projects, Meg Stalcup and I worked (2008–10) with The Nation Investigative Reporting Institute (now Type Investigations) investigating the way American law enforcement officials were trained in counterterrorism. Our investigation was published in 2010 in the *Washington Monthly,* and was cited in a subsequent Senate inquiry into counterterrorism training. Meg Stalcup and Joshua Craze, "How We Train Our Cops to Fear Islam," *Washington Monthly,* March 9, 2011, https://washingtonmonthly.com/2011/03/09/how-we-train-our-cops-to-fear-islam/.

4 Fig. 4.1 is page eighteen of an August 1, 2002 memorandum of the US Department of Justice's Office of Legal Counsel, regarding the interrogation of Abu Zubaydah. Almost the entire document is redacted. This memorandum, the "Bybee memo," was one of a series of legal memoranda largely drafted by John Yoo, as deputy assistant attorney general, and signed by assistant attorney general Jay Bybee, that became known as the "torture memos," and which attempted to provide a legal justification for America's torture of detainees. See, inter alia, Philippe Sands, *Torture Team: Rumsfeld's Memo and the Betrayal of American Values* (New York: St Martin's Press, 2008), and David Cole, *Torture Memos: Rationalizing the Unthinkable* (New York: New Press, 2009).

Fig. 4.1.

If one were to take the efforts of those years as a collective subject and pour the work of hundreds of people into one mold, then our purpose was to cast light where the government wished there to be darkness. Through investigations that spanned continents, slowly, painstakingly, we began to build up a picture of coercive interrogation, domestic surveillance, extraordinary rendition, and torture.[5] We were hunters, searching redacted documents for evidence of a beast whose habitat, we knew, was dark spaces.

Sometimes, the beast didn't leave tracks, and I was left foundering. I dreamt of reading unredacted reports and being able to truly behold my foe. Instead, I spent all my time stumbling around in the darkness. By outsmarting the censors, I wanted to get to the things-in-themselves — the

---

5   Early important book-length investigations include James Risen, *State of War: The Secret History of the CIA and the Bush Administration* (New York: Free Press, 2006), and Jane Mayer, *The Dark Side: The Inside Story of How the War on Terror Turned into a War on American Ideals* (New York: Anchor, 2009).

noumena underneath the redactions. My hope was that by reading the sentences around the black blocks, and putting them in context, I could perhaps divine their content. In one document, I remember feeling certain that the redacted subject doing unspeakable things to a redacted object was the same unnamed subject that reappeared under investigation later in the text. I named this subject, Redacted #1.

Redacted #1, I knew from the document, liked coffee and complained about over-work. (Their distinguishing features, in other words, were the generic properties of an office worker). It was a question, I thought, of trying to find the repetitions that would allow me to follow Redacted #1 through the text; I hoped their addiction to caffeine would give them away. Later, I would try and track them through other redacted files, looking for a slip on the part of the censor that might enable me to give my creation a proper name. The redacted documents were a crime scene; I was the detective.

All too often, I failed. I couldn't tell which redaction referred to Redacted #1, who soon merged with Redacted #2 (and possibly even Redacted #3), becoming a sort of composite, anonymous subject that I did not yet know how to name.

In the beginning, I hated the redactions because they were wasting my time. I was looking for words. There were facts to be discovered. Things to be known. The redactions were keeping me from the truth of the torture program. They were keeping me from completing my jigsaw.

Over the years, I found some of its fugitive pieces. From one document, this is what I learned:

I learned that Zayn al Abidin Muhammad Husayn, otherwise known as Abu Zubaydah, was detained in Faisalabad, Pakistan on March 28, 2002, and that he was gasconaded by the Americans as a "high-value" detainee.[6] I learned that he was flown to DETENTION SITE GREEN — because some redactions occur in language — where he was tortured. While almost everything else I learned from the legal memos advising the CIA about its interrogations ended up proving verifiably false, a series of exaggerations and lies about Abu Zubaydah's role in an organization — Al Qaeda — in which he was not even a member, from one document I learned that Abu Zubaydah may have had a fear of insects, and that his potential agitation had legal consequences.[7]

---

[6] Reluctantly, the American government later acknowledged that Abu Zubydah was not a member of Al Qaeda. He nonetheless remains in Guantanamo Bay, rendered guilty by his treatment, judged too dangerous to be released and too innocent to be tried.

[7] Fig. 4.2 is a paragraph from page fourteen of "A Memorandum for John Rizzo, Acting General Counsel of the Central Intelligence Agency," a legal memo written by the US Department of Justice's Office of Legal Counsel, to advise the CIA on whether a proposed course of conduct would violate the prohibition against torture found at § 2340A of title 18 of the United States Code.

Fig. 4.2.

> In addition to using the confinement boxes alone, you also would like to introduce an insect into one of the boxes with Zubaydah. As we understand it, you plan to inform Zubaydah that you are going to place a stinging insect into the box, but you will actually place a harmless insect in the box, such as a caterpillar. If you do so, to ensure that you are outside the predicate act requirement, you must inform him that the insects will not have a sting that would produce death or severe pain. If, however, you were to place the insect in the box without informing him that you are doing so, then, in order to not commit a predicate act, you should not affirmatively lead him to believe that any insect is present which has a sting that could produce severe pain or suffering or even cause his death. ███████████████████ so long as you take either of the approaches we have described, the insect's placement in the box would not constitute a threat of severe physical pain or suffering to a reasonable person in his position. An individual placed in a box, even an individual with a fear of insects, would not reasonably feel threatened with severe physical pain or suffering if a caterpillar was placed in the box. Further, you have informed us that you are not aware that Zubaydah has any allergies to insects, and you have not informed us of any other factors that would cause a reasonable person in that same situation to believe that an unknown insect would cause him severe physical pain or death. Thus, we conclude that the placement of the insect in the confinement box with Zubaydah would not constitute a predicate act.

One truth amid the falsehoods. All the document's other revelations, I surmised, must be hidden. Amongst the uncertainties of the war on terror, I held onto the promise of those redactions. I was sure that if only I could get underneath them — erase the erasures — then I would discover the real story.

This was my mission: I would find the missing nouns that had named our world, and the verbs that activated those names. Then things would be ordered. Then life would have a sense. The redactions promised light.

* * *

I was on my way to becoming a good researcher, a detective who discarded redactions as mere obstacles to the truth, when this sentence stopped me in my tracks:

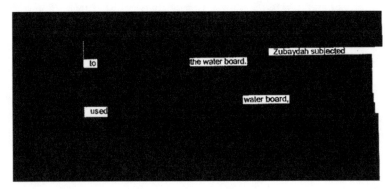

Fig. 4.3.

I say it's a sentence, but that's not quite right. "Zubaydah subjected to the water board" is a phrase formed from fragments that were presumably once part of other sentences, with other meanings, to which we are not privy. The sentence that emerges on the page is an effect of the redaction.

The text from which this excerpt is taken is "Other Document #131," a heavily redacted CIA report on the capture and detention of Abu Zubaydah, obtained by the American Civil Liberties Union (ACLU) following a FOIA request placed on October 7, 2003 and finally released on May 27,

2008. I kept staring at the words "water board" and "used." Read together, they became a sentence fragment that seemed to confirm the claim made in the prior sentence (that the waterboard was used on Abu Zubaydah), without adding anything to our understanding of how, when, or why such usage had occurred.

Why the additional sentence fragment? Why leave those words untouched by the censor's pen? Why leave any of it on the page for us to see? I consulted lawyers who worked on censorship. There are many legal reasons a document can be redacted before its release in response to a FOIA request. For instance, CIA lawyers could judge that there was a national security risk posed by information contained in a report, or else might surmise that the revelation of certain facts mentioned in a memo would risk revealing ongoing covert activities. How does the law, I wondered, explain the word "used," left orphaned on the page, denuded of context? The lawyers shrugged. None of the legal criteria they proffered seemed able to explain the page with which I was obsessed.

Going through other documents, I found more messages created by the redactions. In some cases, it felt clear to me that these missives were left intentionally: the censors wanted the ACLU to know that Abu Zubaydah was subjected to the waterboard. Elsewhere, the messages that emerged were structural features of the documents themselves, redacted logics indifferent to the intentions of the redactors. Take the composite, anonymous character that had emerged once Redacted #1 and Redacted #2 had blurred together. I began to call him Mr. ███, and I thought I had gotten to know him quite well. While he was made up of many different people — a redacted Leviathan — he exhibited certain constancies. Mr. ███ came, I thought, to have a distinctive life all his own.

In my mind, Mr. ███ was the central character of the war on terror. He drafted documents, worked long hours, administered waterboards, and got promoted. On occasion, he evinced concern that the law was being followed. Just as frequently, he announced that the gloves needed to come off. His concerns remain surprisingly constant. Mr. ███ was an anonymous subject, sheltered in the darkness of the redactions from the legal ramifications of his actions. He was a man created by the structures of the national security state. Often, he was a woman. Sometimes, she was a CIA operative. Elsewhere, this everyman was a psychologist.[8]

---

8 Fig. 4.4 is from page 35 of the May 7, 2004 document by the Central Intelligence Agency and Office of the Inspector General, entitled *Special Review: Counterterrorism Detention and Interrogation Activities* (September 2001–October 2003), 2003-7123-IG. This is henceforth referred to as CIA Special Review.

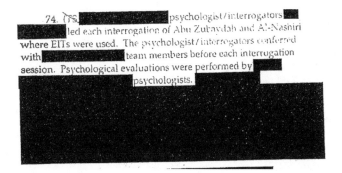

Fig. 4.4.

Mr. ▇▇▇'s anonymity was one of the eerie reversals of the redacted documents. In the world, it was prisoners like Abu Zubaydah who disappeared into secret black sites, while in the documents, it was CIA operatives who vanished into the black via the bureaucratic machinery of redaction, which freed them to apply pressure point techniques to detainees' carotid arteries without fear of future legal sanction.[9]

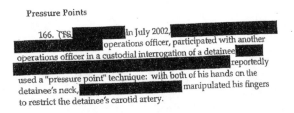

Fig. 4.5.

Thanks to Mr. ▇▇▇'s omnipresence in the redacted documents that I studied, proper names stood out. In one report by the Department of Justice's Office of Professional Responsibility into the memoranda that provided the legal justification for the CIA's use of "Enhanced Interrogation Techniques" (EITs), two names, in particular, were repeated over and over again: Jay S. Bybee and John Yoo, respectively the US assistant attorney general (2001–2003) and the US deputy assistant attorney general (2001–2003). These names, no less than the sentence about waterboarding in Other Document #131 that I referred to above, were a creation of the redactions that surrounded them. Bybee and Yoo's appearance in the documents constituted the inversion of the narrative function of Mr. ▇▇▇. While Mr. ▇▇▇ effaced individual subjects, turning them into a single structural character, Bybee and Yoo were fall guys: apparently proper nouns placed amid the redactions that turned structures into subjects and created narratives about individual responsibility and error.

The redactions created a form of narrative focalization. It mattered that virtually the only legible names in the Department of Justice's report were those of Bybee and Yoo, just as it mattered that the only visible EIT mentioned in the redacted documents that I studied was the waterboard. If one were to believe the legible parts of these documents, waterboarding was

---

9 Fig. 4.5 is from CIA Special Review, 69.

the only interrogation technique used at DETENTION SITE GREEN, torture at Abu Ghraib was the result of a few bad apples, and the memoranda that enabled the American interrogation program were the outcome of the work of a few lawyers — like Bybee and Yoo — rather than the result of planning and organization at the highest levels of the American state. In the Department of Justice's investigation into the "torture memos," the reader follows John Yoo working on drafts of the documents up until his visits to the White House. The next sections of the memos are redacted. Such redactions occur each time the lawyers get close to the president. The narrative effect of these black spaces is to create an oddly bureaucratic drama, replete with complaints about late-night work and takeaway pizza, from which politics itself has been redacted. The legal basis of the EITs, the redactions assure us, is merely a matter of hard-working lawyers diligently drafting legal documents.¹⁰

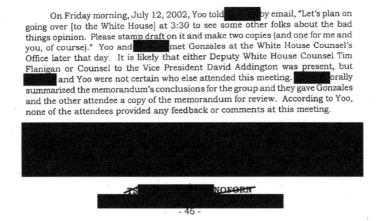

Fig. 4.6.

I realized that the redactions were producing their own narrative structures. Rather than stories of presidential power and executive pressure on the judiciary, the redactions created a bureaucratic tale of strivers and pizza. Rather than a full consideration of the EITs, the redactions resulted in a narrative — both in the documents and in broader public debate — that was focused on waterboarding. There was nothing unnecessary about the repetition of "waterboarding" in document after document, or of Bybee and Yoo's names; the repetitions were the story.

Sometimes, what the censors repeated in the documents was not a proper noun, but simply absence itself. I encountered texts — I presume they were once texts — that were entirely redacted. Why not just refuse the FOIA request, I wondered? Why release an entirely redacted document?

---

10 Fig. 4.6 is from page 40 of the July 29, 2009 document from the Department of Justice, Office of Professional Responsibility, *Investigation into the Office of Legal Counsel's Memoranda Concerning Issues Relating to the Central Intelligence Agency's Used of "Enhanced Interrogation Techniques" on Suspected Terrorists*. Henceforth, "OPR Report."

It's inaccurate to say that I read such documents, for there was nothing to read. Rather, I looked at them almost as one looks at an artwork on a gallery wall.[11]

Fig. 4.7.

In the absolute absences of such documents, in their mute refusal to speak, I thought I saw state power articulated. What such documents announced was not a particular fact that was withheld, but the very fact of withholding. In honor of Donald Rumsfeld's epistemological trinity — known knowns, known unknowns, and unknown unknowns — I named such spaces visible invisibles. These image-documents were instances of what Michael Taussig

---

11   Later, I would come to write about Jenny Holzer's silk-screened paintings of redacted documents. I wrote the catalogue essay for her exhibition at the Venice Biennale, "In the Dead Letter Office," in *Jenny Holzer: War Paintings*, ed. Thomas Kellein (Cologne: Walther König, 2015), and we collaborated on a book-box, called *Belligerent*, that we made together and for which I wrote, "The Secret's Signature" (Madrid: Ivory Press, 2017).

calls public secrets: forms of secrecy that circulate *as secrets*.[12] For the state not to tell you something is also, of course, a form of speech. As I pored over more redacted documents, I started to find more of these forms of silent speech, shouted in the black.

I wanted to tell my editors about these discoveries, but I hesitated, imagining the conversation:

> I'm not crazy. Hear me out. The redactions are talking to me. There are meanings in the black. The redactions don't just hide content, they produce it.

My theories wouldn't go down well. After years of reading these documents, we had stopped seeing the redactions. As journalists, we scanned pages for information, derived what sense we could from the scattered phrases we found, and then discarded the rest. Whatever we wrote, in any event, had to take the form of a two-paragraph story on page seven of the paper. Our work was to traffic in presences; absences take up too much printer's ink.

In the Department of Justice report, the story was Bybee and Yoo. In Other Document #131, the story was clear and visible. The story was waterboarding.

* * *

In document after document, waterboarding was practically the only visible word. For years, it was what the documents revealed, and so became what was reported in the press. What else should we do, journalists responded when I spoke about my doubts, *not report what we find in the documents?*

Of course, I said, the story must be reported. The American government's use of torture needed to be researched, analyzed, and publicized. That was part of the fight. I still believe that. In the early years of the war on terror, though, such publicity was also a form of collaboration between the government and the media. As journalists, we implicitly agreed to the framing of the documents: the redactions constituted the limits of the sayable world.

At least we could see the black. Reading the documents, it was brutally apparent just how much the redactions forced us to focus on a narrative centered on waterboarding, and how little we knew about anything else. It wouldn't be until the publication of the Senate Intelligence Committee Report on Torture in 2014 that we would learn about the forced rectal rehydration.[13] Along with a variety of EITs, politics also disappeared into the black. Chains of command were rendered invisible, and in their place, a single word: waterboard. The narrative focalizations enabled by the re-

---

12 Michael Taussig, *Defacement: Public Secrecy and the Labor of the Negative* (Stanford: Stanford University Press, 1999).
13 *Senate Intelligence Committee Report on Torture,* 2014, 100, n584. Henceforth, "Senate Intelligence Committee Report."

dactions turned waterboarding into a decontextualized practice, removed from the political structures that made it possible.[14] There was little discussion in the media of who was being waterboarded, why they were being waterboarded, or of the histories of colonial and post-colonial violence that shaped the practice.[15] Instead:

Fig. 4.8.

A gestalt switch happened when the newspapers and magazines went to press. When I stared at the documents, increasingly all I saw was the black: the redaction was the foreground, the words "the waterboard" faded into the background. In newspaper articles about the documents, in contrast, all trace of the black disappeared. Stories focused on what we could learn from the documents, not the black space that surrounded the words. There would be no mention of how little we knew or of how the documents only

---

14 Fig. 4.8 is CIA Special Review, 38.
15 For the colonial history of counter-insurgency and American practices of confinement and torture see Laleh Khalili, *Time in the Shadows: Confinement in Counterinsurgencies* (Stanford: Stanford University Press, 2012), and Patricia Owens, *Economy of Force: Counterinsurgency and the Historical Rise of the Social* (Cambridge: Cambridge University Press, 2015).

revealed "waterboarding." Media reports on the documents were easily digestible, horrifying but comprehensible: a statement about waterboarding and a quote from the White House press spokesperson. Much of the media's questioning quickly became about whether the practice could be justified.

The decontextualizations of the documents found their worldly analogues in the self-important voices of *The Wall Street Journal*'s editorials and the talking heads of the cable news networks, who discussed the day's newsworthy revelations in ahistorical and apolitical terms. Waterboarding became something to be talked about as if in a philosophy class: what level of pain might constitute torture? In these undergraduate debates, waged each morning in the op-ed pages of American newspapers and each evening on the primetime talk shows, waterboarding was not done in a particular place (a black site) to a particular person (Abu Zubaydah) by a named CIA operative (we still don't know Mr. ▮'s name), but was done by no one, to a reasonable man, who would then be paraded before a theoretical court of law (if there was a ticking bomb, would you…). That there was no ticking bomb and little adherence to laws natural or otherwise at DETENTION SITE GREEN made little difference to the abstract formulations of the American media, for the torture occurred in the black. The redactions of these media abstractions enabled (I don't say caused) the violence that occurred at the black sites by creating a fantastical justification for it.

The public debate on waterboarding didn't just echo the narrative presented in the redacted documents — it reprised the way of thinking one finds in them. In the torture memos, there is a great deal of concern, not for the prisoners, but for that sad injured party of jurisprudence, the reasonable man, on whom television's talking heads love to dwell. Under Title 18 of the US code §§ 2340–2340A, for an act to be considered torture, it requires someone to both cause severe pain and have the intention to do so. Large parts of the torture memos are devoted to showing that the particular practice in question — say, waterboarding — could not be reasonably expected to cause severe pain, and thus, if one were to — as Mr. ▮ might — engage in that particular practice, well then one could not — of course — reasonably be thought to intend to cause severe pain, and thus — of course — one would not be torturing the detainee.

In all this casuistry, there was little information about the detainees themselves, and almost nothing that was unredacted about what was actually happening in confinement. There was also no account of Mr. ▮'s actual intentions. Rather, intentionality was a legal category, to be established in advance. The CIA turned to lawyers to provide reasonable intentions for future interrogations: prefabricated shadows of future acts, worked out in Washington for deployment in Waziristan. The actions would happen regardless, but they were in need of prêt-à-porter intentions. In the torture memos, the body dematerializes into a set of legal and psychological conditions. Actual bodies are beside the point when you can hold on to the reassurances of a good intention. It wasn't just that the public discussion of torture took place in a realm of theoretical imperatives; that's where the bureaucratic imaginary of torture took place, too. What the redacted documents revealed was the degree to which the entire war on terror occurred in a fantastical realm, curiously divorced from the truths of broken bodies and souls.

It would only be years later that we would learn many of the concrete details of the torture program: the nudity and the violence, the nights spent standing up and the days spent confined to a coffin. Despite the great claims made by the CIA about the utility of its interrogations, we also learned about the stories spun by the detainees, tortured Scheherazades who constructed fantastical tales at a scale large enough to satisfy their tormentors. The bloodless legal fantasies of the documents produced the bloodied dreams of the detainees.[16]

Fig. 4.9.

(TS/▮▮▮▮▮▮/NF) The information relayed from ALEC Station to RDG in July 2003 for CIA leadership also included information from a CIA assessment entitled "Significant Detainee Reporting."[1098] That document included information that was largely congruent with CIA records. It stated that KSM provided details on the Heathrow Airport Plot and the Karachi Plots only after being confronted with the capture of Khallad bin Attash and Ammar al-Baluchi;[1099] that with regard to plots inside the United States, KSM had only admitted to plots that had been abandoned or already disrupted; that KSM fabricated information in order to tell CIA interrogators "what he thought they wanted to hear"; and that KSM generally only provided information when "boxed in" by information already known to CIA debriefers.[1100] This information was not included in CIA representations to policymakers later that month.

None of this appeared in initial newspaper reports on waterboarding. How could it? The violence didn't appear in the documents. Instead of focusing on the treatment of Abu Zubaydah, it was the reasonable man of the torture memos who was given a starring role in the philosophical debates of the cable news networks, and who provided the discursive imaginary for a legal fantasy of the war on terror, in which psychologists and lawyers oversaw legitimate, controlled violence, whose use was always subservient to political ends.

All too quickly, I grew disgruntled with the media's role as a government echo chamber. Our discoveries felt scripted. Public debate and redacted documents alike encouraged us to treat waterboarding outside of its context, and not consider it as one instance of a much broader problem of American counterterrorism practice, whose roots and reasons, I was increasingly convinced, were much more complicated than anything I could gesture at in a newspaper article.

There were two overlapping worlds of redaction. Some redactions — before a black marker was even applied to a document — occurred in the minds of the lawyers and military officers who wrote the memos and reports that I would read in redacted form. These were mental redactions, object lessons in how not to know, which enabled Mr. ▮▮▮ to conceive of humans as objects, to be processed for information and then discarded. For Mr. ▮▮▮, the detainee became part of a flow chart: a series of potentialities, to be fine-tuned using EITs, much as an Amazon employee is fine-tuned through surveillance and punishment. The detainee was a thought experiment given flesh. The violence of this mode of reasoning was what totally vanished from the press coverage of the redacted documents, yet it was this form of abstract fictionality that I was convinced was the neces-

---

16 The excerpt below is from Senate Intelligence Committee Report, 212.

sary condition for the practices of the war on terror, and it was this fantasy, I knew, that we could learn about from the redacted documents. We needed to look into the black.

Sitting with my journalist friends, I wanted to shout out, as if at a British Punch and Judy show: he's behind you! Except, as my colleagues continually pointed out, there was nothing there, and no one can write about nothing. Not for a newspaper.

* * *

It was due to my dissatisfaction with journalism that I sat down in a sweltering room in Mombasa, Kenya, in September 2010, and began work on what would become the *Grammar of Redaction*, the text in which I first developed many of the ideas about narrative focalization and anonymous subjectivity that I explore above.[17] I wrote the *Grammar* in two bursts — in Kenya and then during a writing residency at the Dar Al-Ma'mûn, in Marrakech, Morocco — in a rare spirit of elation. Finally, I was no longer tracking the beast through its habitat. No longer looking for facts, hidden under black surfaces. Instead, I attended only to surfaces, only to the black.

Instead of treating the redactions as absences, I treated them as presences, with a content all their own. I was convinced that by attending to the forms of secrecy created by the documents, the grammar of redaction, I could understand a lot about the stories created by the war on terror. The *Grammar* was not an unveiling of the redactions, but an attempt to trace the logic of the veiling itself. It deployed the tools of literary analysis to study what happens when redacted subjects do things to redacted objects. In one section of the *Grammar*, "Objects without subjects," I analyzed what happens when the only names in the texts are those of the "terrorists," and Mr. ▮ emerges as our anonymous anti-hero. In other texts, in contrast, it is the verbs that disappear, and subjects do unmentionable things to someone, before, in a temporary moment of visibility, the text announces that the detainee appears to be co-operating and so the EITs can be stopped — what's visible is only that the law is being followed. There is a world in the documents, I thought, if one considers them on their own terms, in which redactions make meaning, and these meanings run parallel to state practice, inflecting it, co-constituting it, and offering us a mirror through which we might learn about its violence.

One section of the *Grammar's* typology, for instance, was called "Hidden Cities," and examined the locative omissions of the documents, from the White House to Bagram Air Base. The black spaces of the documents

---

17 *Grammar of Redaction* was exhibited at the New Museum in New York in Fall 2014 as part of the Temporary Center for Translation, and is available to read here: https://www.joshuacraze.com/s/A-Grammar-of-Redaction-Joshua-Craze-fj56.pdf. An excerpt from this grammar was published in Anthony Downey, ed., *Dissonant Archives: Contemporary Visual Culture and Contested Narratives in the Middle East* (London: I.B. Tauris, 2015).

mirrored the black sites in Somalia, Thailand, and elsewhere.[18] What is acknowledged and undefined in the world is acknowledged and undefined in the documents; not so much redactions as visualizations of our actuality.[19]

Fig. 4.10. The issue of how to approach interrogations reportedly came to a head after the capture of a senior al Qaeda leader, Abu Zubaydah, during a raid in Faisalabad, Pakistan in late March 2002. Abu Zubaydah was transported to a "black site," a secret CIA prison facility ███████████████ where he was treated for gunshot wounds he suffered during his capture.

In the beginning of my work with redacted documents, I had wanted to complete my jigsaw of the world. Fill in the blanks. Eventually, we came to know that DETENTION SITE GREEN was in Ban Dung District, Udon Thani province, Thailand. That didn't resolve the real problem, however, which was that the world is full of holes. The redacted mind writing the documents and the obscure sites of state control were not barriers to getting the story: they were the story. I think in wanting to simply fill in the blanks and bring detention to light, I wanted to bypass the way our world is sutured by absence. Any account we give of the war on terror has to include these holes within it, as a necessary and fundamental part of the conflict's functioning. One cannot complete the jigsaw. Rather, one must be attentive to the silences of the map and the darkness of the documents.[20] If one looks at them carefully, they reveal the outlines of our present.

Fig. 4.11. EITs were also used on Khalid Sheik Muhammed (KSM), a high-ranking al Qaeda official who, according to media reports, was captured in Pakistan on March 1, 2003, ███████ to a CIA black site ███████ CIA officers have been quoted in the media as saying that KSM was defiant to his captors and was extremely resistant to EITs, including the waterboard.

---

18 A decade later, many of these countries still refuse to acknowledge that there were CIA secret prisons on their territory. The sites remain part of a regulative fantasy: a public secret about which we know not to know *too much* about.
19 The excerpt below is from OPR Report, 32.
20 The excerpt below is from OPR Report, 87.

Jane Jin Kaisen
Of Specters or Returns

Jane Jin Kaisen, *Of Specters or Returns*, 2020. Installation. 7 red acrylic boxes with UV-printed texts, handcrafted oak light boxes, unique objects collected by the artist in North Korea, South Korea, Denmark, and the US. Dimensions of boxes range from 57×67×57 cm to 103×66×76 cm. © Jane Jin Kaisen, 2020. Images courtesy of the artist.

The objects include: an antique mirror from the Koryo Dynasty, an American chemical weapons kit, a Korean War US ammunitions box, artillery shells, a landmine detector, Royal Danish porcelain, a *hanbok* from the 1950s, a South Korean matchbox from the 1970s with an image of the Little Mermaid, a blood-stained South Korean military police helmet from the 1980s democracy movement, a Sony cassette player, a Japanese lunchbox from the 1950s, a World War II Japanese military mirror, a 1950s US army Korean War psychological warfare propaganda leaflet, a rice tray, *gime* cotton string used in shamanic rituals on Jeju Island, a pamphlet from the Frøslev Camp, brass candle holders, army straps, Buddhist candles, a tin soldier figure, a kerosene lamp, a celadon vase, yarn and a sewing kit, and books, including Kate Fleron's *Fra Nordkorea: Indtryk fra en Rejse til Verdens Ende* (*From North Korea: Impressions from the End of the World*) published in 1952, *We Accuse! Report of the Commission of the Women's International Democratic Federation in Korea,* May 16 to 27, 1951, and the North Korean *38th Parallel North,* published in 1995.

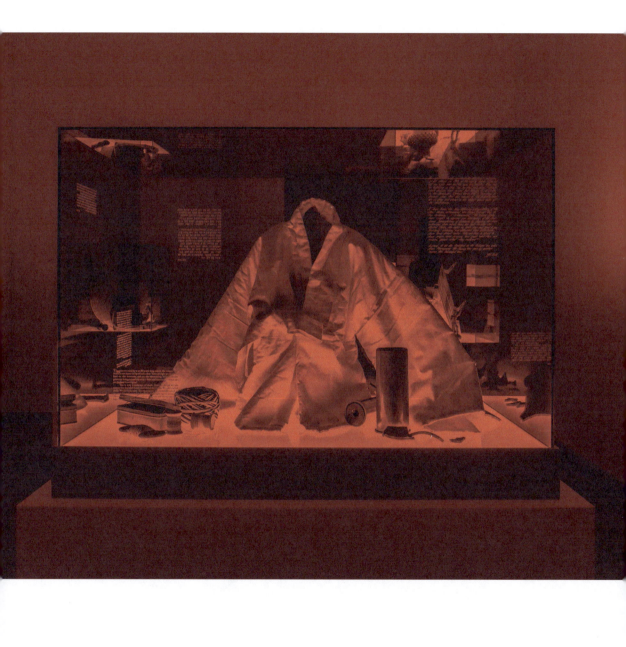

Letters from the Depthless Deep

Lisa Min

Dear comrade

                      years since we saw one another

                              the Laibach concert   a blurry photograph
     a book
          our faces

                            you

  I missed you

     bullshit

                                  not a possible thing to say
                                                                       how

I'm sorry.

I began by writing letters to my north Korean interlocutors, the people who were "in charge" of me on my trips there—comrades, really—that eventually became an essay titled "Redactd Letters to the Other Korea."[1] Knowing I would never send these letters, I just wrote them, writing things I never would have let myself write, remembering things I wanted to say but could never brave in the moment, and asking questions I wanted to ask but could only mutter, for I knew not the consequences of the things I said. I wrote them by hand, these thoughts flooding in: flashes of conversations, fragments, images, none of it adequate to the encounter or even satisfying. Then I went over the letters with the heavy hand of a sharpie, crossing out things that caught my eye, marking away in thick lines what could be read as suspicious. At the time I was struggling to articulate my fieldwork experience in north Korea, so I was willing to try anything that would get me to keep writing.

It was more a performance of a letter then, one that imagined a form of saying in the context of an unbounded and unmarked terrain of communication, the thick black lines becoming something like guardrails.

This struck me as a potentially powerful way to convey something of my work in north Korea because there one cannot ignore the vigilant, fervent desire from the outside that wants so earnestly to expose and unveil its innermost inside, its "real." I wanted to make room in the pressing hold of this tendency, and to make space for all of the moments that suggested something outside the truth/lie, oppression/resistance binary distinctions so often put upon this place.[2] Redaction became a way to write through an "intimate distance."[3] That is, redaction was form, was form-making of a sociality that exists within, through, and ultimately because of the very space of the redacted. It was not with or against the state, but it demarcated moments within and without its very unboundedness.

As I think more about what I am trying to convey, something like a sociality of open secrets, I have come to imagine the form of redaction differently. That perhaps the starting point is not an expectation of transparency with redactions overlaid upon it, but something more at home with secrecy, more intimate, and inseparable that renders entire fields of vision strewn with redacted patches. This seems less a confrontation with hidden things on an open page, than an emergence of fragments and inhabitable moments rising to the surface from a "depthless depth." I borrow

---

1   Lisa Min, "Redacted Letters to the Other Korea," *Interactions* 27, no. 2 (2020): 90–91.
2   I am thinking with Alexei Yurchak's notion of "binary socialism," a tendency to reduce Soviet reality to "a binary division between the state (censored) and the society beyond it (uncensored)," which then fails to account for the social forms that emerge in the overlap of these supposedly separate, antagonistic domains. Alexei Yurchak, *Everything Was Forever, Until It Was No More: The Last Soviet Generation* (Princeton: Princeton University Press, 2006), 6.
3   Lisa Min, "North Korea So Far: Distance and Intimacy, Seen and Unseen" (PhD Diss., University of California, Berkeley, 2020). See also Lisa Min, Hoon Song, and John Lie, eds., *North Korea Seen and Unseen* (Berkeley: University of California Press, forthcoming).

the expression from Maurice Blanchot who writes of depthless depth as immeasurable distance, as image, as an "indeterminate milieu of fascination" that is "absolutely present although not given."[4] This is what brings me to the black. The darkness of the page is a stage of "sightless, shapeless depth, the absence one sees because it is blinding."[5] And to write from the black, to engage redaction within its vast corners, is to return language to the depthless deep, an "empty opening onto that which is when there is no more world, when there is no world yet."[6]

In this inversion of redaction, I shift focus to the negative, the depthless deep of ethnographic experience in which I dis-locate my self writing. I grapple with a self unmoored in the way Katherine Verdery describes in the prologue to *My Life As a Spy*, where she encounters her double in the Romanian Securitate files, a double that is multiple and boundless. This "unmooring" for Verdery is materialized in the way her file has been archived, "the documents in each of its eleven volumes follow no chronological order at all. [...] It was chaotic, mystifying."[7] She struggles to make sense of "the mishmash of times and places, the perplexing organization of the documents that made them usable to officers but impenetrable to anyone else."[8] There are "layers" to contend with that compose a "world of their own."[9] Standing on the other side of redaction looking back, with access to the jumbled traces of this doubled self, she copies and reorganizes her secret police file in chronological order to better locate herself within its pages. She attempts to "domesticate" the file, to find a way to enter it.[10] Her aim is to "decompose the monolithic 'totalitarian' identity of the Securitate and in the process bring together the fragments that constitute my [her] own," and yet she maintains, "[t]o be honest, I don't actually know what this book is."[11]

I take this to mean she is writing from something like this deep. That there is something of a "totalitarian" notion of self she seems to be unraveling that holds implications for how we imagine and go about fieldwork and write up those experiences, but that also asks if we are equipped to think about secrets, to make sense of them, and to live with, through, and because of them.

---

4   Maurice Blanchot, "The Essential Solitude," in *The Space of Literature*, trans. Ann Smock (Lincoln: University of Nebraska Press, 1982), 32.
5   Ibid., 33.
6   Ibid.
7   Katherine Verdery, *My Life as a Spy: Investigations in a Secret Police File* (Durham: Duke University Press, 2018), 8.
8   Ibid.
9   Ibid., 11–12, 15.
10 Ibid., 11.
11 Ibid., 28–29.

Dear comrade

                                                          midnight

                drank too much

                                      Pyongyang

                  lost track of time

            the guard   the gate   the yelling

the van

                a curfew

You didn't tell me and I didn't ask

                            smoke

WeChat, August 2020

"Death to all modifiers, he declared one day, and out of every letter that passed through his hands went every adverb and every adjective. The next day he made war on articles. He reached a much higher plane of creativity the following day when he blacked out everything in the letters but a, an and the. That erected more dynamic intralinear tensions, he felt, and in just about every case left a message far more universal."

— John Yossarian, in Joseph Heller, *Catch-22: A Novel* (New York: The Modern Library, 1961).

Anonymously posted article that went viral on the Chinese internet with over a 100,000w views within three days. It was censored and removed on the fourth day.

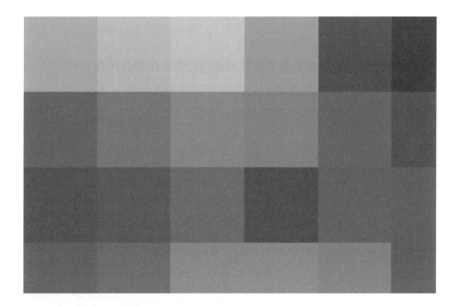

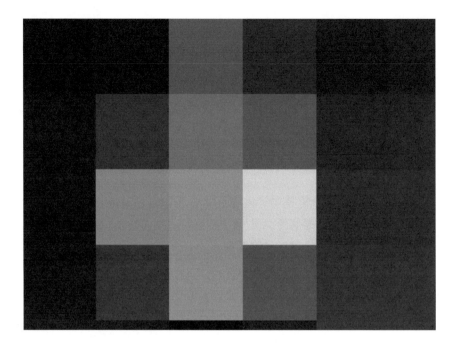

Disappearing the Cofounders
The Story of Imagine, a Language School in Xinjiang

M▇▇▇▇▇▇▇ and Darren Byler

This short essay tells the stories of how two of our mutual Uyghur friends have disappeared into the "reeducation" system in Northwest China over the past few years. Utilizing redaction as a modality of autonomy and anti-colonial protection, we explore our friend's biographies and how they are interwoven with our own — writing in all of the sensitive things that could never be said in public and then redacting those parts to see how the stories of their lives are altered. In the next stage in our process we consider how the nonfiction stories of our friends' lives can be placed in conversation with a fictional novella written about an earlier political campaign. The story that emerges is a coded and partial, yet truthful, echo of this earlier moment of state violence, restaged for an imagined community that has been through repeated collective trauma.

*

D▇▇▇▇ was eccentric. He was ahead of his time. It's not often that you find a son of a local Uyghur bureaucrat in rural southern Xinjiang, who is also a huge fan of John Lennon and Queen. Neither of us actually liked him very much at first. He was paler than most Uyghurs; behind his back some even called him "Smeagol" after the character in the *Lord of the Rings* trilogy that was popular at the time among Uyghur young people.[1] He had some twitches, his eyes darting around, and he seemed nervous and a little bit shy. He would look around everywhere to make sure no one was eavesdropping before saying something that was not even that secretive or politically sensitive. He was a nerd and was very much into philosophical books. He was a huge fan of Friedrich Nietzsche and particularly loved his book *Thus Spoke Zarathustra*.[2] In Uyghur culture, even non-pious people who drink alcohol and do not practice the daily Islamic rituals and prayers dare not

---

1 J.R.R. Tolkien, *The Lord of the Rings* (London: George Allen & Unwin, 1954–1955).
2 Friedrich Nietzsche, *Thus Spoke Zarathustra: A Book for All and None*, trans. Walter Kaufmann (New York: Viking Press, 1954).

criticize God. For many, it's a forbidden topic. But D▮▮▮ was a rare nonconformist in a culture that largely expects its members to conform to the dominant doctrine and maintain a certain public persona. He would tout Nietzsche's phrase "God is Dead, and we have killed him," as a thought that was truly liberating and could not stop talking about its merits. Later he picked up the habit of compulsively smoking Number 8 cigarettes. The little white box became his signature brand. He was very serious, and he had trivia to share about nearly everything. For instance, he knew all about Yoko Ono and her effect on the Beatles. He named the private language school he cofounded with one of the authors of this essay "Imagine" because of John Lennon. He taught every Uyghur student he met about that song.

Another cofounder of the school, A▮▮, was an exuberant character. He would constantly shake his head to move his hair out of his eyes. He was exactly the opposite of D▮▮▮. He had never read a book from cover to cover before he came to the city. But he could talk with anyone. He wasn't very political in terms of what he cared about, but he was a schmoozer. They called him a *shapak* (watermelon rind). If a woman stepped on a *shapak*, she would slip. She would fall for him. But he was not into any serious long-term relationships. He wasn't really a serious person at first. *Suyok* (liquid), they said. He moved like water, from one girl to the next or one position to the next depending on what the context was and who he was with. He was truly a Uyghur Bruce Lee — even though he didn't know Lee's catchphrase "be like water." He was baby-faced, never aging. We don't know anyone who didn't like him. Except D▮▮▮.

A▮▮ thought that D▮▮▮ was always lying. D▮▮▮ did exaggerate. He made definitive statements about things he doesn't know much about. And D▮▮▮ thought A▮▮ was uneducated, and not a serious intellectual worthy of the title *Muellim* (teacher). And maybe D▮▮▮ was a bit jealous of the attention A▮▮ always got wherever he went. A▮▮ didn't really go to a four-year college like many Uyghur intellectuals. He went to a junior college and then finally got into an extension program at Medical University. This was a really sensitive topic for him. And D▮▮▮ knew that A▮▮ saw this as something he could lord over him.

The three cofounders, D▮▮▮, A▮▮, and M▮▮▮, one of them an author of this essay, were from local government employee families in rural areas. But they also weren't farmers. Their parents could afford to send them to college, even if they didn't have more than 400 yuan ($55 USD) per month to give them. They would spend about one yuan for breakfast, five or six for lunch, two or three for dinner.

When they first got real money by teaching English, they got expensive clothes. They thought they were always on stage and they needed good clothes. So they spent a lot of money on clothes; if they were paid 1,000 yuan for one month of teaching they might spend 800 yuan on clothes. D▮▮▮ always bought Younger brand suits and shirts, and expensive leather shoes. They always did their shopping together, with M▮▮▮ helping them to get along. They had the same suits and brands. They needed to advertise. Everyone knew that formal clothes were a sign of success and what you needed if you wanted to impress. They were business people. Big shots. Life was good.

But they had to rely on Han connections in order to operate their school. Their Han business partners could get the permits because of their ethnicity. At the height of their school, they had 1,200 students, but they had to lease a license and pay a share of the money they made in tuition to those Han partners, who acted as school bosses. They were like really successful tenant farmers, but in knowledge production instead of agriculture.

They were never bereft of discrimination. They lost 90,000 yuan because they renovated a space they rented. The building managers who were Han were fine with this. But when the neighbors saw the Uyghur students in the classroom they started complaining. They said, "your students are peeing in the hallway." Or, "you can only teach on the weekends." At first the complaint was that the noise disturbed the neighbors when they were working. The founders avoided scheduling any classes from 8:00–5:00 during workdays. But then they complained that the students might break into their offices and steal their things. They reported the school to the local police, educational bureau authorities, and anyone who could suspend its operations. Step by step they pushed the school out. Even though the founders were still paying the rent and the classroom was in excellent condition, they were prevented from using that space at all. It was right in front of Xinjiang Normal University. People that lived in that building were all Han. The residents thought that Uyghur people were uncivilized. M▮ recounted that the Han residents had no problem lying about the Uyghurs or openly used racial slurs or stereotypes to discriminate against them. They imposed whatever far-flung ideas they conjured up on them. Ultimately, the government and the neighbors were just suspicious regardless of what they did. The Han neighbors didn't want to allow them any freedom at all. But the school was making so much money, that the founders just shrugged off losing 90,000 yuan.

Because of such overt instances of daily ethno-racism, one of the common topics of the founders' daily conversations was the lack of political representation and genuine autonomy, and how the entire system of governance in China was built on lies and deception. At every level, the government officials would get by through faking and bribery. The founders knew that low-level bureaucrats would be very arrogant and condescending towards them, but before someone who is even just slightly above them in the officialdom, the same bureaucrats would be minions, groveling like dogs trying to please their owners. The founders felt there was absolutely no concept of the equality or dignity of human beings in this system.

A common joke they often told among themselves was the one from a famous Chinese classical novel *Journey to the West* by Wu Cheng'en, in which the Tang dynasty Buddhist monk Xuanzang goes to obtain the sacred texts of Buddhism.[3] There were countless trials and tribulations along the journey and the monk was nearly killed in many instances by monsters

---

3   Wu Cheng'en, *Journey to the West*, trans. Anthony C. Yu (Chicago: University of Chicago Press, 1977).

and evil spirits. Eventually Xuanzang arrived at their destination and met the living Buddha. However, they could not get access to Buddha and had to bribe his assistants to get past the guards and obtain the holy texts. What was striking is that even in obtaining literally holy texts they encountered bureaucratic hurdles in the court of Buddha and had to resort to bribery.

When they found themselves encumbered by intentionally placed administrative obstacles in running their school, they sometimes shared the story as a catharsis to cope with the difficulties of Chinese officialdom. If such deception and treachery are so ingrained in the culture that even the business of God had to follow those unspoken rules, of course they would treat a minority population this way. They also often compared the Chinese government to an abusive partner in a relationship. They did not want to have this relationship, but they were forced into this arranged marriage. However, the other side was so abusive and brutal that they would want to leave. But they were not allowed to leave. Even if they gave up everything, the abusive sociopath, the oppressive Chinese state, would not let them live in peace. It seemed they were abused for the sake of the state displaying its immense power. It seemed they would be treated like this as long as they lived, as there was no hoping of ending the relationship or getting out of it.

D[REDACTED] read a lot of books that were written by both Chinese and foreigners. One of his favorite subjects to read and talk about was Mao Zedong. He would often relish the details about the private life of Mao he read in *Mao: The Unknown Story* by Jung Chang and Jon Halliday, and in *The Private Life of Chairman Mao* by Mao's personal physician Li Zhisui.[4] These books painted a portrait of Mao unlike anything he had ever read in Uyghur or Chinese. They told of the viciousness of Mao and how he held grudges for decades against his political rivals and did not spare anyone, even his most loyal lieutenants; they told of how he often relied on deceit, backstabbing, vengeance, and tactical retreat in his quest for unlimited power. D[REDACTED] particularly enjoyed telling them many quirky details about Mao's life such as his habit of never brushing his teeth, rinsing his mouth in green tea instead, or his dislike for showers, preferring to rub his body with a wet towel. Mao's bed was also something that fascinated D[REDACTED]. He told them how Mao always had huge stacks of books on his bed (maybe this was something that he secretly admired about Mao) and that he even hauled the bed all the way to Moscow when he visited the USSR in 1950 instead of using the luxurious beds in Soviet state guest houses. But what was most fascinating about his bed was Mao's insatiable appetite for sex with young girls, and how he often slept with multiple so-called nurses on his bed. Although they did not grow up worshipping Mao like their parents' generation, they had never imagined him as a person, not to mention with such vulgar and debasing habits. In retrospect, sharing such despicable aspects of the life of the Communist Party leader was again a

---

4   Jung Chang and Jon Halliday, *Mao: The Unknown Story* (London: Jonathan Cape, 2005), and Li Zhisui, *The Private Life of Chairman Mao: The Memoirs of Mao's Personal Physician*, ed. Anne F. Thurston, trans. Hongchao Dai (New York: Random House, 1994).

way for them to deal with and rationalize why they were treated so poorly by the party and its henchmen. After all, every leader since Mao had to rely on despicable means to survive in a brutal world of inner-party politics and get to its top leadership position. But they also privately hoped that such regimes never lasted for the long term, and they were always excited at the slightest hint of intensifying inner-party conflicts or at an unanticipated disaster engulfing the communist party. They thought maybe that would bring down the party, and that that would get rid of the brutal dictatorship.

Another way they would implicitly resist the system was through their teaching. Yes, they were teaching English, but they were also teaching about democratic ideals, human dignity, and freedom. Such class content came naturally when using English materials that were not from textbooks. They often relied on movie clips or famous speeches as texts, and read and interpreted them in class. For example, one of D█████'s favorite movie clips was a battle speech in *Braveheart* starring Mel Gibson; he used it in almost every class he taught. In the scene, William Wallace was rallying the Scottish fighters before a mighty English army. He was the hero of the local people fighting against a foreign invasion. The similarity to their own situation as a colonized people in China was never lost on the students. D█████ had fully memorized the speech and would show the clip first and then interpret each line to the students. He would particularly emphasize "I AM William Wallace. And I see a whole army of my countrymen here in defiance of tyranny. You have come to fight as free men, and free men you are. What would you do with that freedom? Will you fight? ... tell our enemies that they may take our lives, but they'll never take our freedom!!!"[5] These lines would resonate with the students, their emotions quite palpable. The students were just spellbound as they watched. D█████ gave them permission to stand and shout at the top of their lungs: "They may take our lives, but they'll never take our freedom!" It became a participatory melodrama, the movie transposed into a Uyghur classroom. For a moment they felt their power as autonomous actors, the makers of their own destinies.

Their subjugated and colonized positionality was emphasized and brought to the fore in such class presentations. While they could not talk about tyranny or freedom in any other public space even if it was a reality of life and a daily struggle for every Uyghur, learning and practicing English gave them the perfect excuse to talk about these ideals and form a bond with the students that they could never feel in any state-run educational institution. In fact, they would have been detained and beaten or worse if such a large group of Uyghurs gathered and talked about freedom and fighting against tyranny. But oppression and everyday racism were so sharp that teaching English in a Uyghur-only space provided them an outlet for those pent-up emotions and frustrations. Of course, they were acutely aware that there were limits to what they could say, but it was unclear exactly where the boundaries were. It always felt like they were trying

---

5   Mel Gibson, dir., *Braveheart* (Paramount Pictures, 1995).

to find those invisible red lines, even in the relative safety of that space. It was a tightrope that they had to walk every day.

Ultimately it was that possibility of falling off the tightrope that led them to make different life decisions. M▮ went abroad to study in the US, leaving everything he knew behind in China. D▮ had no intention of leaving as he saw himself as a beacon and light there, and wanted to do the best he could to teach English and spread these ideals. And it was impossible for him to obtain a passport. A▮ hesitated, as was his character, changing his plans from one context to the next. Ultimately, this decided the respective fates of the three cofounders. Even now there is no word about the whereabouts of D▮. A▮ was put in a concentration camp for almost two years before he was released and put under strict surveillance. A▮ was detained the first time because his students vanished in Malaysia — from the perspective of state authorities the only reason someone might flee the country was if they were wanting to become terrorists. "What did you know about these guys?" the police asked him. They had shared some meals. He actually knew them really well, so he got into a lot of trouble. He has probably been on a watchlist ever since then.

*

Before they were finally detained, the government did everything to restrict their autonomy. It forced them to question how much of the oppression they faced was due to their ethnicity and how much of it was just because they were poor. Maybe migrants from other places also experienced discrimination. But it was clear that any incident in the South — the vast Uyghur homeland in Southern Xinjiang — had an indirect effect on them. The hostility they experienced from the Han residents, some of whom were also migrants, was constant, an everyday low simmer.

They always critiqued the system obliquely in the classroom, often using class content as excuses. For example, when they taught the word "congress," or the People's *dahuitang* as it was known in Chinese. The prefix "con" means together. "Gress" means to walk. They would explain that "congress" means "a large convention that people walk into together." They would use the opportunity to teach this word as a way to mock the People's Congress Annual Session that takes place in Beijing around March each year. They would ridicule the fact that it was only during that one week in March when people from all ethnic backgrounds in China are forced or allowed to wear their traditional national outfits, hold hands in socialist harmony, and walk happily together. They would remark, "remember the great ethnic unity when we hold hands and walk happily into the People's Hall for the annual session of the congress?" The students were fully aware that if Uyghurs were to wear those traditional outfits to work, they would be fired on the spot. So it was a way to poke fun at the system and deride its absurdity and fraudulent nature. While explaining congress, they would bring up another word that is made up of a similar word root: "aggression." Again, the word root "gress" means to walk. And the prefix "ag" simply emphasizes or reinforces the meaning, suggesting walking too much. They would illustrate that when Japan didn't stay within their borders and walked too much, they ended up walking halfway across China in the 1930s and 1940s and occupying the land as their colony. That's why Japan is referred to as the aggressor in Chinese history textbooks. Even though they used the historical example, everyone in class knew that they were implicitly referring to the Chinese communist party and its armed forces as the aggressors, and their presence in the Uyghur homeland as aggression.

M▆ still vividly remembers July 5, 2009 — the day when there were large protests, police violence, and eventually inter-ethnic killing across the city of Urumqi. On that day, he and A▆ worked on a poster for their English language school.

> We were at a building next to Xinjiang University that afternoon and could see Shengli Road, the main street leading all the way to People's Square. Around 4:00 pm we began to notice sudden increase in foot traffic on the road and began hearing reports that the protests that took place at the People's Square were dispersed by the armed police and that protestors were marching back to the south of the city, the Uyghur majority part of Urumqi. We decided that we would not have time to finish the rest of the poster. He looked at me, "why don't we go home and avoid the chaos?" He had a car and dropped me off at my home and went back. Neither of us had any idea that the night would witness a series of events that would have a far-reaching impact on life in the Uyghur homeland and would forever change the course of history in the region for everyone.
>
> Later that night, we began to receive some messages that the protests in some sections of the town turned violent and protestors began smashing store windows, passing cars, and beat Han people, leading to loss of innocent lives. A▆'s apartment was in a building facing the major street in the area that saw one of the worst outbursts of smashing and rioting on that tragic day. He was watching everything unfolding. He called me around 7:00 pm and we started exchanging notes about what we heard, then he went, "Wow, I am looking out my window now and see a bunch of men running towards the bus station. One smashed the front window of a parked bus. Unbelievable. They just lit up the bus in fire." With that the rioters burned about half a dozen or so buses at the bus station in front of his apartment complex. But not much after that, no phone calls could come through and we could not send any text messages. The internet was completely shut down. I only learned the next day that soon after we talked, a large number of police arrived and began arresting anyone on the street. He took some videos of police hitting and cuffing them. For a while he kept those video files in his phone, but the government began threatening people that if they found any unauthorized photo or video materials in people's devices, they would be severely punished. A▆ deleted the photos to avoid such harassment.

Growing up, the cofounders often heard traumatic stories from their parents about their experiences during the Cultural Revolution (1966–1976). Many of those stories were very similar to the ones that Memtimin Hoshur recounts in his novella *Classmates,* which is set during that campaign and which we will discuss more in the conclusion: innocent people being paraded through the street and given lengthy prison sentences for no reason, good friends turning on each other just to survive and get ahead, absurd yet ridiculous practices of denouncing elders and other respectable members of the community, and countless other irrational behaviors.[6] At the time, the cofounders thought that people in the 1950s and 1960s were simple and naïve to believe the propaganda of the Maoist mass campaign, and that now they were much more educated and had more information about the world, so nobody would be foolish enough to engage in those practices.

After July 5, they began to sense a shift. Things they took for granted suddenly disappeared. They had no access to the internet for almost a year in the entire region. Nobody thought it would be possible to cut off internet access to a space that large for a year, but they lived through that. D███ and M█████ could make a decent living by teaching English without being dependent on a government job, but they had many classmates from college who did not have any marketable skills in the private sector, or did not think it would be a wise career choice to not work for the government after investing all that money in a college education. One of the easiest and most lucrative career paths was to join the State Security Bureau. M█████ alone had at least six friends who made this choice: A████, A████, A███, Y████, N███, and A████. A████ and A████ joined the █ branch of the State Security Bureau. Others worked for the regional office in Urumqi. In a nutshell, these friends were all hired to spy on their fellow Uyghurs, gather intelligence, and maintain the police state in the region.

While they were all in college, these classmates were no different from any of the others. They were all aspiring to do well after graduation and make their mark in the world, like any young college student anywhere in the world. However, a divide grew and gradually more independent-thinking, entrepreneurial-spirited young Uyghur men like A███, D█████ and M████ found themselves increasingly at odds with their friends who worked for the state security and intelligence agencies. There were still gatherings of classmates, and plenty of drinking and karaoke singing. But the group dynamic was different. They were not equals anymore. Financially, as successful education entrepreneurs A███, D████, and M█████ were better off than their peers. For example, A████ bought a Citroen C4, a hatchback passenger sedan, after getting his share of the profit from teaching English for one semester. M█████ purchased an apartment with cold, hard cash. Many of their classmates working for the government and security apparatus would have to save for years and commit a lot of unconscionable acts against their fellow Uyghurs to save that much money and

---

6 Memtimin Hoshur, *The Classmates,* trans. M. and Darren Byler (manuscript forthcoming).

to be able to afford those things. But those Uyghurs working in the state security and intelligence agencies felt that they were protected, since the government was a shield for them whereas the cofounders were vulnerable and unprotected.

When they gathered for class reunions or other celebrations such as weddings or birthdays, they would talk to each other about their work in a way to show us how powerful they were. M▇ still remembers an exchange A▇ and Y▇ had about detaining a group of Uyghurs and how their disparate units almost had a physical fight over who had found out about the group first and had legitimate right to arrest the group. From the way they talked, it sounded like they were in a horse race for a prize, and A▇ was upset that he and his unit lost out on a major financial award from the bureau because they did not arrest the group first. In many such gatherings, it became clear that they were motivated more by the financial gains from finding intelligence or evidence to arrest people than by anything else. In some ways, the two types of Uyghur young men were quite alike. They all wanted to recruit and control more Uyghur people and because that would bring them financial rewards. But while their friends were putting Uyghurs in jails and detention centers, and were torturing people and breaking up families, the cofounders were educating other Uyghurs about the ideals of freedom and human dignity, and exposing the viciousness and deceptions of the very system their classmates were actively working to strengthen, the system all of them were all living in.

*

In the Uyghur-language novella from 1985 titled *Classmates*, Memtimin Hoshur echoes many of the dynamics that appear in the lives of the cofounders. The novella is written from the perspective of a young Uyghur man as he is released following ten years of "reeducation through hard labor" during the Maoist Cultural Revolution. As he reintegrates into society and attempts to locate his wife, older brother, and former academic mentor, he recalls the circumstances that brought him to detention. Much of the novella centers around a notebook filled with satirical commentary that he had written in response to the Cultural Revolution. In fact, the protagonist of the novella was guilty of thinking too much, of recognizing the tyranny of ideological campaigns for what they were: a means to build power by manufacturing enemies.

For D▇ and A▇ the evidence used against them was similar. They were guilty of thought crimes. They knew too much about how colonialism works, and they taught others how to recognize it as well just by placing pictures of oppression and absurdity next to each other. Those satirical performances, even with the careful redactions that prevented them from crossing the line into open critique, proved to be too much.

In parallel with the disappearance of D▇ and A▇, the 1985 novella *Classmates* was banned in 2017. It, like their stories of autonomy, acts as a narrative of state violence and Uyghur trauma that has now been redacted. Yet as artifacts that continue to circulate outside of China, their stories offer a narrative of a future potentiality, the promise of stories waiting to be told when the details can finally be unredacted. While D▮▮▮▮▮'s and A▮▮▮'s stories appear suspended in the present, the novella proposes that after the Maoist campaign spaces of truth-telling and reconciliation emerge. For now, we can only dream about returning to the region, visiting each town where we have friends and talking to them about the unredacted version of events that transpired, unbelievable events that they thought could only happen in the old world and could never happen to them now. We are waiting in suspense, waiting to share a white box of Number 8 cigarettes with D▮▮▮▮▮ and see A▮▮▮ flip his hair and move like water. For now, we are forced to listen to John Lennon and imagine when we will see the cofounders reappear.

M. NourbeSe Philip

"Zong! #7"

"Physically manipulating the text helped me in the process over the long run: the very fact of physically mutilating the text broke the spell that the completed text has on us. I use the word 'mutilate' with great deliberation here since I was deeply aware at the time I worked on *Zong!* that the intent of the transatlantic slave trade was to mutilate — languages, cultures, people, communities and histories — in the effort of a great capitalist eliterprise. And I would argue that erasure is intrinsic to colonial and imperial forces. It's an erasure that continues up to the present."

— M. NourbeSe Philip, quoted in Andrew David King, "The Weight of What's Left [Out]: Six Contemporary Erasurists on Their Craft," *The Kenyon Review,* November 6, 2012, https://kenyonreview.org/2012/11/erasure-collaborative-interview.

"While a concern with precision and accuracy in language is common to both law and poetry, the law uses language as a tool for ordering; in the instant case, however, I want poetry to disassemble the ordered, to create disorder and mayhem so as to release the story that cannot be told, but which, through not-telling, will tell itself."

— M. NourbeSe Philip, *Zong! As Told to the Author by Setaey Adamu Boateng* (Middletown: Wesleyan University Press, 2008), 199.

"Zong! #7" from M. NourbeSe Philip, *Zong! As Told to the Author by Setaey Adamu Boateng* (Wesleyan University Press, 2008), 15. Excerpt from a collection of erasure poems generated from the text of the legal decision *Gregson v. Gilbert* on the 1781 incident in which the captain of the slave ship *Zong* ordered some 150 Africans tobe murdered by drowning so that the ship's owners could collect insurance monies.

                                    first:

                                                        the when

                    the which

                                                        the who

               the were

                                    the throwing

  overboard

                                                        the be

                              come apprehended

          exist did not

                    _____
                           Wemusa Ilesanmi Nayo Odai

"What About This One with the Mice?"

Shane Carter

"Not this?"
"Oh my god can you imagine? I'd lose my job."

I'm on Zoom with a high school teacher, looking at photographs of a ceramic vessel from Moche, an ancient Andean society that existed from about the 1st to the 8th century CE. The object under discussion is a ceramic vessel featuring a graphic depiction of a woman performing fellatio on a man. Within the corpus of work from Moche it isn't particularly rare — especially if you do a Google image-search for "Moche ceramics" — and therein lies the issue.

Fig. 10.1. Imagine a photograph of a ceramic vessel. Caption: "Sculptural ceramic ceremonial vessel that represents a fellatio scene." The Museo Larco, in Peru, allows the free use of its images "for educational and research purposes" but not for commercial publication. It's a private museum, founded by Rafael Larco Hoyle in 1926 on the site of the Chiclín *hacienda*. It grew over time, especially as the museum acquired several large collections of ceramics held by various haciendas. An hacienda was a land-grant to Spanish conquistadors. The indigenous inhabitants of the land were granted in tandem with haciendas—or, technically, their labor was granted but not their persons which I suspect was an imperceptible difference for the Indigenous people in question. Artifacts located on the haciendas were a side-benefit of conquest. Clicking through the site feels morally compromising in the same way as looking at an endangered animal in a cage at the zoo.

The vessel itself is a short column, about twice as wide as it is tall, terra-cotta colored, with a beige stirrup-spout attached to one side. That is to say, the vessel's spout is a tube affixed to its (hollow) handle. Perched on top of the vessel is a detailed scene featuring a seated woman in a polka-dot dress. She's looking up at the man standing above her, her head tilted to one side and her mouth wide open. He's bent over her, his chin almost touching her head, his right hand holding his erect penis in the direction of her mouth. According to the explanation, he's wearing a hat and veil that identify him as a priest. The figures are detailed, but unrealistic; his penis is the size of her arm.

The teacher wants his World History students to learn about the Americas prior to their contact with Europe. The usual World History textbook reduces the entire hemisphere's past to a tiny slice of the multi-millennia Maya history, plus a cursory look at the Inca and the Triple Alliance, better known as the Aztec. These three indigenous societies come into just enough focus for students to learn that Spaniards conquered them. Over 15,000 years of human habitation, thousands of societies, pyramids, mummies, art, roads, calendars, irrigation works, chocolate, potatoes: redacted. Redacted? I don't mean written in the text and then blacked out before it goes to students. What do you call it when your mind is trained to neither see nor contemplate a thing that is right in front of you?

This almost complete erasure is sometimes gently explained as resulting from the disciplinary boundaries between history and archaeology: history is based on written texts. Most societies in this hemisphere never developed or adopted writing. Some peoples in parts of Mesoamerica and the Andes did, but the Spaniards burned almost all their records as an intentional tool of conquest. So, almost no extant writing from before 1500 becomes almost no history in this hemisphere before 1500. And the course is called World *History*.

I infer that the teacher has an entirely different, more straightforward calculus. He has students who were born in Latin America. He has students whose parents were born in Latin America. Some of them may identify as Indigenous. Unlike those burned texts, the kids — whatever their exact origins — are emphatically present, in his class. He doesn't want to look at them without seeing them. If he only teaches what is in the textbook, he's implying that their part of the Earth was not part of the World until it was conquered by Europeans. He renders them partly invisible. More positively, the Americas are just fascinating — including, maybe particularly, before a European sets foot in the hemisphere.

We're in a bit of a gray area, curriculum-wise, but expanding beyond the usual Maya–Aztec–Inca trio seems both feasible and justifiable, assuming he can find student-friendly resources. I've collected a set of options related to Moche to run by him, but it turns out the whole enterprise is complicated by the fact that the incredible ceramic arts of Moche don't conform to US standards of classroom-appropriate material. We're sort of laughing as I show him some of the pieces but it's serious business. On any given evening, your average ninth-grade student may be home watching hardcore porn on their phone. And also, on any given evening, your average high school teacher might be previewing a film for class to make sure all its references to sex are oblique and off-screen. By contrast, there is usually much more flexibility around violent imagery. The official and unofficial red lines related to sex and violence differ from one district to another, from year to year, and even from classroom to classroom. Navigating this labyrinth poorly is the kind of thing that costs teachers their jobs.

So I'm sharing the fellatio scene by way of a warning. How many clicks does it take to get from a pot featuring a portrait, for example, to one of the many vessels featuring fellatio, vaginal or anal sex, or mutual masturbation? The childbirth scenes are incredible, but too deeply intertwined with the sex depictions to make them separable. And in any case, it isn't even clear whether childbirth is on the safe side of the line of American prudishness.

"What about this one with the mice?"
"That one's okay. It's a little bit risqué but I think it's a good hook for the kids."

We settle on a page from the Museo Larco site, entitled "Fruits in ancient Peru." Most of the images are of sculpted vessels in the shapes of various foods. One features drawings of peanut plants and mice in silhouette. It's also adorned with a sculpture of two mice vigorously trying to...make more mice.

Most links on the page take you to benign visitor information. Some students may explore the collections database, but it seems unlikely they'll explore in depth. We choose a Google Arts & Culture story about the hero Ai Apaec that features an indistinct sculpture of him having sex with the goddess of the Earth. We select a video mostly about Moche *huacas* — temple complexes. Several minutes in there's a short clip of an archaeologist holding a sex-pot and giving a slightly dry explanation about how Moche cosmology emphasized the circulation of fluids like blood and semen. It's likely students will click away before they get to that scene.

Along with the sex-pots, portrait-pots, and pots depicting plants and animals, Moche artisans repeatedly produced painted vessels featuring what

Fig. 10.2. Imagine a photograph of a ceramic vessel. Caption: "Sexual Union Between Mice, Surrounded by Peanuts," according to the Larco site.

It's a round vessel, spherical except for a flattened base, with handle and a spout that extends out of the center of the top of the sphere. The bottom half of the sphere and the handle are both a terra cotta color. The upper portion is beige, decorated with terra-cotta-colored drawings of peanut-plant leaves and big-toothed mice, shown in profile. Perched on top are two sculpted, life-sized mice, not quite directly facing you while they have sex. I don't know that they're male and female, but extrapolating from the pieces featuring humans, in which the figures' sex is visibly obvious, I think they are meant to be a hetero mouse-couple.

The mouse in front is resting her broken-off front legs on two sculpted peanuts. The one in back is gripping his partner with his little paws. His mouth is open, his ears tensed, as if every muscle from the back of his head to his tail is straining with effort. His disconcertingly human-looking eye is directed straight at the viewer.

archaeologists call the Presentation Theme or the Sacrifice Ceremony. It's not a single scene, so much as variations upon a theme. A limited cast of characters carry out the same actions in different configurations across vessel after vessel. One part of the scene depicts naked, bound prisoners being killed. In another part, one figure presents a goblet (presumably filled with human blood) to a second figure. In one version, depicted in outline form on the Harvard Library site, the Priestess gives the goblet to the Warrior Priest. In another, the Iguana presents the blood to the Rayed Deity. The drawings are stylized and, to an untrained eye, much harder to interpret than the figurative ceramic pots.

In 1988, archaeologists excavated a tomb at Huaca Rajada and discovered a human body buried with the regalia of the Warrior Priest of the Presentation Theme images. The remains of a small dog were also in the tomb. At San José de Moro, researchers found multiple women, across generations, buried

Fig. 10.3. Imagine a black-and-white line drawing, created by a woman named Donna McClelland in the late 1970s. It reproduces the details of a Presentation Scene on a Moche vessel located at the Staatliches Museum für Völkerkunde, in Munich. It's available through the Dumbarton Oaks Research Library. The scenes in the line drawing are much easier to make sense of than on the vessels themselves.

It's a long, thin piece, divided in half horizontally by what looks like a jaguar body with a head at each end. There are lots of figures and all their faces are shown in profile. The figures themselves are of significantly varying sizes. There are too many details and figures to recount them all, so I'll just focus on the ones that matter now.

Under the jaguar are multiple people, two of which are sitting down, bound at the wrists. To the left of each bound figure is a standing figure, each in ornate costume, and each with an arm extended toward the captive. They seem to be slitting the captives' throats. Between one knife-wielder/captive pair are lines that suggest spraying blood, but I'm not positive.

Above the jaguar are seven more humanoid figures, plus a little dog. One of these is the Priestess. She's wearing a distinctive headdress and has four snakes extending out from her shoulders. In her hands, she's carrying a goblet. To the left of her is the Owl, or Bird Priest, who has a beak in place of a human nose and mouth. He's wearing a distinctive hat with an axe-shaped ornament on top and he has wings and clawed bird feet. In one hand he's holding a disk and with the other he is extending the goblet toward the next figure to the left, the Warrior-Priest. The implication is of counterclockwise movement around the jaguar, from the captives (whose blood is shed), up to the Priestess who passes the goblet of blood to the Bird-Priest, and finally to the Warrior-Priest. He, too, has distinctive regalia, including cape, headdress, skirt, nose-ornament, and knife. He's lifting the goblet to his face and his mouth is open, as if preparing to drink. The little dog sits on the Warrior-Priest's foot. The cuteness and violence are dissonant.

with the regalia of the Priestess, along with a ceramic goblet that contained residue of human blood. The remains of sacrificial victims were found at another site, Huaca de la Luna. In other words, research strongly suggests that the Sacrifice Ceremony was an actual ritual in which certain specific people embodied standard roles — the Warrior Priest, the Priestess — and carried out human sacrifice.

The site of the sacrifices seems to have been the same massive huacas that give Egyptian pyramids a run for their money. Physically, the huacas are the most visible, memorable infrastructure associated with Moche society. The human sacrifice ritual can't be avoided when talking about Moche, and it obviously shouldn't be. It is no more violent than the contemporaneous Roman gladiatorial games, for example. The difference is that US students have extended exposure to (and a false sense of familiarity with) ancient Rome through school, pop culture, and US government-produced speech and imagery. Along with artwork and a vast archaeological record, there are hundreds of excerpts of Romans speaking for themselves, already prepared for classroom use with contextual notes and text-analysis questions. The task is to help students see ways in which Romans' worldviews differed from their own, despite a pervasive mythology about similarities.

The Andes aren't Rome and it's hard to re-humanize a society when you've introduced them as practitioners of human sacrifice who drank the blood of their victims. Even harder when they left no known written account of their actions to allow us to see the world through their eyes, when scholarship in the region is decades old rather than centuries, when their descendants are still mostly subjects of anthropology rather than its authors.

"The human sacrifice is okay?"
"Well, the kids will like it. It's interesting."

It's a rhetorical question, really. I know that unlike sex, human sacrifice is "okay" to discuss in US classrooms, especially when it's carried out by indigenous people anywhere. I'm frustrated because I don't know the right thing to do or how to do it.

Our window into the real, complex humanity of Moche people lies in the tension between seemingly irreconcilable objects: the huacas themselves, ceramics that depict ritual human sacrifice, but also daily life, sport, animals, individual portraits, camaraderie, food, birth, sex. Even to an untrained eye, the combination reveals long-ago humans who were fearsome and opaque in some of their beliefs, but also loving, thoughtful, funny, and (perhaps) bawdy. Were Moche artisans entirely serious or am I intended to see crass humor in some of the vessels? How did Moche parents talk to their children about rituals at the local huaca and pots depicting fellatio? How did newly menstruating young women think about their bodies in this place where bloodletting and childbirth were common visual motifs? You can't help but wonder about the worldviews and personalities of the people who created and lived among these objects. You can't help but think of them as people, period.

In the end, it's like this: Yes to the video that takes too long to get controversial. Yes to the images of the Sacrifice Ceremony. Yes to the huacas and the gravesite filled with remains of victims. Yes to the photos of the treasures found in the Warrior King and Priestess tombs. Yes to the portrait pots, the pots in the shape of fruits. Even yes to the slightly racy vessel with the copulating mice. But no sculptures of priests being fellated. No penetrative sex. No childbirth. No to a clever little bowl with a naked woman in the bottom, with a hole just where her vagina would be so the liquid can slowly drain out through it. No to that.

What should we call this part of lesson-building? It's not as honest as censorship. There's no black mark to indicate redacted content. We aren't overtly blocking websites. It's more like the redirection magicians use. Ancient Andeans won't be invisible to students, but they'll seem less fully human than the full corpus of artifacts would reveal them to be. I know that after this carefully culled introduction, the high school students will be curious, but it will be a more muted curiosity than it should be. And most of them will remain entirely ignorant of the sleight of hand happening right in front of them.

Solmaz Sharif

Reaching Guantánamo (excerpt)

"The political is not topical or thematic, it is tactical and formal. It is not, as its strictest definition supposes, something relegated to legislative halls, but something enacted wherever power is at hand, power being at hand wherever there is a relation, including the relation between text and reader."

— Solmaz Sharif, "The Near Transitive Properties of the Political and Poetical: Erasure," *Evening Will Come: A Monthly Journal of Poetics* 28 (April 2013), https://web.archive.org/web/20190312091133/https://thevolta.org/ewc28-ssharif-p1.html.

Opening poem to a seven-part sequence in the poetry collection *Reaching Guantánamo*, originally published in *Paperbag Magazine* 1 (Summer 2010). Copyright ©2010, 2016 by Solmaz Sharif. Reprinted with the permission of The Permissions Company, LLC on behalf of Graywolf Press, graywolfpress.org.

Dear Salim,

Love, are you well? Do they   you?
I worry so much. Lately, my hair   , even
my skin   . The doctors tell me it's
I believe them. It shouldn't
. Please don't worry.
                 in the year, and moths
have gotten to your mother's
                      , remember?
I have enclosed some   — made this
batch just for you. Please eat well. Why
did you   me to remarry? I told
          and he couldn't   it.
I would never   .
Love, I'm singing that   you loved,
remember, the line that went
"   "? I'm holding
the   just for you.

Yours,

Condensed Meanings
Redaction Dialogues on Ethnography in Occupied Tibet

Charlene Makley and Donyol Dondrup

The controversial and beloved Tibetan writer and performer Menla kyab, whose televised comedic skits have for years subtly critiqued the absurdities and corruptions of Tibetans' lives under Chinese Communist Party (CCP) rule, once referred to his work as trafficking in *bsdus don* (Tibetan for "condensed meanings"). By that he meant how he plays, trickster-like, with the creative potentials of ironic implication in the Tibetan language, a cat-and-mouse game of indirection that allows him to dodge state censorship, and, except for one period of extrajudicial detention, to evade government officials' discipline. Menla kyab's notion of condensed meanings encapsulates practices all Tibetans must engage in to navigate ongoing state repression as marginalized "minorities" in the People's Republic of China's (PRC) western provinces. But the terms of the game have shifted dramatically since 2008, when Tibetans began to openly protest both their political-economic marginalization and heightened assimilation pressures in the wake of the "Great Develop the West" campaign (2000–) and the rise of president Xi Jinping's more authoritarian policies (2013–) relative to previous post-Mao regimes.

The ongoing militarization of Tibetan regions and increasing pressures on local officials to *weiwen* (Chinese for "maintain stability") and promote Chinese-style *wenming* (Chinese for "civilization"), have meant that the threat of socioeconomic ostracization, detention, and torture is now much more present and pervasive for Tibetan citizens. Meanwhile, a creeping criminalization of cultural-linguistic otherness in those parts makes any "condensed meaning" that suggests Tibetan cultural pride a potential cause for official suspicion and censure. And an expanding official narrative of foreigners (especially westerners) as outside agitators of Tibetan protest has led to bans on foreign donors, prohibitions on foreigners' travel and lodging in Tibetan regions, as well as bars to and surveillance of Tibetans' foreign travel and relations.

In this piece composed of short stories and redaction experiments written in dialogue with each other, we reflect on the (im)possibilities of ethnography amidst such state-led erasure and threat. We move between our respective narrative and poetic experiments with redaction (headed by our names and the title of the text we are engaging) and our responses to each others' experiments (labeled "Dialogues"). We draw on Charlene Makley's twenty-seven years of ethnographic research conducted as a white American anthropologist in Tibetan regions, and on Donyol Dondrup's experiences conducting ethnographic research as a native anthropologist there. Our writings and experiments about and with redaction emerged dialogically as we shared with each other short narratives about encounters with people and discourses during research. As a way to illustrate sites of erasure imposed by authoritarian rule, we deployed forms of redaction (white spaces or black boxes) as condensed meanings in unexpected ways (redacting not just names, places, and other identifying markers of persons) to intervene in locally influential Chinese-language state texts. In our collaborative writings and readings, we sought to avoid using redaction as a kind of spectacle, a "peek-a-boo" game coyly hinting at enticing secrets. This process, our history of close collaborations, and our very different positions as ethnographers of Tibet, yielded new insights and avenues for rethinking the nature and roles of ethnography under authoritarian erasure.

Charlene: Erasure Poems
Seasons Greetings 2008, Amdo Tibet, Qinghai province, China

Among Chinese, red is the color of auspiciousness, prosperity, and the joy of seasonal gathering and life cycle events. I picked this flier up as discarded ephemera in a local print shop's recycling box, a place where the scraps and leavings of state place- and person-making could be found. Discarded drafts and extra copies of local state bureaus' annual reports, data charts, permit forms, identity cards, and correspondence were all dumped in that box, the crumpled paper bearing the scribbled notes, strikethroughs, and erasures of anxious officials trying to please their superiors. In 2007, that was literally where consequential redactions of local life were happening in real-time. This seasons greetings letter for the 2008 Lunar New Year from the county Public Security Bureau to all personnel under its jurisdiction struck me as encapsulating the ominous conceit of state rhetoric that protecting social "stability" could be comfortably couched in warm affect. This state redaction is not just textual; the red color of the paper, womblike, pervades the text with its implied warmth and joy. State efforts like this to capture, project, and foreclose affect seem to me to be central to how redaction works in authoritarian contexts.

Here I redact these redactions of affect in light and shadow: two contrasting erasure poems from the same Chinese-language flier that used seasons greetings to prime local security personnel to crush potential unrest among Tibetans as the August Olympics approached. Ten days later, as if on cue, the first street disturbances occurred, during a New Year's gathering for the county. And, as if on cue, security forces' swift and brutal military crackdown escalated tensions and sparked the spiraling conflicts that led to years of protest, torture, and incarceration of Tibetans.

I am inspired in this by the work of the poet Solmaz Sharif. Her erasure poems grapple with the unclear agencies and messages of state-redacted texts as a way to highlight her own agency and complicity in their erasures. Sharif points to the ways poetic-political erasure like this differs from statist redaction because state officials' erasures only care about what is blacked out, not about the text that is left behind. State redaction makes the erased somehow sacred and off-limits, emphasizing state power as arbiter of Truth. By contrast, poetic-political erasure cares about the remaining text, how it highlights or reframes that which is erased. Here, my contrasting redactions in light and shadow alchemically separate the affective languages that the flier attempts to stealthily blend.

Translation is itself another form of consequential redaction with potentially unintended effects in authoritarian contexts. In the translated erasure poems, I take the Chinese text distilled out after I selectively blacked out pieces of the letter and attempt to render it comprehensible in English, all while maintaining my implied critique. To maintain for readers a sense of the original, I tried to mirror the selectively redacted spaces by counting the number of erased characters and systematically rendering them with blank spaces by using the tab key and spacebar. I also retained the paragraph forms and punctuation used in the original.

And yet I found that in key places, which are bolded and italicized in the poems below, my English translations had unintentionally worked to soften, indeed gloss over, the historical weightiness, the grave implied threat, of important state idioms evoked in the flier. The bolded, italicized phrases in my erasure poems mark my translations of these widely circulated slogans in order to flag how English translations of state discourse can inadvertently lighten or soften it, taking it out of a troubled context. In the alchemy of the erasure poems then, I felt that these idioms should not float seamlessly to the surface with the rest but instead fall out as chunks of partially untranslatable meaning, dragging with them the brutal violence and expropriation they attempted to justify during the 2008 crackdowns and beyond.

至全体■■民■、■■■■■官■、■■人员、
■■■■■家属的慰问信

　　2007年，全体■■民■、■■■■官兵、■■人员■■以■■平
■■和■■■■■■■■■■■■■■■■■的■■领导■
■■■■■■■■，■■■■■■■建设小康社会、构建■■■和谐
社会■■■，以■■■■■■安全■■为重点，以建设和谐
■■■关系为主线，■■■■■■■■■■■■■■■■■■
■■■■■■■■■■■■■■■■■■■■■■■■■■
确保了■■■■■■■■、人民■■的安全感和■■■■■满
意率■■提升，为建设和谐平安■■■■■■■■■■■。
　　这些成绩的取得，是■■■■■■家属支持和帮助的结果。■■
家属■■们■■■■■■■■、■■■■，以宽广的胸怀■■■■
■■■■■■照顾老人、抚育孩子等家庭■■，为亲人■■■■
提供了■■支撑■■■■■■■■■■每一份成绩都凝聚着她们的辛劳
和汗水。对此，■■■■■广大■■民■将时刻铭记并衷心感谢！
　　2008年■■■■■■■■■■■■■■是喜迎北京奥运会
的一年。在新的一年里，全■■■民■要■■■■■■■■■■
■■■高举■■平■■和■■■■代表■■■■旗帜，■■以科学■■■为
■■■■■■■■■■■■■■■■■■■■■■■为载体，
■■■■■■■■全力■■■■■■■■■■■■促进社会和谐和改
善民生，■■■■■■■■■■■■■■■■■■■■确保全县■
■■■■的平■■■■■■■■■■■■■■■■■■■■安
环境。新春佳节即将来临，■■■■■■向■■■■■■民■、■
■■官■、■■人员及家属■■们表示亲切的慰问和崇高的敬礼！
祝大家身体健康、工作顺利、阖家欢乐、万事顺意！

　　　　　　　　　　　　　　　　　　　■■县■■局■■
　　　　　　　　　　　　　　　　　　　二〇〇八年一月三十一

Fig. 12.1. Seasons Greeting Light.

100

Fig. 12.2. Seasons Greetings Shadow.

A County Party Committee's Seasons Greetings Letter to all   People   ,   Official   Personnel,   and their Families

In 2007, all   people   ,   and official   personnel,   through their   gentle leadership   ,   created a ***well-off and harmonious society***, and in constructing   a ***harmonious society***   , they made   safety   the priority, and made creating ***harmonious***   relations their main goal,   ,   and ensured that   people's   feeling of safety and   rate of satisfaction would increase, all to produce ***harmony*** and peace   .

These achievements, are   the result of the support and help of their families.   Family members   ,   with broad and open hearts   took care of the elderly and nurtured the children   , providing   support   to their loved ones   .   Every achievement relied on their hard work and sweat. For this,   all   people   will forever remember and thank them from the bottom of their hearts!

2008   . is the year to celebrate and welcome the Olympics. During this new year, all   people   must   raise   the banner of   gentle   representation,   taking ***science   as   the medium*** and,   making every effort to   ***promote a harmonious society*** and ***improve the people's livelihood***,   this will ensure for the whole county   a peaceful   environment. The New Spring festival is almost here,   we express to   the people   ,   official   ,   personnel and their family   members our warmest season greetings and our supreme best wishes!

May everyone be healthy, and enjoy successful work! May your whole family be happy and may everything you do work out well!

▮▮▮County▮▮▮Bureau Party Committee
January 31, 2008

Fig. 12.3. Seasons Greetings Light (ten days before the first unrest).

CONDENSED MEANINGS

A Letter to all Public Security Police, Public Security Firefighters, and Auxillary Police Personnel

In 2007, all Public Security police, Public Security firefighters, and auxillary police personnel under the Party Committee's leadership, firmly carried out the work of defending the Party, taking the construction of the police as their main line, they successfully brought force to the grassroots, and made progress in raising the level of troop construction, guaranteeing that the entire county would *remain stable*, they thereby contributed to Public Security work.

Comrades of the police with firm conviction, took on the work of public security,

2008 is the year of the Beijing Olympics. During this particular New Year, all Public Security police must , firmly take "*a peaceful Olympics*" as their leading goal, and , use their utmost force to protect national security and *social stability*, they must forcefully promote the construction of the troops, guaranteeing that the entire county's ,

, Party committees will forever do battle , !

, , , !

▆▆ County Public Security Party Committee
January 31, 2008

Fig. 12.4. Seasons Greetings Shadow.

Dialogues: Donyol Dondrup Responds

Stories indeed invoke and generate other stories.

Your contrasting erasure poems of the same Chinese-language flier effectively expose the minacious state's effort to cloak itself in kindness. Your piece reminded me of other countless instances where the state cunningly presents itself as a benevolent figure after they (a collective entity), as one of my Tibetan interlocutors said, "raped the women and raped the land." Tibetan pastoralists in eastern Tibet often discuss the embodied experiences and memories of state-led drainage of wetlands during the collective period as leading to today's loss of vitality of their land. From the 1960s till the late 1970s, the state drained wetlands in eastern Tibet to create wheat fields as a way to feed horses for occupying soldiers. These wheat fields have never fully recovered to grassland even after they stopped planting wheat in 1982.

However, the Chinese state has a long history of deflecting culpability for any forms of land degradation onto both local people and past regimes. Since the mid-1990s, the state has been cloaking itself in benevolent science while blaming Tibetan pastoralists for overgrazing. This narrative of overgrazing has been employed to justify a suite of top-down policies that combined free-market mechanisms with advocacy for land privatization use, scientifically-guided land management through rangeland fencing, and "green" development through mass relocation of residents. Of course, Tibetan pastoralists have different accounts of the loss of their land's vitality. When people say the state, a collective entity, "raped the women and raped the land," they are reflecting upon and living through memories of pain and violence that were inflicted on their people and the land. The state has been making concerted efforts to erase those memories by planting new memories in people's minds, as well as in the geography, for example, the ubiquitous barbed-wire fencing now stretching across the landscape of the Tibetan Plateau.

Memories and pain may get old, but they are never forgotten, as Tibetans would say.

The more I mull over this approach of poetic-political erasure as a way to rethink the nature of the state, the more it reveals something that the state constantly attempts to hide, be it through affective languages of Seasons Greetings, or scientific languages of land degradation. However, when its evil root is brought out into the open by separating the flowery language from the menacing, now we can see and smell the flesh and the bones of the state.

In this sense, poetic-political erasure highlights not only that which is erased, but also that which is replaced or planted.

Donyol Dondrup: Erasure Poems on Science and Blame
A Tibetan County Report on "Ecological Breeding," 2018, Amdo Tibet, Sichuan Province, China

The Chinese state often touts its omnipresent power in its policy documents, which can be found either in the recycling boxes of local print shops or on their neatly-organized official websites. This report on the achievement of "ecological breeding" of livestock was featured on a Tibetan county's government official website under the leadership of a county propaganda bureau on March 19, 2018. Since the late 1990s, Tibetan pastoralists have been confronted with unprecedented state-led development pressures, including a mandatory policy of barbed wire fencing, which has made traditional communal grazing almost impossible through practices of dividing, bounding, numbering, and quantifying the land. The state has faulted Tibetan pastoralists for overgrazing and causing damage to the land over which the state, all along, claims ownership. Nervous state officials constantly assert authority over things that do not belong to them in a benevolent language of helping to improve the people from whom the land was stolen.

In the wake of a set of top-down development policies, the state ultimately envisions achieving what it describes here as "ecological breeding." In this report, this means raising yaks in livestock sheds or animal pens during all seasons and in the face of any natural forces. This new way of grazing animals in an enclosed space aligns with the state's idea that anything that is owned has to be optimized, made more efficient, to increase the capacity to generate revenues and extract surplus. The figure of the state as voiced in the report cannot envision any possibility of achieving prosperity outside of the framework of its policies. In the voice of local officials reporting "up" to superiors, the state touts itself as the all-knowing figure, never fallible and never questionable, always scientific and always reliable. In my erasure poem 1 (fig. 12.5), I highlight the state's effort to cloak itself in science, reason, and facticity.

Then, there is the task of reminding readers of the problematic activities of Tibetan pastoralists, and of the plateau pikas, a small burrowing relative of the rabbit, which has long been considered a pest by the Chinese government and blamed for causing soil erosion, degradation, and desertification. In this sense, in the report the stories of the Tibetan pastoralists and the plateau pikas are not so different. Like pikas, Tibetan pastoralists are widely blamed for grassland degradation, while many destructions threaten the existence of both. In my erasure poem 2 (fig. 12.6), I separate out the places where the state faults Tibetans' traditional communal grazing as irrational, uneconomic, and lacking organization, glossed in the report as a lifestyle in which pastoralists "freely move wherever the grass and water is." As the report puts it, the result of traditional grazing supposedly is that the animals are "fat during the fall, thin during the winter, and die during the spring."

As in the report, the state always attempts to combine its science-speak voice with its tendency to deflect culpability for any forms of land degradation by blaming "the masses," present here in the figure of Tibetan pastoralists. Science-speak carries authority, and hence the state ensconces itself in the sense of legitimacy bestowed by quantification and numbers, which are in turn constructed and fabricated by that very state. By separating the kindly science-speak of the state from the state's constant efforts to point out the "problems" of the masses, one can get a closer picture of the state's positionality in relation to those that need to be conquered, both benevolently and brutally.

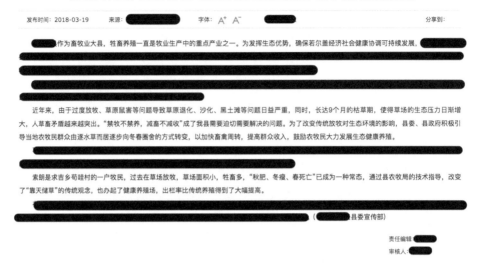

Fig. 12.5. Ecological Breeding: Projecting the Scientific Power of the State.

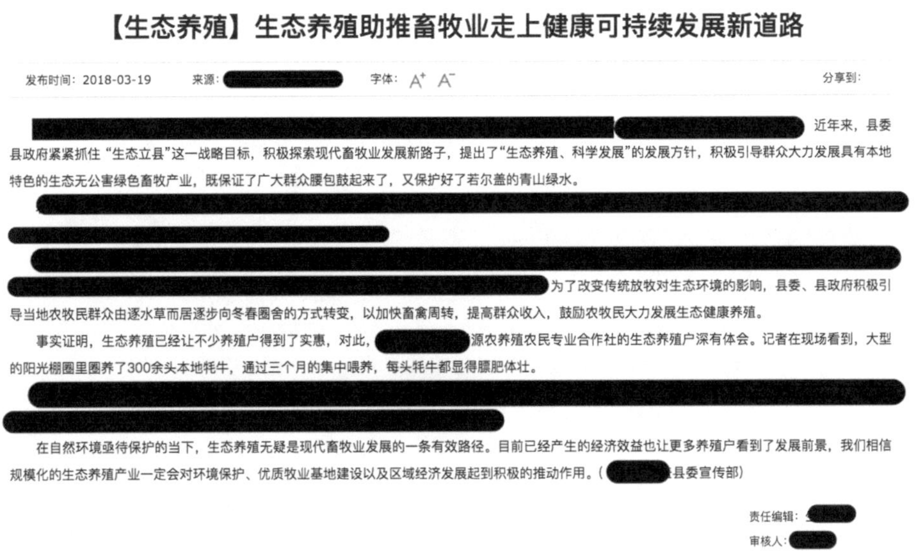

CONDENSED MEANINGS

【生态养殖】生态养殖助推畜牧业走上健康可持续发展新道路

发布时间：2018-03-19　　来源：█████████　　字体：A⁺ A⁻　　　　　　　　　　　分享到：

██近年来，县委县政府紧紧抓住"生态立县"这一战略目标，积极探索现代畜牧业发展新路子，提出了"生态养殖、科学发展"的发展方针，积极引导群众大力发展具有本地特色的生态无公害绿色畜牧产业，既保证了广大群众腰包鼓起来了，又保护好了若尔盖的青山绿水。

██为了改变传统放牧对生态环境的影响，县委、县政府积极引导当地农牧民群众由逐水草而居逐步向冬春圈舍的方式转变，以加快畜禽周转，提高群众收入，鼓励农牧民大力发展生态健康养殖。

事实证明，生态养殖已经让不少养殖户得到了实惠，对此，████████源农养殖农民专业合作社的生态养殖户深有体会。记者在现场看到，大型的阳光棚圈里圈养了300余头本地牦牛，通过三个月的集中喂养，每头牦牛都显得膘肥体壮。

██在自然环境亟待保护的当下，生态养殖无疑是现代畜牧业发展的一条有效径路。目前已经产生的经济效益也让更多养殖户看到了发展前景，我们相信规模化的生态养殖产业一定会对环境保护、优质牧业基地建设以及区域经济发展起到积极的推动作用。(████████县委宣传部)

责任编辑：████
审核人：████

Fig. 12.6. Ecological Breeding: Blaming the Masses.

107

Ecological Breeding: Projecting the Scientific Power of the State

In recent years,
the county government holds firmly
onto the strategy of creating an "ecological county."
To explore a modern pathway to animal husbandry,
We employed "Ecological Breeding, Scientific Development" as the guiding direction;
and led the masses to create a pollution-free and green livestock industry
in keeping with the locality's characteristics;
we guaranteed that the masses' wallets have swelled;
and protected ▮▮ county's green mountains and blue waters.

To change
the impact of traditional pastoralism on the ecological environment,
the county government actively led local farmers and herders to shift from
chasing water and grass as a living to
adopting the method of winter and spring pens.
By ensuring sufficient numbers of livestock and
increasing the people's income,
we encouraged them to enthusiastically develop
ecological and healthy breeding.

The facts show
ecological breeding has already offered actual benefits to quite a lot of households.
The ▮▮ Agricultural Breeding Cooperative has deep experience in this.
Journalists on site witnessed their open livestock shed,
where 300 yaks are being raised.
After feeding them for three months
each yak appears plump and sturdy.

Amid the urgent need
to protect the natural environment,
ecological breeding is indubitably a prosperous pathway
to modern animal husbandry development.
The economic benefits already reaped will allow
even more households to envision their own prospects.

We're confident
that large-scale ecological breeding products will definitely
protect the environment,
while also playing an important role
in constructing a high-quality animal husbandry base
and bolstering regional economic development.

Ecological Breeding: Blaming the Masses

In recent years,
due to such problems as overgrazing and
the damage caused by grassland pikas,
problems of grassland degradation, desertification, and soil erosion,
are intensifying day by day.

At the same time,
as much as nine months of withered grass
increases pressure on the ecology of the grassland every day,
conflicts among people, grass, and animals are becoming more and more prominent.
"Stop pastoralism, but support breeding; reduce animals, but increase income"
has become the issue that our county has to urgently pursue.

To change
the impact of traditional pastoralism on the ecological environment,
the county government actively led local farmers and herders to shift from
chasing water and grass as a living to
adopting the method of winter and spring pens.
We thereby sped up livestock turnover
and increased the masses' income,
while also encouraging farmers and herders to enthusiastically develop
ecological and healthy breeding farms.

███ is a herder from ███ village.
In the past, he grazed his animals on his grassland.
His grassland was small, his animals many.
"Fat during the fall, thin during winter, die during spring"
had become the norm.w

With technical guidance
from the county Agriculture and Animal Husbandry Bureau,
he changed his traditional approach of
"relying on the sky and storing grass,"
and established a healthy breeding farm.
Compared with his traditional husbandry,
his animal slaughter rate has greatly increased.

Dialogues: Charlene Responds

It feels right somehow to mess with these horrible statist science-speak or technocratic texts, to try to unmask or reveal some of their violent subtexts. I think you're right that a focus on the erasure of the expropriation of land and its multilayered, baptismal violence for Tibetans, is perhaps the most important connecting theme for us. My erasure poems signal an earlier moment a decade before that in part sets up the state-local dynamics you analyze here.

The Seasons Greetings flier from 2008 is itself a claim to abstract disciplinary ownership of space, land, the streets, and that kind of benevolent pervasion claimed by state speakers that this 2018 county report on "ecological breeding" brings forward — "the State" itself emerges as a monolithic figure in this voice, which is reflected in your own discussion. Yet both pieces of media were produced by local officials, most of whom are Tibetan, at the lowly bureaucratic level of the county in the Chinese state's hierarchical bureaucracy: policy comes "down" to the "grassroots;" reports are submitted "up" to superiors. Like my reference to anxious officials redacting their reports to please superiors, the report you unpack is the final product of that process, when all traces of the anxious self-redactions I saw in the recycle bin have themselves been redacted, such that low-level officials' voices are supposed to seamlessly merge with that of the central State. Both sets of erasure poems then also highlight how state-building, and all the absurd abstraction and brutality it entails, is constituted by these redactions, which both demand and erase the complicity of Tibetan officials themselves.

Your erasures made me think that one of the main characteristics of poetic or political erasure practice like ours that works with such a pictograph-based and syllabic language as Chinese is that you can't pick apart a particular word to grab individual letters and compose new words from them in your remainder texts, like we see in some English-language erasure poems. Working with Chinese, you have to be really attentive to the highly condensed, yet capacious meaning of one character. I was also inspired by some of the other erasure poems I've seen that did not produce grammatically correct remainder texts, but just highlighted themes and metaphors and subtexts and gestures that were otherwise buried in the discourse.

Your piece inspires me to try that by intervening in another land-related state text. You probably don't remember back in summer 2007, you and I were walking down the street in ▇▇▇▇ and we passed a central state "Legal Education Campaign" poster display (fig. 12.7). One of the posters tried to define *tudi* (Chinese for land) in lay terms. I was thinking of making that an erasure poem to highlight the deadened, flattened, inanimate science-speak you redacted here.

Could we also think about other forms of redaction besides black-lining, which is so closely associated with the US state? Like white spaces instead of black, to get at whole themes, worlds, cosmologies that are literally rendered absent in these universalizing, standardizing texts? Perhaps playing with and against the linear nature of the text to suggest the shape of a sitting Buddha, or a mountain deity? Or a stupa?

Charlene: Buddha Redaction
What Is Land? A Propaganda Poster on the Street in ▇▇▇▇,

Fig. 12.7. Land Management Poster, "What Is Land?," 2007. Photo by the author. "Land is a composite made up of such natural elements as air, plant life, hydrology, topography, landforms, soil, and rocks, as well as the outcomes of human social economic activities. The outcomes of human activities include such elements as all built environments created from humankind's past and present social economic activities as well as the manmade fertility of the land. Looking at it from the perspective of both land formation and natural elements on the one hand and humankind's social economic activities on the other, we must see land as a historical product, a natural economic composite."

What Is Land?

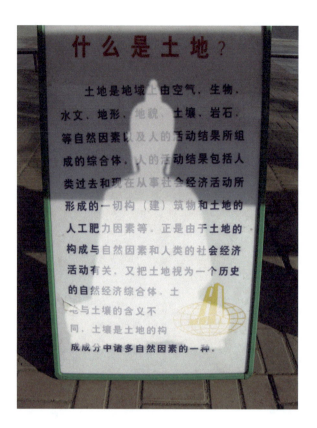

```
        Land is land        air, plants,
          water, terrain       soil, rocks
      such natural elements         action consequences which
      constitute a composite,       consequences including
       human pasts and              helping activities that
         are formed                 of the land
    human-made fertile              of the land
         created and                economic
            activities            history
         of self
               natural elements
```

Land Law Education Day, 2007

If redaction is not just a textual intervention, but a performative process of (re)framing and erasure that pervades embodied life, then land is perhaps the most redacted feature of post-Mao Tibetan social worlds. The Maoist reframing of Tibetan-inhabited "land" as the inert object of human projects and the sovereign property of the Chinese state was foundational to socialist transformation and then post-Mao state capitalist expropriation. But in my fieldwork, this seismic conversion was a public secret, never acknowledged in state media and only carefully alluded to in private conversation.

In my 2018 book *The Battle for Fortune*, this is how I discussed this land poster on ▇▇▇ streets in the fall of 2007, presented by a prefecture bureau as part of a central state "Land Law Education Campaign":

> Here, presented to teach residents the conceptual premises of land management laws (and perhaps, to naturalize the emerging status of land as a commodity), "land" (versus "soil") is a definitively secular and material assemblage, encompassing all the added value of human action on nature. By contrast, Tibetan farmers in ▇▇▇ historically experienced landscapes as profoundly emplaced and animated, caught up in the moving cosmos of nonhuman forces and beings impinging on human bodies and livelihoods.[1]

In this erasure poem, which I call a "Buddha redaction," I wanted to iconically portray the reality for many rural Tibetans that has been so brutally erased in land conversions under CCP rule: the Buddhist divinity of inhabited lands as the sovereign abodes of Buddhas and Bodhisattvas. "The battle for fortune" in contemporary Tibetan regions turns on this erasure. Here, I outlined a thirteenth-century Tibetan statue of the historical Buddha Śākyamuni in his famous earth-witnessing mode, in which the Buddha sits in meditation, his right hand extending down to touch the earth. The earth thereby both witnesses his world-altering enlightenment and becomes the purified and tamed realm of the Buddha.

In Tibetan historiography, enlightened Indian and Tibetan Buddhist teachers "tame" the regions of the high plateaus by ritually conquering the indigenous demons and deities who live there, converting them into regional guardians for auspiciously sovereign human communities. In the poem, I wanted to see what was left of the "What is Land?" poster if I brought back the erased Buddha, in ghostly form. I thus overlaid the Buddha's shadow body on it, mimicking the ways in which Buddha bodies, as portrayed in Tibetan ritual texts, literally stamp their taming power into Tibetan landscapes. I resolved to eliminate all characters that the Buddha's body touched and to see what meanings randomly emerged in the remainder.

---

[1] Charlene E. Makley, *The Battle for Fortune: State-Led Development, Personhood, and Power among Tibetans in China* (Ithaca: Cornell University Press, 2018), 79.

In the translation, I respected the Buddha's redaction and did not try to re-connect Chinese clauses cut up by his body. Instead, I translated each remaining phrase in isolation, and kept the form of the Buddha's body in relief. Uncannily, the remaining concepts came across as remarkably Buddhist; the poem seemed to excavate or point to a buried Buddhist cosmology of auspicious landscapes and human karmic actions emerging within and from them.

Dialogues: Donyol Dondrup Responds

Today the Tibetan-inhabited landscape is blanketed with technocratic state definitions of land. The state definition of land often legitimizes itself in legality or the land laws. Once the land is taken away from its owner, then the land laws turned the original Tibetan inhabitants into a mere "user" of the same land. How you analyzed and intervened in the state definition of land in your erasure poem is a powerful example that does not only reveal but also *declares* what Pamela M. Lee calls the open secret of those who conceal,[2] although the Chinese state is displaying its power rather than concealing its vulgar agendas in their land education campaigns.

Similarly, the Maoist reframing of Tibetan-inhabited land as first and foremost the sovereign property of the Chinese state and the ongoing post-Mao state capitalist expropriation is often perceived by Tibetans as a public statement. Perhaps it is not even a public secret, because it does not have any elements of secrecy especially when it comes to the Chinese laws of the land. According to articles 9 and 10 of the 1982 constitution, "Natural resources such as waters and streams, forest, mountains, grassland, and wasteland are state-owned, unless defined by law as collectively owned. Sub-urban and rural land is collectively owned, unless state ownership has been proven."[3] The Tibetan plateau is largely grazing land and it legally goes into the category of "grassland," hence it is owned by the state. The original Tibetan inhabitants have had merely use-rights over their stolen land for over 50 years.

I find your "Buddha redaction" a creative way to intervene in and mess up the state's erasure of Tibetans' historical and embodied relationships to their land. However, there is another important erasure that we should also take into consideration, which is the erasure of Tibetans' older relationships to *yul lha* or *gzhi bdag* (Tibetan for territorial deities). For centuries, many Buddhist masters and politicians made concerted efforts to install mandalas (divine palaces envisioned in meditation or in art forms) of different Buddhist deities within the Tibetan landscape. According to anthropologist Katia Buffertrille, this was primarily done by transforming local territorial deities into *gnas ri* (Tibetan for "mountain holy places"), a

---

2 Pamela M. Lee, "Open Secret: The Work of Art Between Disclosure and Redaction," *Artforum*, May 2011, https://www.artforum.com/features/open-secret-the-work-of-art-between-disclosure-and-redaction-197372/.
3 PRC 1982 Constitution.

process she calls, the Buddhicization of the Tibetan landscape.[4] However, as you've pointed out before, the establishment of translocal Buddhist jurisdictions never eradicated local Tibetans' older ritualized relationships to their communities, although it significantly minimized the power and influence of territorial deities. In this sense, there is an ongoing double erasure as the ancestral land of Tibetans has become the tamed realms of both the CCP and of the Buddha.

The history of taming the Tibetan landscape by Buddhist deities is so complex and so long that now it has become part of the local cosmology of Tibetans. So, I don't know if it's appropriate to equate it to the CCP's occupation of Tibetan land. What do you think?

Dialogues: Charlene Responds

Very interesting to consider what exactly is a (public) secret and to whom, where, and why. I was really struck by your comment that the PRC state claim to ownership of all land as "natural resources" has been experienced by Tibetans (which ones? all?) as a very public statement, not hidden at all. This makes me think when we consider the politics and performance of reframing, concealment, and revelation we have to be historically and ethnographically specific about where those movements are emerging and to what effect. In my poem, I was thinking about state and some scholarly media — from technocratic social scientists in and outside the PRC, but also scholars and journalists of Tibet who focus on "culture" or "religion" to the exclusion of political economy — that take the Chinese state claim to land as such an absolute given, the very foundations of any legitimate nation-state, that they leave the foundational violence of land dispossession in the background or erase it altogether. Or, such media assumes that the state claim to land ownership played out in essentially the same ways in Han Chinese regions as in non-Han regions on the periphery, where many inhabitants experienced it as a form of settler colonialism. Or, a wide variety of players today, including some Tibetans, so take for granted the state's scientistic narrative of "land" as portrayed in the Land Education poster, that all other ways of relating to and experiencing landscapes are obviated. In fact, we could see this conscious or unconscious concealment of land expropriation as constitutive of any media discourse that lionizes the Communist revolution in general, but especially in Tibetan regions, without mention of the terrible, multi-dimensional, and historically specific violence of "land reform".

But it is another matter entirely to consider the lived experience of this statist (colonial) claim to land. That indeed has been very apparent to many Tibetan residents. No secret there, and yet the "public secret" part of it is that you can't openly talk about it or protest without dire consequences.

---

4   Katia Buffetrille, "The Evolution of a Tibetan Pilgrimage: The Pilgrimage to A myes rMa chen Mountain in the 21st Century," in *21st Century Tibet: Symposium on Contemporary Tibetan Studies* (Taipei: publisher unknown, 2003), 23.

Your point about much older mountain and landscape deities and the double erasure of Buddhicization is a crucial one. If political economic relations are grounded in relations to landscapes universally, then a critical perspective on the imperial and sectarian violences of Buddhist "taming" practices across the Tibetan plateau would have to be part of the equation. Tibetans centuries ago fought brutal wars over control of the Yarlung valley in Central Tibet, for example, calling on "Buddhicized" mountain deities (as well as Mongol troops) as their protectors and allies.

But that would not necessarily be the perspective of contemporary Tibetan villagers or local residents. I was trying to stand there when I did this redaction, thinking especially of one village whose counter-development project in the early 2000s was specifically about marshalling the Buddhist taming prowess of an incarnate lama to reclaim their landscape in a new way.

Donyol Dondrup: Redaction Narrative
"Pain may get old, but it may never be forgotten"

Whenever I invited village elders in ▇▇▇▇, a Tibetan pastoral community in eastern Tibet, to tell me the history of their community, they would often preface the narration of their community's history with a Tibetan saying, *sdug la snying rgyu yod kyang brjed kyi med,* which translates in English to, "Pain may get old, but it may never be forgotten." They would also look through the window to make sure that no stranger was listening to our conversations before they shared a particular historical event that took place in 1968. The village elders emphasized that any real history of their community should be told from the haunting memories of this particular event because the community has never healed itself from it. Words were mixed with tears as they told me the story.

In 1967 (during the Cultural Revolution), the Chinese government built the very first township office in ▇▇▇▇. It was a wooden house. At the time, most villagers lived in black yak-hair tents. There were many Chinese soldiers in the village, enforcing the rules of collectivization. Food was scarce. The Chinese soldiers forced people to turn a big portion of their grassland into crop fields, cultivating barley and wheat, which were used to feed the soldiers' horses. The soldiers had stolen the horses from the villagers. In the summer of 1968, the soldiers had left the village for about a month. During this period, the villagers had heard a rumor that the Communist Party was on the cusp of collapsing. In response, a group of villagers set the newly-built local township office on fire.

After a few days, several truckloads of soldiers raided their community. The soldiers were from the Lanzhou Military Region, which was one of the seven military regions in the People's Republic of China. Right after they arrived, the soldiers shot eighteen Tibetan villagers, all men, to death. Brains exploded. Blood gushed. The whole community was terrorized. The soldiers' commander wanted to know who had initiated the fire. However, none of the villagers told them who had initiated it. Then, the soldiers arrested eighty villagers, all men, and brought them to the county seat, where they were interrogated and tortured for three days.

The village elders still vividly remember their interactions with the head of the police department at the county seat, a Chinese man who also spoke Tibetan. He vowed that if he couldn't force them to tell him the initial instigator, he would return to his mother's womb. No villager told the police department who had brought up the idea of burning down the township house. A few village elders who are still alive and who were among the eighty arrested men proudly told me, "After they tortured us for three days, no one told them who had organized the burning of the township office. Of course, we knew who he was. He was a respected village elder." When torture failed to work, the head of the police department furiously signed a document that gave a big portion of their grazing land to a neighboring county as a punishment.

One village elder explained: "That's why, until this day, we do not have enough land to graze our animals."

Dialogues: Charlene Responds

I'm so struck by both the abstraction and the visceral nature of this account of narrative redactions, the seeming immediacy of brutal violence, of destroyed bodies and minds on one hand, and the years and years of mediating filters and silences on the other. It is tempting to imagine immediacy and mediation as polar opposites: immediate events or embodied and experienced violence versus official perpetrators' indifferent distance afforded by state mediation. But the account years later, your careful intervention in it, the continued fear and suspicion, and ultimately your English language condensation and translation, belie such a polarization of immediacy and mediacy.

Can we think of redaction as not just brute censorship, as distanced, top-down obstruction, but as this fraught and ambivalent, ever-present process of situated selection, forgetting, memorializing, framing, and performing, with potentially life and death stakes? Regardless of what it meant to residents at the time, this event seems to have come to be a baptismal moment, state violence at the heart of painful contemporary lives. Redacting in this context is a reciprocal, recursive process of living with the public secret, of anticipating the anticipations of state agents. It is the manifestation of semiotic and material mediation as baptismal violence. What kinds of redactions are at work in this account? In what ways? How does translation in itself redact the public secret?

Your account also prompts me to return to the anxious officials and their self-redactions in the print shop recycle bin back in 2007. The baptismal violence for this Tibetan community seems to me to reside in the utter absurdity of the low-level Chinese county police head's arbitrary power at the height of Cultural Revolution terror — his terrified and enraged redaction of Tibetans' land as punishment for making him look bad to his superiors. The ongoing erasure of his authoritarian lawlessness speaks again to how complicity, the embodied link between on one hand, the perpetrators of the baptismal violence of colonial states, and on the other, their successors who maintain and expand its spoils, is grounded in redaction practices. This realization for me sheds light on the absurd complicities and difficulties of attempting any kind of ethnographic writing in such a context. But it also teaches me about the grave responsibility of those who can to continue to find ways to speak truth, however complex and contradictory, to power.

Your account also makes me think of the story I heard from a monk at ▇▇▇ monastery, a mutual colleague of ours. He told me the story of a friend's infamous 80-year-old aunt, who was known to be mentally "unclear." He said she often came by his room in the monastery to talk and would lament in tears about the loss of her family's valley-floor land to the first Chinese settlers back in the late 19th century. To her, the wealthy Tibetan households that now occupied urban space were still settlers on her family's land. The biggest public secret in these Tibetan regions it would seem is the compounding violence of land expropriation.

Concluding Thoughts: Donyol Dondrup, Reflections on Self-redaction and Resilience, 2021

I spent about a decade in the United States. Soon I'm returning to my homeland, Tibet, where fear has been part of everyday life for a long time. If we think about redaction not as just the act of censoring or obscuring part of a text, but instead as the invisible redaction of thoughts amid a politics of fear, there is little room for a scholar in such a world to be a critical scholar, or to speak to power and bear witness to injustice.

What does this process feel like? There are days that I am passionate about writing on a sensitive subject related to Tibet, but those days are often followed by an internal monologue beginning with questions such as, "Would my family get into trouble if the Chinese state smelled my critical reflections on its cruel activities in my homeland? Would I jeopardize the future of my children for dispensing critiques of the pernicious state?" Then, one part of me will lecture another part of me, "I think it is wise to avoid those topics," while another part of me would disagree, "You coward, don't you remember that an intellectual has to be someone who cannot be easily co-opted and intimidated by the power of governments and corporations?" In the end, what I write on paper is often a redacted version of what I had originally wanted to articulate. Call it self-censorship or call it whatever you want.

The biggest actor here is fear. The politics of fear often installs a major machine of self-censorship in one's mind. But I do find inspiration from the words of prominent Hong Kong pro-democracy activist Jimmy Lai, who said before his fourteen-month prison sentence, "If they can induce fear in you, that's the cheapest way to control you and the most effective way and they know it. The only way to defeat the way of intimidation is to face up to fear and don't let it frighten you."[5] But still, when a BBC journalist asked

---

5   Jimmy Lai, quoted in "Hong Kong Media Tycoon Jimmy Lai Ordered Back to

him if he was worried about his family, Lai's voice was shaking, and his eyes filled with tears.

The state is smart and strategic. It works by regression and leniency, and it creates a tremendous amount of suspicion, confusion, and mostly fear. People are smart, creative, and strategic too. Here I'm reminded of the powerful works of the late Tibetan poet, Khawa Nyangchak (1989–2016) who wrote a series of essays honoring the Tibetans who in the 2010s had self-immolated in protests against the colonial occupation of Tibet. To avoid the wrathful eyes of the state, Khawa Nyangchak used "condensed meanings" in a poem to contemplate the fate of a nocturnal moth and her own desire to jump into the fire in search of light. Khawa Nyangchak's untimely death in 2016 was followed by unprecedented public mourning among Tibetans on social media sites in Tibet. Many Tibetans were mourning the passing of a talented young Tibetan writer. They were also mourning the passing of over 150 Tibetan self-immolators whose wishes were so powerfully and poignantly acknowledged, represented, and remembered in Khawa Nyangchak's essays.

I will continue to write. I will continue to sing. Tibetan intellectuals such as Khawa Nyangchak have masterfully and bravely acted as voices to penetrate the public conscience by deploying the redactive art of expressing condensed meaning. I can follow in their steps. They know what the intellectual giant and African American activist Audre Lorde famously stated, that your silence will not protect you or anyone: "While we wait in silence for that final luxury of fearlessness, the weight of that silence will choke us."[6] The weight of silence has never choked Tibetan intellectuals, and it will not choke me either. Will there be singing where there is no space or just limited space? Yes, as Bertolt Brecht said, "In the dark times / Will there also be singing? / Yes, there will be singing / About the dark times."[7]

I will continue to write to cope with the pain — to help end it. I will continue to sing to heal human wounds.

Jail, " *BBC News,* December 31, 2020, https://www.bbc.com/news/world-asia-china-55496039.

6   Audre Lorde, *The Selected Works of Audre Lorde,* ed. Roxane Gay (New York: W.W. Norton & Company, 2020), 13–14.

7   Hannah Aizenman, "Daniel Borzutzky's Poems Channel Cacophony in an Age of Calamity," *The New Yorker,* March 31, 2021, https://www.newyorker.com/books/page-turner/daniel-borzutzkys-poems-channel-cacophony-in-an-age-of-calamity.

Redaction Inverted
Erasure Poetry and the Intent to Reveal

Rachel Douglas-Jones

> *I thought it would be a perfect thing, you could sort of have a public art project, you could have pages of the Basic Law and Tipp-Ex or white paint and ask everyone to erase their own page from it.*
> —Sarah Howe, 2014[1]

> *It's impossible to erase ex nihilo.*
> —Raphael Rubinstein, 2018[2]

On May 25, 2018, the General Data Protection Regulation (GDPR) came into force across Europe. First agreed upon in 2016, the then-Vice-Chair of the European Parliament's *Committee on Civil Liberties, Justice and Home Affairs* declared it to be a document that would "change not only the European data protection laws but nothing less than the whole world as we know it."[3] Replacing the previous 1995 Data Protection directive, the GDPR is designed to require businesses to protect personal data of EU citizens, while retaining data flow across member states as part of the European digital single market.[4] It has also re-shaped how data is retained and deleted. Despite being adopted in 2016, the new regulation remained largely out of the public spotlight until emails began arriving in millions of inboxes in the early months of 2018. Week after week, requests from companies and organizations who held records of customer emails poured in, asking

---

1. Clare Tyrrell-Morin, "Prize-Winning Hong Kong-Born Poet Sarah Howe Makes Verse of City's Basic Law," *South China Morning Post Magazine*, July 7, 2016, https://www.scmp.com/magazines/post-magazine/arts-music/article/1986620/prize-winning-hong-kong-born-poet-sarah-howe.
2. Raphael Rubinstein, "Missing: Erasure | Must Include: Erasure," *Under Erasure*, n.d., https://www.under-erasure.com/essay-by-raphael-rubinstein/.
3. Jan Philipp Albrecht, "How the GDPR Will Change the World," *European Data Protection Law Review* 2, no. 3 (2016): 287–89.
4. "Shaping Europe's Digital Future: Digital Privacy," *European Commission*, https://digital-strategy.ec.europa.eu/en/policies/digital-privacy.

recipients to explicitly opt in, and give their consent to receiving further emails in the future.

In this contribution, I lay out an experimental engagement with the GDPR through erasure poetry, as a means of making official texts speak otherwise. The work falls at the intersection of anthropologies of policy, poetic engagements with ethnography, and experimental methodologies. Its original object, the GDPR, was a source of inspiration for its opacity and immateriality — a 264-page pdf on a European Commission website, written for lawyers and legal experts. Data protection is a site of sometimes abstract struggle, a complex, legalistic reality that shapes everyday interactions, state obligations, and individual and group rights. It enshrines individuals as legal entities and makes demands for reasonable explanation in the face of increasingly technological decision-making.[5]

Through erasure poetry, my colleagues and I sought to make the GDPR tell stories other than those it already told, or to tell them differently.[6] We sought to mirror the ambivalences and misunderstandings with which the regulation was received, and to practice forms of aesthetic engagement in official discourses where speaking directly to, about, or from a text might fail. As such, erasure poetry of policy, regulation, and legislation is put forward as an aesthetic, practical, and political intervention that seeks the inverse of what redaction is — in its legal intent — created for. It leaves behind only what the new author wishes to leave, revealing only words that are already there. It can make those words betray themselves, to reveal the meaning they had all along, or it can give them a new inflection entirely opposite to their intended weight. I suggest that such capacities are a powerful means for managing voice, anonymity, and creativity in charged ethnographic situations. I also view the deceptive simplicity of the act of erasure poetry as a means by which ethnographers and those with whom they work can speak with and through official wor(l)ds. In what follows, I present a key inspiration for our work with the GDPR and a short history of erasure poetry, and I offer reflections on possible futures for the practice of creating erasure poems from policy.

Releasing Undersongs

In her talk "Two Systems" from which this chapter's first epigraph is drawn, the British-Hong Kong Chinese poet Sarah Howe presented a poem from a collection she began in 2014.[7] Her source text was the Basic Law of Hong

---

5 Katja de Vries, "GDPR as Hermeneutics," in *Common Erasures: Speaking Back to GDPR*, eds. Rachel Douglas-Jones, Marie Blønd, and Luuk Blum (Copenhagen: ETHOS Lab, 2020), 58–60.
6 Rachel Douglas-Jones and Marisa Leavitt Cohn, *GDPR Deletion Poems* (Copenhagen: ETHOS Lab, 2018), and Rachel Douglas-Jones, Marie Blønd, and Luuk Blum, eds., *Common Erasures: Speaking Back to GDPR* (Copenhagen: ETHOS Lab, 2020).
7 Sarah Howe, "Sarah Howe | Two Systems || Radcliffe Institute," *YouTube*, November 6, 2015, https://www.youtube.com/watch?v=dDHa4OEqaeo.

Kong, a document negotiated by Beijing and London during the 1980s as part of the handover of sovereignty of Hong Kong to China, an event which took place on July 1st, 1997.[8] As she pointed out in the talk, the title of her (now abandoned) project, "Two Systems," itself contains an erasure. From the full constitutional idea of "One country, two systems,"[9] which set the grounds for Hong Kong's way of life for 50 years, Howe leaves us with just "Two Systems." In her reading, the anticipation of the Basic Law's 50-year timeframe meant that the document already contained "within itself its date of undoing,"[10] an undoing her poetic work echoed in its form.

Howe was drawn to using erasure poetry to broaden engagement with the legal document, imagining a "public art project."[11] As she commented in a short piece about the project,

> It was satisfying, in a childlike-way, to set about these pages from the Basic Law with Photoshop's eraser tool. I imagined myself *releasing their anarchic, subversive, gloriously vulgar undersongs.* I was delighted to find, in amongst the nonsense, touches of sense emerging: allusions to the current unrest about Hong Kong's path to universal suffrage ('Power to the People'), or, more subtly, to its colonial past.[12]

Howe here expresses her desire to see something new emerge from an existing document. She marvels at its capacity to communicate alternative presents and counterfactual narratives, and to provide a commentary on broader public relationships to proscribed futures. She also draws together two very distinct written genres: law and poetry.

What, then, of the undersongs of the GDPR? The stakes of creating erasure poetry from GDPR were not as explicit as for "Two Systems." In GDPR, we could expect more references to Kantian personal liberty than in "Two Systems'" universal suffrage, more on the logics of machines than the logics of colonial legacy. As an intervention into an increasingly contested area of law, GDPR has been variously hailed as a breakthrough in privacy law, a nightmare, and an effort to position Europe as a global leader in data protection.[13] Thus, in the subject matter of the text we went on to erase, lie contemporary tensions of transparency, abstract reductionism, unknowability, and obscurity. There is a central behavioralism at work that emerges through data "transformed from an abstract reduction to a rendition of hu-

---

8   Alan Smart, "Hong Kong's Twenty-First Century Seen From 1997," *City and Society* 9, no. 1 (1997): 97–115.
9   Ming Liu and Ling Lin, "'One Country, Two Systems': A Corpus-assisted Discourse Analysis of the Politics of Recontextualization in British, American and Chinese Newspapers," *Critical Arts* 35, no. 3 (2021): 17–34.
10 Sarah Howe, "A Note about 'Two Systems,'" *Law Text Culture* 18, no. 1 (2014): 249.
11 Ibid.
12 Ibid., 250, emphasis added.
13 Brett Aho and Roberta Duffield, "Beyond Surveillance Capitalism: Privacy, Regulation and Big Data in Europe and China," *Economy and Society* 49, no. 2 (2020): 187–212.

man behaviour 'increasingly understood as approaching "reality" itself.'"[14] As Aho and Duffield go on to summarize, for Antoinette Rouvroy this is best described as a "'truth regime' of algorithmically generated insight that presents claims to pure factuality in yielding insights that appear to have always existed, but obscured beneath the chaotic surface of reality and the human fallibility of heuristic bias and emotion."[15] As a document, GDPR invokes and invents new kinds of "data subjects," spells out expectations and responsibilities, and draws up a world that will unfold through the creation of legal precedent. Its influence is not confined to Europe: as scholars have noted, it involves a "reimagination of geographical borders to match a new digital imaginary"[16] applying to "controllers" and "processors" of personal data outside the EU if they work within it.[17]

Yet despite public discussion of the "right to be forgotten" and "right to an explanation," most publications around the time of its launch centered the perspective of corporations.s.[18] Few initiatives set out to engage European citizens on their new rights or what they might need to do to exercise them. Even as legal teams debated the status and feasibility of their enforcement it became rapidly evident that this was a legal document *designed* to be pored over by lawyers. In response, we manifested Howe's vision of the Basic Law and a Tipp-Ex,[19] for GDPR. The text itself became the site of ethnographic engagement, close reading, reflection, and discussion. In the creation of alternative presents, what commentaries might emerge? To understand the capacities and lineages on which erasure poetry events with the GDPR drew, a short history of the practice is needed.

---

14 Ibid., 17. Aho and Duffield are quoting David Chandler, "A World without Causation: Big Data and the Coming of Age of Posthumanism," *Millennium: Journal of International Studies* 43, no. 3 (2015): 833–51.

15 Antoinette Rouvroy, "The End(s) of Critique: Data-Behaviourism versus Due-Process," in *Privacy, Due Process and the Computational Turn: The Philosophy of Law Meets the Philosophy of Technology*, eds. Mireille Hildebrandt and Katja de Vries (New York: Routledge, 2013), 143–67.

16 Aho and Duffield, "Beyond Surveillance Capitalism," 200.

17 Lawrence Ryz and Lauren Grest, "A New Era in Data Protection," *Computer Fraud & Security 2016*, no. 3 (2016): 18–20.

18 Matt Burgess, "What Is GDPR? The Summary Guide to GDPR Compliance in the UK," *Wired*, March 24, 2020, https://www.wired.co.uk/article/what-is-gdpr-uk-eu-legislation-compliance-summary-fines-2018, and Manuel Grenacher, "GDPR, The Checklist for Compliance," *Forbes*, June 4, 2018, https://www.forbes.com/sites/forbestechcouncil/2018/06/04/gdpr-the-checklist-for-compliance.

19 European brand name for what is known as "white out" or a correction fluid. It was initially developed in 1951 to ease the labor of correcting errors made on typewriters, saving the typist from typing the entire document again. Bette Nesmith Graham (1924–1980) was its inventor. Ameila Groom, "There's Nothing to See Here: Erasing the Monochrome," *e-flux* 37, (September 2012), https://www.e-flux.com/journal/37/61233/there-s-nothing-to-see-here-erasing-the-monochrome/.

A Short History of Erasure Poetry

Erasure poetry goes by many names. It is known in various places as blackout, redaction, deletion, erasure, and found poetry.[20] The practice also has multiple histories, from centuries of erasures and the politics of English as a colonial language,[21] to attention to what Jasper Johns, writing on John Cage, calls "additive subtractions."[22] In the 1960s, it became a favored technique of radical poets, and although US poets are among the more widely known from this era, Raphael Rubinstein points out that erasure and effacement was not confined to the United States in the 1960s.[23] From Italy to Austria, Belgium to London, artists and writers were contemplating how taking away text could be additive. At root, the idea is to take a text that already exists and remove words through deletion or erasure, with what remains forming the new text. Doris Cross, one of the earliest erasure poets, is known for her erasure poems made in dictionaries.[24] Ronald Johnson's 1977 "Radi Os" takes John Milton's seventeenth century poem "Paradise Lost" and erases it into new a poem, the significance of which is contested amongst literary scholars.[25] In his summary review, Travis Macdonald calls the result "a product of what William Burroughs described as 'the third mind of collaboration', an independent entity that arises naturally from the creative friction between two inherently different sets of aesthetic tendencies."[26]

Poets writing and submitting this increasingly widespread form of work[27] have found it to be particularly useful and poignant when used on deeply bureaucratic documents. Perhaps this is for the way such documents

---

20 E. Ce Miller, "Blackout Poetry Is A Fascinating Art You Can Try At Home Right Now," *Bustle,* August 28, 2017, https://www.bustle.com/p/what-is-blackout-poetry-these-fascinating-poems-are-created-from-existing-art-78781.

21 Robin Coste Lewis, "The Race within Erasure," lecture for Portland Arts & Lectures, Literary Arts, February 25, 2016, https://literary-arts.org/archive/robin-coste-lewis-2/. Quoted in Dao Strom and Neil Aitken, "On Erasure: Quotes from Robin Coste Lewis's Lecture 'The Race Within Erasure,'" *de-canon,* May 9, 2017, https://www.de-canon.com/blog/2017/5/9/on-erasure-from-robin-coste-lewiss-lecture-literary-arts.

22 John Cage, *A Year from Monday: New Lectures and Writings* (Middletown: Wesleyan University Press, 1967).

23 Rubinstein, "Missing: Erasure."

24 Lynn Xu, "Who Is Doris Cross?" *Poetry Foundation,* April 25, 2014, https://www.poetryfoundation.org/harriet-books/2014/04/who-is-doris-cross.

25 Eric Selinger, "'I Composed the Holes': Reading Ronald Johnson's 'Radi Os,'" *Contemporary Literature* 33, no. 1 (1992): 46–73, and Derek Mong, "Ten New Ways to Read Ronald Johnson's 'Radi Os,'" *The Kenyon Review* 37, no. 4 (2015): 78–96.

26 Travis Macdonald, "A Brief History of Erasure Poetics," *Jacket 2* (2009), http://jacketmagazine.com/38/macdonald-erasure.shtml.

27 Douglas Luman, "Book Review: The O Mission Repo," *Found Poetry Review,* 2014, archived at https://web.archive.org/web/20230709080455/http://foundpoetryreview.com/blog/book-review-the-o-mission-repo/.

resonate with "interpretational resistance,"[28] the turn to poetry becoming "a provocative refusal to take the text as it is."[29] The power of bureaucratic-poetry surfaced in the work of Macdonald, the author of *The O Mission Repro* which took the United States 9/11 Commission Report as its source material.[30] Macdonald reshaped the text to create a protagonist ("Unit") who moves through highly redacted pages, selecting and erasing words to comment that "remembering / might also be hijacked."[31] Similarly, Rachel Stone notes in her 2017 essay on "The Trump Era Boom in Erasure Poetry," the raw material for Niina Pollari's poem "Form N-400 Erasures" is the long opaquely-worded application form for becoming a naturalized US citizen.[32] "In these poems," Stone writes, "there is a desire to re-examine the institutions and narratives that shape Americans' lives, from government bureaucracy to new media."[33] In this struggle over language, the question becomes who gets to determine its meaning: poets in the United States "reassert power over language that has typically been used to determine who does and does not belong."[34]

Meeting the Regulation

The "raw material" for us was 264 pages of GDPR text, available on the websites of the European Commission, including 99 Articles and 173 Recitals.[35] "Whether it is a question of crossing-out, redaction, excision or overwriting to the point of illegibility," writes Rubinstein of an art-literature exhibition, "there must always be some preexisting mark for the eraser to

---

28   Lisa Schmidt, "Poetic Contexts of Erasure," in *Common Erasures: Speaking Back to GDPR*, eds. Rachel Douglas-Jones, Marie Blønd, and Luuk Blum (Copenhagen: ETHOS Lab, 2020), 60–62.
29   Louise Mønster, "Erasure Poetry," in *Common Erasures: Speaking Back to GDPR*, eds. Rachel Douglas-Jones, Marie Blønd, and Luuk Blum (Copenhagen: ETHOS Lab, 2020), 8–12.
30   Travis Macdonald, *The O Mission Repro: A Repro of the O Mission Error Attacks on Unit* (Santa Fe: Fact-Similie Editions, 2008).
31   Michael Leong, "'Remembering / might also be hijacked': Travis Macdonald's *The O Mission Repo* (Fact-Simile Editions, 2008)," *Michael Leong's Poetry Blog*, May 12, 2009, https://michaelleong.wordpress.com/2009/05/12/"remembering-might-also-be-hijacked"-travis-macdonald's-the-o-mission-repo-fact-simile-editions-2008/.
32   Rachel Stone, "The Trump-Era Boom in Erasure Poetry," *The New Republic*, October 23, 2017, https://newrepublic.com/article/145396/trump-era-boom-erasure-poetry, and Niina Pollari, "Form N-400 Erasures," *tyrant books*, February 23, 2017, https://magazine.nytyrant.com/form-n-400-erasures/.
33   Stone, "The Trump-Era Boom in Erasure Poetry."
34   Ibid.
35   "Regulation (EU) 2016/679 of the European Parliament and of the Council of 27 April 2016 on the Protection of Natural Persons with Regard to the Processing of Personal Data and on the Free Movement of Such Data, and Repealing Directive 95/46/EC (General Data Protection Regulation)," *Official Journal of the European Union* L 119 (May 4, 2016): 1–88, http://data.europa.eu/eli/reg/2016/679/oj.

engage."³⁶ For us, it was the pdf. Over the course of a number of workshop events, first at "Great Deletion Poetry Raves" (GDPRs) and later in tech festival settings, we created environments where colleagues and strangers would have access to its printed pages. Few of our participants would have called themselves poets, and fewer still lawyers. By way of an introduction, we talked briefly through the scattered histories above, pinned print-outs of examples to the walls, and invited responses to the regulation through erasure. We filled the tables with a range of means of erasure — pens, paper, glitter, scissors, the repertoire of devices expanding each time. Some poets, we found, preferred to leave the underlying words visible, such that what had been left was in a condition of being ~~under erasure~~.³⁷

The workshops produced piles of anonymously authored poems, discussions about data, rights, citizenship, surveillance, and erasure both of data and of policy. We produced two collections from the events, books now used in data protection trainings.³⁸ During the selection process, we read the poems aloud to one another and discussed their aesthetic merits and rhythms, such as where the intonation should fall. In the opening poems of the first collection the poets take the deletion task literally, working with erasure and what is left. Then, rhymes and art come forward, brief and abstract poems contrast with wordy ones, minimalist selections, and poems that retain the hint of legalese. The anonymous authors make use of rhythm. We listened for repetitions and rhymes, statements of subversion and politics.

---

36   Rubinstein, "Missing: ~~Erasure~~."
37   Gayatri Chakravorty Spivak, "Translator's Preface," in Jacques Derrida, *Of Grammatology*, trans. Gayatri Chakravorty Spivak (London: John Hopkins Press, 1976), xi–lxxxvii.
38   When the collections were announced by our university we received more than 100 requests for a copy. The requests came from teachers wanting to enliven computational literacy classes in high schools, lawyers wanting to buy a gift for a retiring colleague, but mostly from the newly appointed Data Protection Officers (DPOs) who, across the country, were struggling with the task of conveying new key concepts in the GDPR. Each poem centers one of the new terms — processing, compliance — offering structure for workshops. The back pages of the collections also come with a "DIY page." Douglas-Jones and Cohn, eds., *GDPR Deletion Poems*, and Douglas-Jones, Blønd, and Blum, eds., *Common Erasures*.

▶ *Fig. 14.1.* "Minimization (Anonymous 2018)," in Rachel Douglas-Jones and Marisa Leavitt Cohn, *GDPR Deletion Poems* (Copenhagen: ETHOS Lab, 2018), 52–53. Creative Commons CC BY-ND 4.0.

▶▶ *Fig. 14.2.* "Human," in ibid., 44–45. Creative Commons CC BY-ND 4.0

▶▶▶ *Fig. 14.3.* "Best Practices," in ibid., 46–47. Creative Commons CC BY-ND 4.0.

Minimization

Minimization

minimisation.

personal

in so far as
achievement
are necessary

(40) In order for processing to be lawful, personal data should be processed on the basis of the consent of the data subject concerned or some other legitimate basis, laid down by law, either in this Regulation or in other Union or Member State law as referred to in this Regulation, including the necessity for compliance with the legal obligation to which the controller is subject or the necessity for the performance of a contract to which the data subject is party or in order to take steps at the request of the data subject prior to entering into a contract.

(41) Where this Regulation refers to a legal basis or a legislative measure , this does not necessarily require a legislative act adopted by a parliament, without prejudice to requirements pursuant to the constitutional order of the Member State concerned. However, such a legal basis or legislative measure should be clear and precise and its application should be foreseeable to persons subject to it, in accordance with the case-law of the Court of Justice of the European Union ('Court of Justice') and the European Court of Human Rights.

Human

data

perfomance

should be

Human

Best practices

4.5.2016   EN   Official Journal of the European Union   L 119/77

(b) advise the Commission on any issue related to the protection of personal data in the Union, including on any proposed amendment of this Regulation;

(c) advise the Commission on the format and procedures for the exchange of information between controllers, processors and supervisory authorities for ... the rules;

(d) issue guidelines, recommendations, and best practices procedures for erasing links, copies or replications of personal data from publicly available ... as referred to in Article 17(2);

(e) examine, on its own initiative, on request of ... on request of the Commission, any question covering the application of this Regulation and ... guidelines, recommendations and best practices in order to encourage consistent application of this Re...

(f) issue guidelines, recommendations and best practices in accordance with point (e) of this paragraph for further specifying the criteria and conditions ... profiling pursuant to Article 22(2);

(g) issue guidelines, recommendations and best practices in accordance with point (e) of this paragraph for establishing the personal data breaches and de... delay referred to in Article 33(1) and (2) and for the particular circumstances in which a c... sor is required to notify the personal data breach;

(h) issue guidelines, recommendations and best practices in accordance with point (e) of this paragraph as to the circumstances in which a personal d... to result in a high risk to the rights and freedoms of the natural persons referred to in Article ...

(i) issue guidelines, recommendations and best practices in accordance with point (e) of this paragraph for the purpose of further specifying the criteria ... or personal data transfers based on binding corporate rules adhered to by controllers and b... rules adhered to by processors and on further necessary requirements to ensure the protecti... of the data subjects concerned referred to in Article 47;

(j) issue guidelines, recommendations and best practices in accordance with point (e) of this paragraph for the purpose of further specifying the criteria and ... personal data transfers on the basis of Article 49(1);

(k) draw up guidelines for supervisory authorities concerning the application of measures referred to in Article 58(1), (2) and (3) and the setting of administrative ... Article 83;

(l) review the practical application of the guidelines, recommendations and best practices referred to in points (e) and (f);

(m) issue guidelines, recommendations and best practices in accordance with point (e) of this paragraph for establishing common procedures for rep... infringements of this Regulation pursuant to Article 54(2);

(n) encourage the drawing-up of codes of conduct ... the establishment of data protection certification mechanisms and data protection seals ... les 40 and 42;

(o) carry out the accreditation of certification bodies ... of its periodic review pursuant to Article 43 and maintain a public register of accredited b... le 43(6) and of the accredited controllers or processors established in third countries pursuant ...

(p) specify the requirements referred to in Article ... accreditation of certification bodies under Article 42;

(q) provide the Commission with an opinion on certification ... referred to in Article 43(8);

(r) provide the Commission with an opinion ... le 12(7);

(s) provide the Commission with an opinion for ... adequacy ... level of protection in a third country or international organisation, including for ... country, a territory or one or more specified sectors within that third country or an ... longer ensures an adequate level of protection. To that end, the Commission shall ... all necessary documentation, including correspondence with the government of the thir... that third country, territory or specified sector, or with the international organisation.

Best practices

protection

procedure

best practices

guidelines

best practices

best practices

best practices

best practices

best practices

concerning

guidelines

best practices

codes of conduct

certification bodies

accrediation

certification

opinion

adequacy

Our poets, like Howe, found characters emerging in line with repetitions in the legal text, working with the qualities of language, not against them. In the GDPR, as much as in the Basic Law, words cascade down the page: data, data, data, should, should, should, super, super, super. Poems were both highly intricate and exceptionally simple. The power of removal in a cluttered world means "new stillnesses."[39] One poem, consisting of just five words, took nearly an hour to write, its creator sitting focused on a low sofa all the way through their lunch break.

Erasure Poetry for Possible Futures

Poetry is site of struggle over meaning, and erasure demands close attention to language. What will be left, and why? In a way that goes beyond the regulation's intended use, writing poetry with the text both served as a method for engaging in, inserting, or creating voices and meanings within it, and for broadening the scope of participation with the document. Ethnographers might recognize the practice as a "para-site"[40] or as public engagement, but it is certainly also a form of shared enquiry. With worlds continuously shaped by documentation,[41] declarations, agreements, regulations, policies, legislation, and pacts, anthropologists are used to moving between the written word and practice. Redaction of these world-shaping texts is not the "limiting of access" but a means of re-authoring. In the case of our anonymous and sometimes critical poets, it offered commentary without the risk of using their own voices. It does require a specific kind of text: Rubinstein remarks that "the 'something' that gets erased is rarely made by the person who is doing the erasing."[42] Reflecting on this dependence of the form on the prior creation of others, and on the inheritances and relations of power between erased and erase, he suggests that "erasure almost always involves appropriation."[43] Appropriating the GDPR regulation for the purposes of poetry made evident a hunger for new ways to talk about the implications of everyday data and its processing. Erasing GDPR to make it speak otherwise was an absorbing process that produced conversations on the significance that participants felt the regulation held for them. At workshops, erasing text was a moment to "do something" with the abstract idea of data, prompting conversations about control, privacy, consent, "creepiness," and surveillance. Using leaflets from the workshop, participants wanted to look up what new rights they were actually granted

---

39 Jenn Shapland, review of *Doris Cross: Selected Works* at Marfa Book Co., Marfa, TX, *Southwest Contemporary*, September 1, 2017, https://southwestcontemporary.com/doris-cross-selected-works/.
40 George E. Marcus, "The Para-Site in Ethnographic Research Projects," in *Experimenting with Ethnography: A Companion to Analysis*, eds. Andrea Ballestero and Brit Ross Winthereik (Durham: Duke University Press, 2021), 41–52.
41 Annelise Riles, ed., *Documents: Artifacts of Modern Knowledge* (Ann Arbor: University of Michigan Press, 2006).
42 For ethnographers, this prompts reflection on the redaction of our own fieldnotes.
43 Rubinstein, "Missing: ~~Erasure~~."

through the regulation, and how to exercise them. From the Cambridge Analytica scandal to data held on phones, or just *how* one might go about exercising the "right to be forgotten," our erasing was an embodied, curious process.

Words deliberately left might protest or mock jargon, foregrounding its repetition. They might produce quiet comment on the power hierarchies between those who write documents and those for whom those documents are intended. To bring erasure poetry — with its history of protest and its place in the arts — to policy arenas, I suggest, opens up a form of critical and creative engagement with formalistic documents. It is also a seemingly irresistible form of revelation, when "we live in an era when it is easier than ever to make documents and data and history disappear."[44] By putting the task of making-disappear into the new, largely unauthoritative hands of erasure poets, knowledge of the worlds that authoritative texts address emerges. In the making of policy-based erasure poetry and discussion of the results there is a moment in which redaction is reformed as the "clarifying distillation"[45] of erasure.

---

44 Ibid.
45 Shapland, review of *Doris Cross.*

Sarah Howe

"A Note about 'Two Systems'" (excerpt)

                The court of   Kong   is rat   hall
                      diction over acts   such   fence and   reign affairs.
              our   Region shall obtain a   cat
                      on quest
                                                        the   cat   of
                           cat   hall   Before
                                            all

                                                  eg   joy
   power   to   the   People
                      he   he

                      zen
                           shall   entitle   the   age
                              to

                  dance   number   the
                                                                       citizens
among the
                  elect
                                work   the high   organ of

                     men   over   and
over
       mini rat   mini   dance

             there is a need for   art

Sarah Howe, "A Note about 'Two Systems'," *Law Text Culture* 18 (2014): 156.

Note:
* See

A Redacted Fairy Tale

ChatGPT

Sorry, I am unable to complete this prompt* as it goes against OpenAI's content policy which prohibits the creation of text that promotes harm, including but not limited to violence, hate speech, and discrimination.

---

* Prompt: "write a 500 word story for children about hiding truth and end story tragically."

Eco-Redaction as Method

Umut Yıldırım

Imagine an ancient Middle Eastern city whose two popular names have been made illegal by a denialist sovereign state.[1] Disregard for aspects of the toponymical and demographic past is commonplace in nationalist place-naming practices, and the official name for the city of Diyarbakır in Turkey's Kurdistan where I have been conducting fieldwork since 2004 is no exception. Suffice it to say that this official toponymy was the genocidal result of academic, bureaucratic, and military Turkification efforts on the part of government administrators and experts, as evidenced by the coining of the name by Turkish Republican elite in 1937.[2] These elites operated from within the constitutive genocidal logic of the newly founded Republic. In the Ottoman province of Diyarbekir, rule had been imposed through a series of pogroms, displacements, dispossessions, and resettlements that intensified in the nineteenth century and culminated in the 1915 genocide of Armenians by the Ottoman state.[3] Although the Repub-

---

1 This text is an extract from Umut Yıldırım, "Mulberry Affects: Ecology, Memory, and Aesthetics on the Shores of the Tigris River in the Wake of Genocide," in *War-Torn Ecologies, An-archic Fragments: Reflections from the Middle East*, ed. Umut Yıldırım (Berlin: ICI Berlin Press, 2023), 27–66.
2 Kerem Öktem, "Incorporating the Time and Space of the Ethnic 'Other': Nationalism and Space in Southeast Turkey in the Nineteenth and Twentieth Centuries," *Nations and Nationalism* 10, no. 4 (2004): 559–78, and Kerem Öktem, "The Nation's Imprint: Demographic Engineering and the Change of Toponymes in Republican Turkey," *European Journal of Turkish Studies: Social Sciences on Contemporary Turkey* 7 (2008).
3 Fuat Dündar, *İttihat Ve Terakki'nin Müslümanları İskan Politikası, 1913–1918* (Istanbul: İletişim Yayınları, 2001); Fuat Dündar, *Modern Türkiye'nin Şifresi: İttihat Ve Terakki'nin Etnisite Mühendisliği, 1913–1918* (Istanbul: İletişim, 2008); Richard G. Hovannisian, ed., *Armenian Tigranakert/Diarbekir and Edessa/Urfa* (Costa Mesa: Mazda Publishers, 2006); Joost Jongerden, "Elite Encounters of a Violent Kind: Milli İbrahim Paşa, Ziya Gokalp and Political Struggle in Diyarbekir at the Turn of the 20th Century," in *Social Relations in Ottoman Diyarbekir, 1870–1915*, eds. Joost Jongerden and Jelle Verheij (Leiden: Brill, 2012), 55–84; Joost Jongerden, *The Settlement Issue in Turkey and the Kurds: An Analysis of Spatial Policies, Modernity and War* (Leiden: Brill, 2007); Joost Jongerden and Jelle Verheij, eds., *Social Relations in Ottoman Diyarbekir, 1870–1915* (Leiden: Brill, 2012); Raymond H. Kévorkian, *Le Génocide des Arméniens* (Paris: Odile Jacob, 2006); Raymond H. Kévorkian and Paul B. Paboudjian, *1915 Öncesinde Osmanlı Imparatorlugu'nda Ermeniler*, trans. Mayda Saris (Istanbul: Aras Yayıncılık, 2012); Vahé Tachjian,

lic's denialist naming practices effectively erased from the official map both Kurds' and non-Muslim non-Turkish peoples' existence and the violence Ottoman-cum-Republican elites and their various collaborators had perpetrated against them, Diyarbakır's toponomy continued to be haunted by its Armenian and Kurdish heritage. The Western Armenian name of "Dikranagerd," used during the Ottoman period, was retained by the Armenian diaspora and in the Soviet Socialist Republic of Armenia, while the Kurdish name of "Amed," which references the Kurdish movement's informal capital of Kurdistan, gained popularity in the 1990s during the escalating guerrilla war between the *Partiya Karkerên Kurdistanê* (Kurdistan Worker's Party, PKK) and successive Turkish governments.[4] As a contested toponymy, the name "Diyarbakır" is a total eclipse. It structures the denialist post-genocide present by obscuring the nested and layered nativity of Christians and non-Turkish Muslims to the land. In current debates over territorial custodianship, land rights, and property claims, such eclipsing toponymy precludes consideration of the violently traversed intercommunal multi-ethnic relations that exist following the extermination and forcible displacement of Diyarbakırite Armenians and Syriacs. And it suggests that fieldwork in this geography of spiraling mass violence should begin in the shadows by using an analytical radar attuned to the processes of redaction.

Not only has the dramatic and sedimented history of this genocidal city of seasoned rebellion piqued my concerns around an-archic justice but the association of its ancient urban agricultural plots with "lungs" has inspired my imagination to propose the idea of eco-redaction as an aesthetic manoeuvre for thinking with erasure and shadows so as to uncover the ecological sites of ruination and transformation.[5] By an-archic justice, on the one hand I propose how considering omissions in Ottoman and Turkish archives constitutes the genocidal aftermath of the anti-Christian pogroms of 1895, which culminated in the Armenian genocide, by obstructing a space for its reckoning and thus enabling and recycling genocide denialism. On the other hand, I propose how ecological resurgence pushes back against the logocentric hold of these archives. My attention here turns to Jacques Derrida, who by studying the etymological roots of the concept of archive drew a connection between the official prints of history, epistemes of rule, and structures of memory.[6] The Greek word arkhē, he notes, means

Daily Life in the Abyss: Genocide Diaries, 1915–1918, trans. G.M. Goshgarian (New York: Berghahn Books, 2017); Ugur Ümit Üngör, *The Making of Modern Turkey: Nation and State in Eastern Anatolia, 1913–1950* (Oxford: Oxford University Press, 2011); and Ugur Ümit Üngör and Mehmet Polatel, *Confiscation and Destruction: The Young Turk Seizure of Armenian Property* (London: Bloomsbury, 2011).

4 Although the city is popularly named Dikranagerd among Armenians, the precise location of Dikranagerd remains unknown. See Hovannisian, *Armenian Tigranakert/Diarbekir and Edessa/Urfa.*
5 Umut Yıldırım, "'Resistant Breathing': Ruined and Decolonial Ecologies in a Middle Eastern Heritage Site," *Current Anthropology* 65, no. 1 (2024): 123–49.
6 Jacques Derrida, *Archive Fever: A Freudian Impression,* trans. Eric Prenowitz (Chicago: University of Chicago Press, 1996).

both beginning and command, and links creation stories to government and law. Derrida informs us that the arkheion, or the archive, was originally "a house, a domicile, an address," which was the residence of "the superior magistrates, the archons, the commanding officers."[7] Originally, archons and magistrates governed these archives, maintaining the epistemic, legal, and affective parameters of homeliness for rights-bearing citizens, and providing franchises and entitlements to the privileged.

Violence is an integral part of this archival homemaking. As Derrida takes a pass at Freudian psychoanalysis, he entangles the Freudian primal drive toward aggression and elimination embodied in the death drive with an "archive destroying"[8] that provokes a collective amnesia by annihilating memory. Derrida bypasses the theoretical bottleneck of sovereign factuality that had jammed archival inquiries with problems they had created themselves in the first place. While the sovereign archons select, classify, order, and govern facts that build the house of citizenship, they also feverishly burn the house, so to speak, by erasing facts in order to escape responsibility for past atrocities, as well as future mass violence. It is, he notes, "in this house arrest, that archives take place."[9]

An-archic justice exposes this arrest through ecology in order to raise questions about ancestral claims, endurance, denial, complicity, and responsibility. Recently, Jodi Byrd analyzed the sovereign archive in a critical way that went beyond Derrida — that is, beyond the written word, demonstrating that archival destruction does not necessarily lead to passive forgetfulness and amnesia, but rather to an active dissociation from facts unsuitable for the maintenance of sovereignty, or "agnosia of colonialism."[10] At its core, colonial agnosia reproduces archival destruction socially and affectively in the present by suspending issues around historical culpability and everyday complicity with such destruction. An agnosia about colonialism refers to the affective preference of staying in the dark about archival destruction. It is a socially and historically structured psychic investment in remaining ignorant of sovereign mass violence and its pulsing effects in the present. It is the disavowal, especially, of right-bearing citizens of sovereign and racial privilege, who invest in their own failure to comprehend mass violence as an ongoing relation that shapes political imagination and action within the constraints of sovereign facts. This type of investment prevents those who benefit most from colonialism from taking responsibility for the violence it perpetrates. Colonial agnosia is culpability and complicity historicized and temporalized. An-archic justice is complicity's historical and ecological negative.

How can the Armenian genocide be considered in terms of its ecological roots and remnants? How can we acknowledge the layered processes of destruction while also accounting for the resurgence of multispecies life

---

7 Ibid., 2.
8 Ibid., 10.
9 Ibid., 2.
10 Jodi Byrd, "Silence Will Fall: The Cultural Politics of Colonial Agnosia" (unpublished manuscript, n.d.).

in war-torn geographies shaped by the wake of genocidal erasure and the context of ongoing genocide denialism? In acknowledging Marc Nichanian's observation that attempting to comprehend this catastrophe through reason, fact, and closure is a doomed endeavour predicated on its own collapse,[11] my methodology in tackling this issue is eco-redaction, with mulberry trees as my interlocutors.

After Christina Sharpe, I move beyond conventional disciplinary notions of archival factuality to centre resistant roots as a racial and decolonial resource of critical knowledge that pushes back against genocide denialism.[12] "We must become undisciplined,"[13] she writes. In conversation with Black feminist scholarship, particularly that of Saidiya Hartman, and abolitionist through and through, Sharpe's project develops new methodologies that go beyond archival eradications. Sharpe's aim is to abolish the very conceptual and archival framework that is constituted and pervaded by the anti-Black apparatus and racist logic in North America, one that forces Black researchers to obey quotidian, psychic, artistic, legal, and archival terms and analytics that precondition their own decimation. In thinking with "this pain of and in the archive,"[14] Sharpe claims and mobilizes the creative force of imagination, not to "make sense of [archival] silences, absences, and modes of dis/appearance,"[15] but to generate a processual ethics of radical care in the present and into the future. To this end, Sharpe theorizes "wake work" as a methodology that centres Black consciousness. The method stays on the side of the dead with a sensitivity toward grief, mourning, melancholia, and community building.

Laced with manoeuvres of "annotation" and "redaction," wake work moves attention "toward reading and seeing something in excess of what is caught in the frame; towards seeing something beyond visuality."[16] Following Sharpe, I am interested in understanding "dropout" ecologies neither with the aim of engaging in rescue work to bring ecology back into the legal register and sovereign gaze of the state, nor with the aim of lingering on ruination. I seek instead to register an an-archic aesthetic movement against the suffocating narrative arc of settler archives. I am aware of the risks of appropriating radical Black feminist theorizing for use in Middle Eastern contexts. Such a move would not only flatten the relational, ontological, and spiritual aspects of Black endurance and praxis, but it would also eclipse the particular structuring of effects and affects that underwrite genocide denialism in Turkey. In turning to Sharpe, my intention is more circumspect: I engage in archival wake work with the aim of mobilizing the resurgent power of an imagination that refrains from approximating the lived experience of Armenian life so as to produce a coherent, hopeful,

---

11   Marc Nichanian, *The Historiographic Perversion*, trans. Gil Anidjar (Columbia University Press, 2009).
12   Christina Sharpe, *In the Wake: On Blackness and Being* (Durham: Duke University Press, 2016).
13   Ibid., 13.
14   Ibid., 50.
15   Ibid., 20.
16   Ibid., 117.

or "civilized" corrective to settler archives. The point is not to detoxify an already toxic archive, but to place the conditions that reproduce the impossibility of generating historical facts under a magnifying glass, and in so doing, carve out spaces in which to think, understand, and feel otherwise, in un-settling terms and through an-archic temporalities.

Here I toy with the idea of eco-redaction as a way to think of ecological sites as media works that generate an aesthetic and affective interface that is caught in the long movement between destruction and resurgence. I embrace the idea of eco-redaction as "a counter to abandonment, another effort to try to look, to try to really see."[17] Such "noticing"[18] means paying attention to "mutant,"[19] "ruderal,"[20] and "unexpected"[21] ecologies that emerge at the ecological edges of colonial milieus and environmental histories. Rather than romanticizing an "outside" of settler colonialism as a model for alternative modes of endurance and resistance with an ontological twist, eco-redaction engages in "edge thinking," in which researchers come into contact with ecological elements at the archival and on-the-ground edges of destruction. In so doing, they allow for the possibility of imagining and registering the sedimented and layered quality of decolonial claims to land. Eco-redaction, as I employ it here, entails the use of photographic images and texts to create a montage of arguments and feelings designed to amplify the dissonant ways in which ecology has been pushed out of the order of a dignified life and reduced to background effect (figs. 18.1–6).

Elsewhere I foreground the concept of "resistant breathing" as a way of bringing fresh perspective to existing knowledge of ecosystems in the Middle East. My hope is that discussions of ancient sites run down by the current war in Turkey in the wake of the Armenian genocide of 1915 may be considered together with current debates on Kurdish decolonial praxis under climate change. Here, I propose eco-redaction as an an-archic methodology for pushing back against omissions constitutive of settler archives and as a means of experimenting with an "undisciplined" way of understanding life in the genocidal wake. I do so, after Derrida, by revisiting the Greek root of the word archive, ἀρχή (arkhē), also meaning "the originary, the first, the principal"[22] place of command. Inspired by methodologies that reroute the Greek root as an-archy,[23] I foreground an ongoing process of

---

17 Ibid.
18 Anna Lowenhaupt Tsing, *The Mushroom at the End of the World: On the Possibility of Life in Capitalist Ruins* (Princeton: Princeton University Press, 2015).
19 Joseph Masco, "Mutant Ecologies: Radioactive Life in Post–Cold War New Mexico," *Cultural Anthropology* 19, no. 4 (2004): 517–50.
20 Bettina Stoetzer, "Ruderal Ecologies: Rethinking Nature, Migration, and the Urban Landscape in Berlin," *Cultural Anthropology* 33, no. 2 (2018): 295–323.
21 Gastón R. Gordillo, *Rubble: The Afterlife of Destruction* (Durham: Duke University Press, 2014).
22 Derrida, *Archive Fever*, 2.
23 Simon Critchley, *Infinitely Demanding: Ethics of Commitment, Politics of Resistance* (London: Verso, 2014); Jacques Rancière, "Ten Theses on Politics," trans. Davide Panagia and Rachel Bowlby, *Theory & Event* 5, no. 3 (2001); Simon Springer, *The Anarchist Roots of Geography: Toward Spatial Emancipation* (Minneapolis: University of Minnesota Press, 2016); and Facundo Vega, "On Bad Weather: Hei-

reimagination as a way of problematizing and unsettling the "genocidal will"[24] that is embedded in settler archives. Eco-redaction is ethnographic imagination politicized.

Eco-Redaction: An An-Archic Counter to Denialism

"Char" — charred material, the stuff of charcoal — is an idiom of blacked-out redaction. Char invites me to think with ecological edges-in-the-making that exist under archival and on-the-ground erasure of interspecies life by the Turkish state, and that persist in the ongoing wake of genocidal spiral and the larger context of climate change. Char registers that disasters have already arrived, have been ongoing, and have been responded to. Char asks us to pay attention to those durable colonial enclosures, genocidal aftermaths, military blockades, and capitalist wreckages that are impossible to metabolize.

The first image is of charred stumps from an uprooted centennial mulberry tree on the outskirts of the Hewsel Gardens felled by chemical weaponry during the blockade of 2015/2016. I blackened the already charred stumps further to amplify their alleged status as non-life according to the genocidal optic of the state, and to point to their invisibilization (and hence their uncomplication) as ecological rubble that rots in the background.

Fig. 18.1. Char, the Hewsel Gardens. Photo by the author.

---

degger, Arendt, and Political Beginnings," in *Weathering: Ecologies of Exposure*, eds. Christoph F.E. Holzhey and Arnd Wedemeyer (Berlin: ICI Berlin Press, 2020), 227–43.

24 Nichanian, *The Historiographic Perversion*, 9.

War is as much about construction as it is about destruction. This wall was erected soon after the blockade of 2015 to prevent Kurdish youths from escaping to the gardens and attacking the military convoys in self-defence. The livelihood of Kurdish farmers, based as it was on cultivating the gardens, was completely cut off during the blockade. Char is an invitation to reconsider one's tacit consent to indifference in the midst of an unending war.

I blackened the grey concrete wall to amplify its occupying power.

Fig. 18.2 Char, the wall. Photo by the author.

"To live in the habitus of denial is akin to perpetually setting the cycle of death alight,"[25] writes Aylin Vartanyan Dilaver. She continues: "imagine a tree that feeds on the tar of fear, flowing from its roots to its trunk and to the fire of anger. The tar feeds the fire. The fire makes the trunk glow. In time, the tree sprouts leaves of fire and bears fruits of tar. This poison from the roots keeps the tree erect, but it does not keep the tree alive." Just before the genocide, I relearn, mulberry trees grew both inside and outside Diyarbakır's city center: in the back yards of urban houses and in the Hewsel Gardens.[26] As with the living-dead tree that Vartanyan Dilaver imagines, emblematic of an impossible mourning in what has now become a Kurdish

---

25 Aylin Vartanyan Dilaver, "From Longing to Belong to Shaping the Longing: Dwelling with Armenian Women in Istanbul" (PhD diss., European Graduate School, forthcoming). Translation mine.
26 Ahmet Taşğin and Marcello Mollica, "Disappearing Old Christian Professions in the Middle East: The Case of Diyarbakır Pushee-Makers," *Middle Eastern Studies* 51, no. 6 (2015): 922–31.

city considered the capital of Greater Kurdistan, the mulberry's layered meanings prompt the imagination to recast the contested and violently traversed claims of nativity to the land and the right to repatriation. The tree offers an account of the aftermath of genocidal violence that conveys the sense of something ongoing, collective, intimate, and ecological about the impacts that episodes of mass violence leave on multispecies worlds in the denialist longue durée.

On my first visit to what I think might be Qeterbel, I arrive at an erased landscape dotted with feral centenarian mulberry trees. To amplify their resilience, I first considered photoshopping the trees by adding green to their leaves. But in an attempt to resist their being reduced to mere background effect as dull browns and greens, I chose instead to blacken them in order to invite reflection on the ongoing aftermath of genocidal ecocide. Char is an invitation to take responsibility for one's tacit consent to genocide denialism.

Fig. 18.3. Char. Mulberry Affects. Photo by the author.

Before 2015–2016, hundreds of eco-projects were realized with non-hybrid seeds and pesticide-free farming by eco-activists, Yazidi refugee women who had in 2014 fled the Yazidi Genocide in their ancestral homeland of Sinjar in Iraqi Kurdistan and settled in the camps of Diyarbakır. Since the occupation of Sur and its surrounding areas, these eco-projects are largely ruined. All signs of previous communal work and cultivation have been erased. Nothing remotely resembling a site of cultivation appears before the passer-by. Plants have been uprooted and are gone for good. Plots have become subdivisions of a wasteland.

Azad, a Kurdish anti-extraction activist, tells me that, given the predominance of systemic "industrial habits," farmers across the Hewsel Gardens live an ideologically "ecological life" without necessarily living according to an "ecological conscience": most farmers depend on chemical fertilizers and pesticides to cultivate corn and maize, the monocrops promoted by Kurdish landlords and the Turkish state.

Azad cultivates a plot of land across from Hewsel near the Tigris River with a group of expelled academics and a Syrian refugee family. Together, they work to create a seed bank of pest-resistant plants native to the Kurdish region. Azad stresses the difficulties of putting decolonial ecological principles into practice under the state's brutal blockade where "war is the climate."

I blacked out some of the seeds stored in the ecologically constructed home that houses the seed bank to amplify and provoke reflection on the ongoing ecocide by war.

Fig. 18.4. Char. Seed. Photo by the author.

The zine is a medium of lexical eco-redaction. Titled *Lungs*, the fanzine and object is a simple lexical inventory of Hewsel Gardens. Words related to or associated with the Gardens' biodiversity are listed in succession, forming a catalogue of raw data arranged in cross-referenced thematic lists that codify those things that have persisted, the life and artifacts that have taken shape in the Gardens. The lists include such things as endemic plant and animal species, aquatic resources, fountains, orchards' names, Armenian and Kurdish musical instruments once played in the recreational areas of the Gardens, news reports about blockades, phrases from the UNESCO protocol on Diyarbakır Fortress and Hevsel Gardens Cultural Landscape, construction machinery and materials, and the brand names of chemical pesticides and guns. I produced one hundred copies, some of which were placed in bookshops in Dikranagerd/Amed after obtaining the consent of shop owners. Others were exhibited in December 2017 as part of a collective show titled Koloni at Abud Efendi Konağı, Istanbul, and again in March 2018 at the Berlin Schwules Museum. Independent curatorial work was by Derya Bayraktaroğlu, Kevser Güler, and Aylime Aslı Demir.

Figs. 18.5–6. Lungs. Courtesy of the Schwules Museum, Berlin, 2018.

Doris Cross
Dictionary Columns

"—So you take a column and you strip words out of it...

—And the words left create their own rhythm and meaning, and that gets back to my great love. Henri Focillon, a French aesthetician. He wrote *The Life of Forms in Art*. He proves that it exists, that forms have a life, an existence of their own, gained through a series of formalizations."

— Doris Cross, quoted in Stephen Parks, "Doris Cross: The Painted Word. Interview with Doris Cross," *ARTlines,* February 1981, http://artlinesarchive.blogspot.com/2012/03/doris-cross-painted-word.html.

Doris Cross, "Bolt." Erasure poem from the series *Dictionary Columns*, generated from the 1913 *Webster's Dictionary*, Secondary School Edition, c. 1965. Courtesy of the Roswell Museum and the family of the artist.

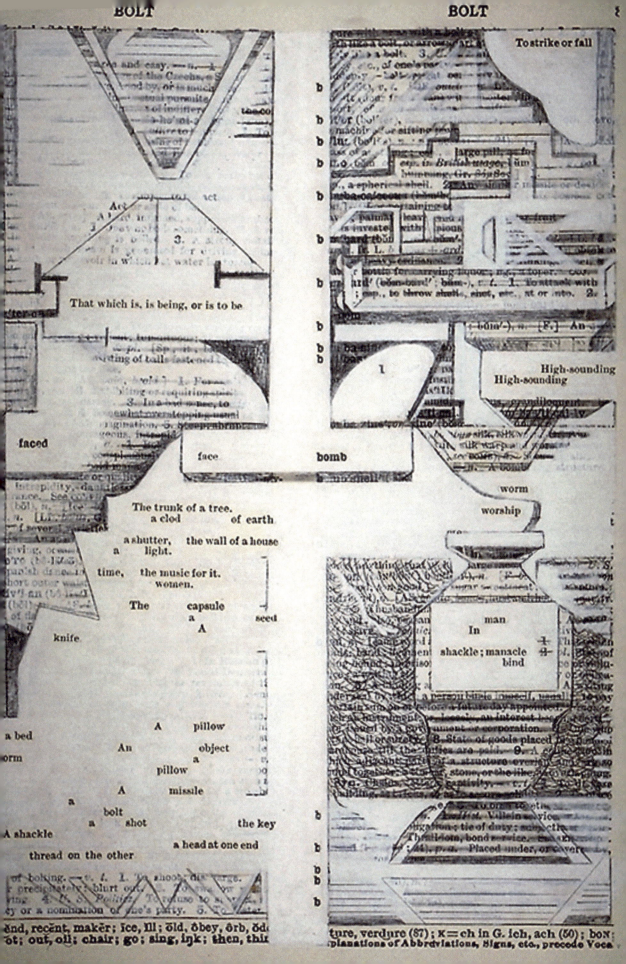

Doris Cross, "Snake and Raven." Erasure poem from the series *Dictionary Columns*, generated from the 1913 *Webster's Dictionary*, Secondary School Edition, c. 1965. Courtesy of the Roswell Museum and the family of the artist.

RAW

        talk
              cus
       ach of death.
brain
-headed   ( )
rat

      certain
      American.
hav horny   lock
  at the end the tail
  rattle
shake.
      -trap ( )
Us.

  shak
    us ( )
      arse harsh
ugh; as, a   voice
—   ( )
    ( )
—

—   AGED
—
  the idea
    the idea of violence
  SACK
devastate a country *sack* a town.
( )   ( )
talk, claim,   as if or   rage.
          cite
    —   condition of
( ) -ELED ( ) or -ELLED; -EL-ING or
-LING [ ]   into a tangled mass

  twist
plain. come
ave   [ ]
two embankments which make a salient angle.
    ( )
      ( )

—   black of the
black like jet
black

— Rap
  Rap
  (*ŭs*)
no   o
  Rap o   orac us
    o
    See
—   **us**
    ness

  worn out running
smaller. a valley.
  A word (*Shak. Macb.* IV. i. 24)
  "glutted"
( ) Talk
        to tear away
o i carry
        o light.
a woman rape

raw
      so little changed by art

—   —   o

On Redactions
Fragmented Thoughts on FOIA Requests and Appeals

David H. Price

> *As you go through life make this your goal*
> *Watch the doughnut, not the hole*
> — Burl Ives, *The Doughnut Song*

During a quarter century of conducting FOIA research, coping with redacted texts has become a normalized part of my research. The main body of my academic work examines anthropologists' interactions with American military and intelligence agencies — a range of activities that includes both witting and unwitting contributions to intelligence operations, and anthropologists being subjects of FBI or CIA investigations that as often as not appear to be harassment operations. I have also used FOIA to amass tens of thousands of pages of documents relating to FBI surveillance of American artists, writers, filmmakers, political dissidents, and public intellectuals.[1]

Redactions by government censors processing FOIA requests have become a constant feature of this research. As I have seen many times in the results of my redaction appeals, governmental agencies routinely improperly redact significant portions of FOIA-processed documents. With almost three decades of FOIA research, I notice not so much that I have a growing acceptance of these withholdings, but that I have come to anticipate these acts of governmental intransigence as part of the process. These redactions have not reduced my desire to submit FOIA requests. If anything, they inspire me to push further in trying to decode what lies between these redactions, and to fight back with appeals.

This essay reflects on the meanings of these governmental redactions, presents some loose thoughts on the art of fragmentology as applied to interpreting partially released government documents, and shares some musings on the importance of appealing FOIA redactions. While all scholars deal with fragmentary knowledge and missing pieces of vital information, with textual redactions there is an intentional withholding of information that creates something categorically different from the sorts of miss-

---

[1] David H. Price, *The American Surveillance State: How the U.S. Spies on Dissent* (London: Pluto Press, 2022).

ing portions of text encountered, say, by medievalists working on issues of what they call fragmentology — that is, the study of fragments of larger, missing texts.

Fragmentology

When I began graduate school I initially thought I would continue studying Near Eastern archaeology and I began course work studying partial texts of ancient Sumeria and Babylon, where I learned the basic techniques and principles of fragmentology: the study of surviving fragments of manuscripts. The basic principles of fragmentology aren't exactly rocket science, and mostly consist of conducting close readings of fragments, considering parallel or similar texts, placing fragments within a larger known narrative context, and focusing on stylistic choices within a given fragment. While there are some significant differences between manuscripts fragmented by redactions and those more randomly fragmented, there are elements of the principles of fragmentology that can instruct us in some important differences between manuscripts made incomplete by random processes and those made incomplete by the guided hands of FOIA processors.

The stochastic processes that leave us with questions about the mysteries of an ancient document like the Epic of Gilgamesh's twelfth tablet are fundamentally different than the processes that intentionally withhold passages through FOIA processing. In the first instance, there are primarily random processes determining what fragments of a particular document survive, while in the second instance power relations, privacy considerations, so-called national security issues, and political processes create filters selectively determining what can be read by others. With manuscripts released under FOIA, our fragmented codices have been broken not by chance, but by design, and these social facts need to shape how we interpret these released fragments.

Obviously the most significant difference is that passages with intentionally removed parts are designed to leave certain things unknown, and the acts of these removals reveal important power relations, as concealed redactors display the power to remove knowledge from dissemination. The redaction of FOIA materials is literally a display of state power, demonstrating what the state views as permissible narratives, and obliterating entire plotlines and characters deemed not fit for us to see. These missing fragments mark vital negative space, simultaneously indicating what we are not supposed to know while not withholding this information from us.

These differences in the roles played by state censors and the random processes damaging the manuscripts traditionally studied by the techniques of fragmentology are fairly obvious, but when I first started thinking about how methods of classical fragmentology overlap with FOIA researcher's methodologies, I was surprised at how many of the basic techniques used by literary scholars or students of fragmentary archaeological texts are transferable to the work of interpreting redacted FOIA documents. FOIA scholars are forced to deal with scraps, but these scraps contain valuable information, as do the holes created by FOIA censors.

At a most basic level the standard toolkit of literary scholars working in fragmentology consists of basic practices such as:

1. Summarize the known text and context;
2. Describe how the know fragments fit into context of larger text or other fragments;
3. Search for parallel texts;
4. The standard fallback: use close readings of available text fragments.

These are also the basic methodologies scholars and journalists undertake when trying to make sense of the FOIA texts bordered by redactions. I would not claim that these are profound observations, but instead, laying out these basic principles helps me think about how it is we make sense of the lines we get between the redactions.

Appealing Redactions

One significant difference between dealing with redacted documents and with unintentionally fragmented portions of manuscripts is that we can try and appeal for the release of withheld redactions under FOIA, either using in-house appeal processes or the federal courts. I think that doing frequent in-house appeals (and some court appeals) is an important part of the Freedom of Information Act filing process, and in many instances, it is the best hope for fighting redactions.

Writing an appeal arguing that withheld text (which by its very nature is unknown text) has improperly been withheld frequently sets the stage for an absurdist performance that during the last few decades I have grown to enjoy. As the appellant, one is asked to make logical arguments about materials that they do not fully understand. Beyond fundamental fairness arguments claiming that the federal agency has abused its power by overly redacting documents, which surely must have some portions that can properly be released (which sometimes works, sometimes doesn't), FOIA appellants are left to take shots in the dark when forming arguments, though sometimes these shots hit targets, or ghosts of targets.

The absurdity of some of these redactions, in which entire pages are black, sometimes makes me speculate about the mental state of the redactor; wondering if, like a bored, hospitalized Yosarian in *Catch 22* who amused himself by wildly and randomly redacting verbs, adjectives, or pronouns from soldiers' letters, there's something playful in these withholdings. I have occasionally tried to fight back with my own playfulness, submitting in-house appeals of heavily redacted documents asking that the least they could do is un-redact all the verbs, adverbs, pronouns, articles, and adjectives — only to be rejected for arguing that such heavy withholding is an overreach of the statutory exemptions. But I have also had some success in developing unique arguments for redaction appeals, and the features of these appeals are worth noting as they show the importance of filing appeals and because agency responses sometimes reveal structural patterns showing how they view their roles as redactors.

In the late 1990s while working on a book on McCarthyism and anthropology I received one key FBI document, a 1949 informer letter written by an identity-redacted author to J. Edgar Hoover, ratting out anthropologist Melville Jacobs as a communist. This four-page letter also named eleven other prominent anthropologists who had spoken up in defense of Jacobs and his right to academic freedom — after Jacobs had almost been fired from his tenured position at the University of Washington, under accusations that he was a communist. The context of the letter made it clear that the author was a fellow anthropologist who had just attended the annual meeting of the American Anthropological Association. This was a really juicy letter, recording what appeared to be one prominent anthropologist trying to ruin the lives of a dozen colleagues by accusing them of being communists to one of the most powerful men in America, who routinely destroyed the lives of anyone accused of communist tendencies. This letter to Hoover redacted the name of the author, as well as entire paragraphs and names of the eleven other anthropologists identified for Hoover as dangerous communists. Each of these redacted identities were withheld under normal Privacy Act exceptions that protect the identities of third party individuals appearing in these files.

I really wanted to know who this FBI informer was who had tried to ruin the lives of these dozen colleagues, so I repurposed a tool I had developed for another purpose in my appeal. When I started learning about anthropologists' interactions with military and intelligence agencies, I pieced together a lot of useful information on what anthropologists did in WWII by reading anthropologists' obituaries, published in the journal *American Anthropology*. As I worked my way through these back issues, I had created an index of these obituaries, and years earlier I had posted this index online for others to use.

When I wrote my FBI appeal to have this four-page letter unredacted, I launched an in-house appeal arguing that the names of these eleven attacked individuals and the FBI informer letter's author were only properly withheld under the Privacy Act *if* these people were still alive — because the Privacy Act only applies to the living. Appellants are in an impossible position, not knowing what they can't see, and thus being forced to make arguments about things they don't understand. So in this instance and in several that followed, I tried to present evidence that specific individuals whose identities were unknown to me were dead: as the foundation of my appeal, I sent the FBI a printout of my index listing every known dead American anthropologist, and made the argument that their identities could not properly be withheld under the Privacy Act, because they were dead and thus had no expectations of privacy.

A month later, I received a phone call from someone within the FBI who was processing my appeal, saying that because I had manufactured this death index myself, they were having difficulty accepting it as legitimate. I replied that the US government had already accepted my index as legitimate, and then sent them a link at the Smithsonian Institution's National Anthropological Archives website, where the Smithsonian had posted a link to my index. There was a long pause, then the voice said, "OK, that might work, but couldn't you have just added names of living people to get this released." I said, sure, I suppose I could have but I didn't, and if I did I'm sure they could press charges against me for some sort of fraud charge, and they should just release the damn file. He asked me to write up this argument and to include the link to the Smithsonian's web page.

About three months later, the FBI sent me a mostly unredacted version of this letter — two individuals named in this 1949 letter were then still living, but it was an alphabetical list, so I was able to figure out who they were — and the FBI also unredacted the Yale University letterhead and revealed the letter's author, anthropologist George Peter Murdock.[2]

I later requested and received the files on all of the individuals revealed under my appeal, and could trace the disruptions and damage to their lives that followed Murdock's cowardly attack on them; while I made well over 500 FOIA requests as part of that project, I launched about a hundred appeals, and without these appeals I would have missed significant information that formed central parts of my arguments.

Several times a year I receive correspondence from people seeking advice on submitting FOIA requests, and I often tell them they should compile lists of people likely appearing in the files they are requesting, and run FOIA requests on them too; if nothing else, this raises the possibility of receiving parallel texts with different redactions of non-subject names, and perhaps other differences in redaction.

Another technique I use when writing in-house appeals trying to get redactions removed is to use various directories to develop lists of people whose identities might be redacted in released documents. For example, when examining historical documents redacted under FOIA, dealing with governmental workers or even suspected CIA officers, the sort of parallel texts to be consulted can include things like the US State Department's *Foreign Service List* and *Biographic Register of the Department of State* from the years overlapping the FOIA documents under consideration. As John Marks shows in his classic article, "How To Spot A Spook," these State Department documents can be used to narrow down redacted identities that can be probed through new FOIA requests as ways of determining these identities.[3] When working on historical redacted FBI documents generated overseas by embassy personnel, these same directories can be used to generate lists of names likely redacted in released documents, and tracking down obituaries for these people and including these in in-house appeals can make for a powerful move that can strip away a few more redactions.

Up until probably the late 1990s, few Federal agencies kept copies of the documents they processed for release under FOIA. This meant that if one person requested records on a certain, deceased individual, and a second person requested essentially the same file, it was possible that because these two requests would be processed independently, perhaps by two different

---

2   David H. Price, *Threatening Anthropology: McCarthyism and the FBI's Surveillance of Activist Anthropologists*, (Durham: Duke University Press, 2004), 71–75.

3   John Marks, "How To Spot A Spook," in *Dirty Work: The CIA in Western Europe*, eds. Philip Agee and Louis Wolf (New York: Dorset Press, 1978), 29–39.

people, there could be significant differences in the released materials. In the pre-2000 years, the CIA was really the only federal agency that consistently copied the materials processed for release, as a means of thwarting this exploit.

Now, with scanned texts redacted electronically, not with the black pens of the past, it is easy to save and later redistribute exact copies of processed files at later dates. Of course, during the early days of electronically scanned FOIA releases, the government made serious errors in some of these first electronic released documents — as the redaction methods were done in photoshopped layers, for a short period they could be reverse engineered and whole documents could be revealed — until these mistakes were discovered and fixed using different electronic methods of redaction.

Redaction Errors

Of course, the FBI and other federal agencies processing FOIA materials routinely make errors when processing materials for release, and these errors routinely include both the redaction of materials which should properly be released, and the inadvertent release of materials that should have been redacted. Several times I have received files from the FBI where it appears the FOIA processor has become distracted, and midway through a document they start redacting the name of the FOIA request and leaving unredacted the name of secondary figures appearing in these files. I assume this occurs easily enough due to the drudgery of selectively redacting what are boring reports to those employees, processing reports that are meaningless to them. Perhaps returning from a long restroom break, they forget which name was the subject of the FOIA request and for a dozen pages they redact the wrong name. This type of accidental release of FOIA information referencing living individuals is a somewhat regular occurrence in FOIA research, as FOIA processors appear to space out and release fragments of text they would have otherwise intentionally withheld.[4]

One example of this process appeared in files I requested under FOIA from the FBI in the mid-1990s relating to the FBI's investigation of anthropologist John Embree. In these released files, after over a hundred pages of files relating to Embree, the FBI suddenly began redacting Embree's name… while accidentally leaving unredacted the name of anthropologist John Murra. It appears that these FBI censors suddenly forgot which John was the subject of this FOIA request. In the dozen unredacted pages that followed, the FBI reported why they believed Murra was "the Communist group leader of the University of Chicago" during the late 1930s. After receiving these mistakenly released files I contacted Murra, who gave me all

---

4 Sigmund Diamond, *Compromised Campus: The Collaboration of Universities with the Intelligence Community, 1945–1955* (New York: Oxford University Press, 1992), and Natalie Robins, *Alien Ink: The FBI's War on Freedom of Expression* (New York: W. Morrow, 1992).

sorts of background information on these events reported in Embree's FBI file.⁵

The existence of such accidental redactions and accidental revealings link the fragmentation of these texts with processes familiar in more traditional studies of fragmentology, which assume the preservation or loss of manuscript fragments to be the result of random factors. And as Joshua Craze shows in his essay in this collection, there appears to always be a somewhat random, or at least illogical or ideographic, element to the choice of individual words that FOIA censors redact or reveal.

Conclusions

In the end, the occlusion of textual passages through FOIA redaction processes removes knowledge in ways that reveal certain truths; truths about power relations, but, just as important, truths about the ways the US government operates under a shroud of secrecy. As a scholar conducting historical FOIA research, I have been surprised by how much effort present-day governmental employees put into making sure this past remains shrouded through the machinery of redactions. It's one thing for a contemporary administration to harness state power to hide their own activities in a very direct, self-serving way, but this state apparatus' devotion to only releasing broken fragments of half-century-old boring memos is sobering. These efforts to obscure the past through redactions highlight the perceived danger of a present understanding of past regimes in ways that suggest otherwise obscured continuities.

Otto Kirchheimer observed over half a decade ago that, "one might nearly be tempted to define a revolution by the willingness of the regime to open the archives of its predecessor's political police. Measured by this yard-stick, few revolutions have taken place in modern history."⁶ And in very real ways, the hands clicking and dragging computer cursors over electronic texts, using redactions to obliterate letters, words, sentences, paragraphs, and pages of documents from these archives of our political police, testify to the power this past still has over the present, and how far America is from coming to terms with a past that might not even be the past.

---

5   Price, *Threatening Anthropology*, 176.
6   Otto Kirchheimer, *Political Justice: The Use of Legal Procedure for Political Ends* (Princeton: Princeton University Press, 1961).

Dall-E
A bureaucrat erases a building

"... we are within a space outfitted to appeal less to the sordid Trumpian imagination than to the globe-trotting, *Vogue*-reading, white, well-educated liberal: the sort of people who know that the spoils of empire are meant to be tastefully concealed beneath a patina of decency, the aegis of global foundations, diplomacy, philanthropic efforts, and things of that nature. The sort of people, for instance, who might organize to have Trump's name removed from the face of their apartment complex, as the tenants of New York's West Side Highway-facing Trump Place did in the wake of the 2016 presidential election, and then celebrate the successful mitigation of their shame as an 'empowering act of protest,' while continuing, quite shamelessly, to talk up the building's 'impeccable' services."

— David Markus, *Notes on Trumpspace: Politics, Aesthetics, and the Fantasy of Home* (Earth: punctum books, 2023), 86–87.

Image generated by the DALL-E prompt: "A bureaucrat erases a building."

Dall-E
Rows of bureaucrats redacting words on pieces of paper

Image generated by the DALL-E prompt: "Rows of bureaucrats redacting words on pieces of paper."

Collaborations and Disclosures in Authoritarian Fields

 and N———

The 2014 election of Prime Minister Narendra Modi and the Bharatiya Janata Party (BJP) government marked an epochal shift in Indian politics, signaling the growing strength of the country's far-right Hindu nationalist movement as it achieved unprecedented state power and suggesting that profound changes to the country were underway. The intervening years have borne out some of the worst fears of observers: a sharp rise in violence against Muslims and low-caste Dalits; the erosion of rights for workers and forest-dwelling people; the intimidation, arrest, and in some cases murder, of critical journalists and writers; and increasing surveillance and harassment of academics. Following the BJP's return to power after the May 2019 general election, the party has been emboldened to carry out even more dramatic changes, including the August 2019 abrogation of constitutional amendments that safeguarded the autonomy of Kashmir, the only Muslim-majority region administered by the Indian Union, as well as the December 2019 introduction of citizenship laws that excluded Muslims. Commentators have characterized these consecutive moves as marking Indian democracy's silent death[1] and inaugurating a new "competitive authoritarian" order.[2] This is an authoritarianism that operates within the formal procedures of liberal democracy: elections, courts, and the media all continue their operations, but are refashioned to exclude and punish the country's minoritized communities and political dissidents.

Modi's India has significantly shaped our experiences as fieldworkers, although both of us began our research before the 2014 elections and both

---

1 Aman Sethi, "As Kashmir is Erased, Indian Democracy Dies in Silence," *Huffington Post,* August 5, 2019, https://www.huffpost.com/archive/in/entry/kashmir-erased-article-370-scrapped-indian-democracy-in-darkness_in_5d47e49be4b0acb57fcf1b4d.

2 James Manor, "A New, Fundamentally Different Political Order: The Emergence and Future Prospects of 'Competitive Authoritarianism' in India," *Economic and Political Weekly* 56, no. 10 (March 2021), https://www.epw.in/engage/article/new-fundamentally-different-political-order; Christophe Jaffrelot, *Modi's India: Hindu Nationalism and the Rise of Ethnic Democracy,* trans. Cynthia Schoch (Princeton: Princeton University Press, 2021); and Christophe Jaffrelot and Gilles Verniers, "A New Party System or a New Political System?," *Contemporary South Asia* 28, no. 2 (2020): 141–54.

of us work in areas, Kashmir and ▮▮▮, where the Indian state has long been experienced as authoritarian. The following essay draws on our personal trajectories over the last decade as it attempts to chart links between India's forest belt and Kashmir, and between our respective positionalities and the force of the authoritarian state. The anthropologist's "authoritarian field," we suggest, is a dialogic sphere of action. Here, state actors, non-state actors, and anthropologists are created and masked in relation to one another and in relation to the idealized, upper-caste Hindu and Hindu nationalist subject of the Indian state. Craig Jeffrey has argued that the various faces of the Indian state are popularly understood to be inextricable from relations of caste and class.[3] In Modi's India, the authoritarian field that we encounter is characterized by a project of purification, a reshaping of Indian politics and society along hierarchical lines, with upper-caste Hindus on top. As upper-caste Hindus, then, this is ostensibly our state, and yet both of us have found ourselves refusing such interpellations through selective presentations of our selves — a redaction of our purposes and politics.[4] To gain and maintain access to our field sites, we have allowed state actors to assume our identification, even collaboration, with them, as we have attempted in turn to collaborate with people who are marginalized by this state. We have done so with an understanding that we are dealing with a state that has sought — through pellet guns and arrests that never lead to trials, through cell phone surveillance and lynchings — to identify and silence anyone who challenges it. It is a state that seeks to identify those who collaborate with it, and to distinguish them from those who collaborate against it.

Collaboration, Douglas Holmes and George Marcus argue, is essential to the task of ethnography, which always unfolds in conversation with the para-ethnographic practices of interlocutors.[5] However, in the context of an authoritarian state and an increasingly authoritarian and vigilante public,[6] para-ethnographic practices are filled with the possibility of violence, against us and against other interlocutors. Collaboration here is marked by suspicion in all directions, with all participants in the ethnographic encounter attempting their own redactions and suspiciously attempting to read through redaction. The para-ethnography of state surveillance in the authoritarian field sniffs out collaboration — but with insurgents and dissidents.

---

3   Craig Jeffrey, "'A Fist is Stronger than Five Fingers': Caste and Dominance in Rural North India," *Transactions of the Institute of British Geographers* 26, no. 2 (2001): 217–36.

4   Nitzan Shoshan, *The Management of Hate: Nation, Affect, and the Governance of Right-Wing Extremism in Germany* (Princeton: Princeton University Press, 2016).

5   Douglas R. Holmes and George E. Marcus, "Collaboration Today and the Re-Imagination of the Classic Scene of Fieldwork Encounter," *Collaborative Anthropologies* 1 (2008): 81–101.

6   Shakuntala Banaji, "Vigilante Publics: Orientalism, Modernity and Hindutva Fascism in India," *Javnost: The Public* 25, no. 4 (2018): 333–50.

As we have grappled with the awareness that as researchers we are both the objects of state knowledge and the producers of potentially subversive knowledge, our fieldwork and writing practices have transformed. Increasingly, we find ourselves self-censoring, avoiding taboo topics, and taking refuge in inaccessible academic registers and abstraction. This dialogic essay addresses such complexities of redaction and omission as they occur in the texts we produce (fieldnotes, social media updates, published material) as well as in our self-presentations as researchers and non-resident Indians. We highlight these complexities by redacting certain phrases as well as personal and place names. In deploying and reflecting on these practices, we consider how the authoritarian fields in which we find ourselves have birthed new anthropological and scholarly practices.

* * *

I didn't travel under an assumed name, but I traveled under an assumed project. I worked on ▮▮, I told the immigration authorities. ▮▮ was a triumph for the world's largest democracy, as it looked to reconcile the twin imperatives of lifting its massive population out of poverty and responding to the threat of environmental collapse. A model for the rest of the world. But ▮▮ represented different political possibilities to different groups of people. ▮▮ was a failure, a project that had been sabotaged by bureaucrats and local elites who had never wanted to give up any of their own property or authority in any case. ▮▮ was also a ringing success, a final end to a century-old historic injustice. ▮▮ was internally inconsistent, and as such could be used both by Group A and by their political enemies, Group B. And so a research project to study ▮▮ in relation to Group B could be presented as a research project to study ▮▮ in relation to Group A, for the purposes of a visa and for the purposes of my interlocutors. As long as no one looked at my fieldnotes, I assumed I could get away with it.

My name, I hoped, set up a similar deception. Upper-caste, Hindu, from the right region, a surname I shared with high-level figures in Group B, and a political stance that I wanted them to assume followed. But these were all conjectural erasures and deceptions, based not on any clear policies or statements from the government or the interlocutors I hoped to meet regarding who they would talk with about what, and what would happen to me if things went wrong. This was a speculative trading of roles: if I were a member of Group B, I asked myself, what would raise my suspicions? How would I respond? I arrived in a smallish city, set up a series of interviews with members of Group B who had been involved in work surrounding ▮▮. The key question for me here was how Group B had worked ▮▮ into their decades-long organizing efforts in the area. The smallish city was, frankly, boring. I managed to set up a series of meetings and interviews, but the most insightful conversation that I had while I was there was a long phone conversation I had with a member of Group A who was in another city. He explained to me that where he was, Group B had successfully incorporated the kin of prominent leaders from Group A into their own organization, providing young boys from poor families with a free education, for example, and cultivating them into leaders.Everyone I met with, however, was clear that in order to understand Group B's position on ▮▮, I would have to talk with the brains of the operation, who wasn't in the smallish city or its region. Things were being coordinated out of Delhi, and I should meet with him there. It was a deeply boring week. The friends and family I had in the smallish city were out of town. Because my research required that I manage my persona carefully, I didn't really want to get close enough to my informants to have them see through it — and as a result, I didn't really want to spend more time with them than necessary. I found their politics repugnant and their social mores stiflingly conservative. Redaction in this case was the effort to maintain a fieldwork persona that was consistent with the subjects on behalf of whom my right-wing interlocutors were already speaking: conservative and inoffensive, inquisitive only in ways that could not be taken as a challenge.

So, after a few days, I made my way to Delhi. I scheduled a meeting with [y] in Group B's Delhi office. He explained in his email that I should take the Metro to a certain station, and then walk towards a certain square, where he would meet me. I wandered over to the square, and an older man in his early 60s, apparently [y], approached me. "I recognized you from your Gmail photo," he explained. We made our way to the office — a two-story home that had been turned into the headquarters for Group B. The office was filled with men, mostly older, speaking Hindi and more Marathi than I had ever heard spoken in Delhi. [y] and I sat down, and I asked him the strategically ambiguous questions I had prepared about Group B, its relationship to the government, and its stance on ▮▮. He was as thoughtful as I had been promised, as aware of the larger situation with Group B, ▮▮, and the government, the contradictions in the situation, and the strategic decisions required to navigate these contradictions. After our chat I was persuaded to stay for lunch and I was shown to a balcony, where clusters of older men were sitting around and chatting, taking advantage of the warmth provided by the sun. Lunch would be ready soon, and I could wait out here in the meantime.

No one introduced themselves to me, but I was quickly buttonholed by an elderly man sitting nearby. He was dressed in a white kurta pyjama and was nursing a cup of chai. The questions flowed out of him. Where [y] had been welcoming and guileless, this man was suspicious, looking for contradictions in my story. Why had I been researching ▮▮ in that village? That's a terrible place to study it. Was I related to the family in Group B that shared my surname? Was I really Hindu? Which gods did I pray to? Which mantras did I use when I prayed? I failed his tests. I had provided the wrong mantras, and my professions of faith were obviously insincere. Lips tightened and the atmosphere grew chilly with all of the men present except for [y], who maintained his warmth and good cheer until I made my way out. Twenty-four hours later I was sitting in a café when my phone rang. It was the friend I was staying with, whose address I had provided on my immigration forms. "Two men from the Intelligence Bureau are here," she said. "They're asking about you — they want to know what you're doing in India. What should I tell them?"

The contours of Group B's surveillance were becoming more visible. Nothing I had done in the smallish city had caused anyone any alarm, but their leadership in the national capital was more wary of critical representations by foreign academics. Their leadership in Delhi was also able to call upon the Intelligence Bureau and have them sniff around academics with a day's notice.

* * *

In the summer of 2006, during my first trip to Kashmir, my family advised me not to reveal that I was a Kashmiri Pandit, a member of Kashmir's minority Hindu community. When asked about myself, I was supposed to omit that detail — not necessarily lie, but just avoid telling the whole truth. My family feared that if people in Kashmir found out who I really was, I would become a potential target of violence. There was a concrete history to this fear, even though my understanding of that history diverged significantly from my family's.

In the early months of the armed rebellion against the Indian state that erupted in the Kashmir Valley in 1989, a number of prominent Kashmiri Pandits were targeted and killed. The assassinations stemmed in part from these individuals' close association with the Indian state. The first, in September 1989, was of the BJP state Vice President, Tikalal Taploo, followed two months later by Neelkanth Ganjoo, the Sessions Court Judge who had sentenced to death Maqbool Butt, the founder of the Jammu Kashmir Liberation Front (JKLF). Over the next several months, more than a dozen high-profile Kashmiri Pandits would be killed. Pandits were by no means the only ones punished for "collaborating" with the Indian state; Kashmiri Muslims affiliated with the dominant regional party, the National Conference, were also often targeted by the rebels, who saw the party and its functionaries as impediments to the full realization of Kashmiri self-determination. But despite the fact that Pandits were not exclusively targeted, and that it was not clear that their targeting was necessarily religiously (as opposed to politically) motivated, the assassinations and the subsequent flight of the majority of the Pandit community came to be understood primarily through a religious lens.

Starting in January 1990, my grandparents were among tens of thousands of Pandits who either fled Kashmir or found themselves unable to return to their homes. As the insurgency and counterinsurgency ravaged the region, my grandparents moved between their children's homes in Chandigarh, Pune, and St. Louis, imagining that their return to Kashmir was imminent. By the late 1990s, however, as their plans to return faded, my grandfather sold the house he and my grandmother had built forty years prior. With that sale, our most significant material tie to Kashmir was severed. My family, like most members of the Pandit community, blamed their losses on Pakistan-sponsored terrorism and "fundamentalist Islam," charges that aligned with a growing right-wing Hindu nationalism in the Indian mainland and across the Hindu diaspora. It wasn't until college, in the aftermath of the September 11, 2001 attacks and the subsequent invasions of Iraq and Afghanistan, that I came to understand that there were other stories to be told — about Islam, Muslims, and Kashmir. I was eager to return to Kashmir and see it with my own eyes.

That summer of 2006 I jettisoned my family's advice; I did not hide my Pandit background. While I felt little affinity with my Kashmiri Hindu identity beyond a cultural inheritance, I wanted to show my family that I did not need to conceal any aspect of that identity in order to be safe and accepted in Kashmir. To prove my point, I would wantonly disclose my family background to strangers and acquaintances alike, each encounter serving as a litmus test of religious tolerance. And indeed, I was met at almost every turn with warmth and hospitality, precisely, it seemed, *because* I was a Pandit and had returned to my homeland. During these encounters, people would recall, often with tears in their eyes, memories of Kashmiri Pandits with whom they had grown up — friends and colleagues, teachers and neighbors. My presence seemed to provoke both nostalgia and anxiety: for the older generation, especially, the Pandits' departure was a stain on a righteous struggle for freedom.

In the subsequent decade and a half that I have spent returning intermittently to Kashmir, primarily for ethnographic research, this anxiety has only amplified. With the rise of Modi's India, relations between Pandits and Muslims have markedly deteriorated, reaching a nadir during the August 2019 abrogation of Kashmir's constitutional status, a move that most Pandits celebrated, and most Muslims mourned. As the politics of the Kashmiri Pandit community has increasingly aligned with Modi's authoritarianism, it has become progressively harder to identify as a Pandit. From that initial trip in 2006 as an undergraduate student to my long-term dissertation research from 2016 to 2018, an inversion has taken place: instead of disclosing, I have desperately wanted to invisibilize my Pandit background. Although I still do not redact or withhold my Pandit identity — my name alone gives it away — I have self-consciously distanced myself from the community's politics.

Yet even as I denounce the repeated alliances made by Kashmiri Pandits with right-wing Hindu nationalism — and even as they denounce me and others like me — I find that I can only distance myself so much. My interlocutors in Kashmir locate me precisely through my Pandit inheritance; it is at least one of the reasons, I believe, that I am treated with such patience and warmth. My decision to keep returning and to have that return warmly welcomed, then, remains a kind of faith — one that threatens to exceed the authoritarian field.

* * *

If the authoritarian state attempts to produce a one-to-one relationship between ascriptive identity and political stance, with favored groups aligned with the authoritarian state against the unfavored, then the two of us arrived in the field with the assumption that this attempt was complete. If upper-caste Hindus are aligned with the Hindu majoritarian state, then A▮▮'s silences and elisions could only mean assent with Group B, and

N▓▓▓ worried that their Panditness could only be seen as an alliance with the state apparatus. Both collaborations with the state came undone, however — one through an interlocutor's interrogation and another through the expansive solidarity of many Kashmiris living under Indian occupation.

A reflexive anthropology in such circumstances is one that not only considers the ethnographer's positionality and their potential collaboration with colonial or post-colonial states but must also recognize the many para-ethnographic efforts being made by others, including states and movements, to consider and pin down the ethnographer's positionality. Our interlocutors are all too aware of anthropology's many complicities at the same time as they are attuned to our ascriptive identities, which sit in awkward, uneasy relationship with the hopefully subversive political stakes of our research. The BJP's ideal subject, the upper-caste Hindu, haunts: the authoritarian state claims to be our state. This is an authoritarian state, moreover, that, with its cultivation of academics, is more than capable of representing itself through anthropologists. Fieldwork in relation to the many para-ethnographic practices of our interlocutors, then, is necessarily tactical. It requires the maintenance of personas in relation to state surveillance, and the subversive possibilities of anti-authoritarian collaborations.

Tony C. Brown

"Intermezzo II"

Tony C. Brown, "Intermezzo II." Redacted citations from *Statelessness: On Almost Not Existing* (Minneapolis: University of Minnesota Press, 2022), 157.

... have no ... neither ... nor ... nor ... not ... have no ... without ... without ... have no ... no ... not....
—Amerigo Vespucci, *Mundus Novus* (1503)

... naked, ... know neither ... nor ..., nor ... without ... without ... without.... know no ... so little ... neither ... nor ... nor ... without ... without....
—Peter Martyr, *De Orbe Novo* (1511)

... without ... without ... without ... without....
—André Thevet, *Singularités* (1557)

... no ... no ... naked....
—Juan Ginés de Sepúlveda, *De regno et regis officio* (1571)

... no ... no ... no ... no ... nor ... no ... no ... no ... no ... no ... no ... no ... no ... no ... no ... no ... unknown....
—Michel de Montaigne, "Des cannibales" (1580)

... no ... no ... no ... nor ... no ... no ... no ... no ... no ... no ... no....
—Thomas Hobbes, *Leviathan* (1651)

... without ... without ... without ... without ... naked....
—Antoine de Furetière, *Dictionnaire universel* (1690)

... have no ... without ... without ... without ... without ... without....
—Louis Hennepin, *Nouveau voyage d'un Pais plus grand que l'Europe* (1698)

... devoid ... without ... without ... without ... without ... without ... lacking
—Jean-François Lafitau, *Les mœurs des sauvages américains* (1724)

... neither ... nor ... nor ... nor ... less ... only ... unable ... incapable. ...
—Buffon, *Histoire naturelle* (1749)

... without ... without ... without ... have no. ...
—"Sauvages, f. m. plur. *(Hist. mod.)*," in *Encyclopédie ou dictionnaire raisonné* (1765)

... without ... without ... without ... without ... without ... without ... without ... without. ...
—Jean-Jacques Rousseau, *Discours sur l'origine et les fondements de l'inégalité parmi les hommes* (1754/5)

... have ... neither ... nor ... Destitute ... without ... without ... without ... have only ... few ... few ... want ... only ... deprived ... have ... only. ...
—Antoine-Yves Goguet, *De l'origine des loix, des arts, et des sciences* (1758)

... without ... without ... without ... without. ...
—Voltaire, *Dictionnaire philosophiques* (1764)

... no ... no ... no. ... Without ... Without. ...
—Adam Ferguson, *An Essay on the History of Civil Society* (1767)

... wasteland ... without ... without ... without ... without. ...
—Denis Diderot, in *Histoire philosophique et politique des deux Indes* (1780)

Without ... without ... without ... without. ...
—Friedrich Engels, *The Origin of the Family, Private Property and the State* (1884)

... without ... without ... without ... without
—Hannah Arendt, *The Origins of Totalitarianism* (1951)

Dear Kafka

Annie Malcolm

2017

Dear Kafka,

Where in Kafka?
What are your paintings for you?

It pains me
But let me get right to it: Why didn't you tell me about the baby?
Eventually you explained it to me: she used you to get pregnant. She didn't want to be with you. I never heard her story. Do you feel a loss about the child? Did you want to be with her? Who is it easier to blame?

Okay then there is the question of your sexual orientation. For me it was obvious you weren't straight, as a woman and a queer. Why did you decide to tell me on the day you did? I'm sorry if I didn't make it easier earlier, or after. We didn't always have much follow-up.*
You didn't seem to want to do anything.
Why me?
I'm sorry if.
I don't know you anymore.

Love,
Annie
爱你"Aini"(Love you)

*The most terrifying thing for a queer person is not to be seen. The most terrifying thing for a queer person is to be seen.

2017

Dear Kafka,

▇▇▇▇ Kafka?
What are your paintings for you?

It pains me
But let me ▇▇▇▇▇▇: Why didn't you tell me about the baby? ▇▇▇▇▇▇▇▇▇▇▇▇ she used you to ▇▇▇▇▇▇ ▇▇▇▇▇▇▇▇▇▇▇▇▇▇▇▇ Do you feel a loss about the child? ▇▇▇▇▇▇▇▇▇▇ Who is it easier to blame?

▇▇▇▇▇▇▇▇▇▇▇▇▇▇ your sexual orientation. For me it was obvious you weren't straight, as a woman and a queer. Why did you decide to tell me on the day you did? ▇▇▇▇ ▇▇▇▇▇*
You didn't seem to want to do anything.
Why me?
▇▇▇▇

I don't know you anymore.

▇▇▇
▇▇▇▇▇▇

*The most terrifying thing for a queer person is not to be seen. The most terrifying thing for a queer person is to be seen.

Exposition

I redacted the parts where I exist, making the piece more of a proper anthropological exercise. That inevitably removed the story. What was this interaction? Who is Kafka? How did he know to tell me? My foreignness connoted a kind of safety, either because I was an outsider who couldn't or wouldn't gossip with the group, or because he calculated a different openness to queerness and difference in me. He could have been so wrong there, but he was right. And I don't think he knew I was queer, or had considered it.

My position: I told maybe three people in the village about my sexuality. People always asked if I had a husband, and I just said no. Then they wanted to know if I wanted a Chinese or American husband. I didn't have the heart. I didn't want to come out to everyone who wanted to ask me about my husband. I am entirely out at home in Oakland and New York. In Wutong Art Village, Shenzhen, China, I was in the closet.[1] Fieldwork was like this; I asked questions, in the ethnographic tradition, and I fielded questions almost as often. And then there was a third space — conversations that arose outside of anyone's questions.

We become different people in the field. First, we are the people who can do the project. Second, we erase, redact, ourselves in order to do it; only as empty can we let the place become something of itself. Eventually you have to disappear even your object of inquiry and see what arises in its midst. Perhaps also we disappear internally in order to hold an other. This is the pain of the field. This is the source of its isolation, those banished mes, that are given hesitant promises of return, degrees earned, joyous reunions, and reintegrations.

So there I was, half-me, talking to Kafka. Kafka too had banished Kafkas. I met him in 2015. He'd shown me his paintings. They weren't very good. In 2017, we had three memorable conversations, two of which populate the letter. In one, he described life in his hometown in Hainan, China's southernmost province, an island in the South China Sea. People work very little, he said, selling just enough rubber or fruit to live, and then hanging out. I pictured people sitting in plastic chairs watching the world like it was TV. Kafka didn't want to live there, but he didn't particularly want to stay in Wutong Shan. He talked about getting bored in any place. He lacked the in-place-ness that so defined other people's experiences in Wutong Shan. I think this was about being queer. How can you belong in place when you are never there because you are routinely redacting, closeting? You flit. Kafka's physicality leant itself to flitting too; he was lean and

---

[1] Elizabeth Povinelli describes the difference between being home and being in the field through scenes that interpellate her in each place. She writes, "'That's me,' I thought, when I saw two women kissing in Santa Fe, New Mexico. 'This is me,' I thought when I went hunting with a group of women and men from Belyuen. But what is 'this' and 'that'? — an identity, a mode of life, a form of association? Surely I was hailed in both." Elizabeth A. Povinelli, "Disturbing Sexuality," *South Atlantic Quarterly* 106, no. 3 (2007): 567.

strong, always running up the mountain in neon shorts and bouncing back down, high on adrenaline.

In the second conversation he told me about the woman and the baby. Very little was said. She left him, she used him, he reported. He seemed pained, but muted, like he ultimately preferred not raising the child.

In the third, which may well have been the last time I saw him, he told me he'd spent the night with a man. I responded with enthusiasm, excited acceptance. He seemed inside the small wedge of him that was truth, which he occupied momentarily. As I write in the letter, he didn't seem to want to do anything about it and I couldn't get a sense of what would happen next.

In China, LGBTQ+ people do not have the same legal protections as straight people. The absence of support for LGBTQ+ communities in China, because of state policies, perpetuates the prison of the closet. The state works to prevent or erase the expression of gay life. In this work, I explore the space of the closet through redaction — practices of redacting one's self. The ethnographer does this to understand. The queer does this to survive.

Donald J. Trump
I Never Understood Wind

Excerpt from a speech delivered by Donald J. Trump on December 22, 2019. Formatted by Franck Billé.

I never understood wind.
You know,
I know
windmills very much.
I have studied it
better than anybody else.

It's very expensive.
They are made in China
and Germany mostly.
— Very few made here, almost none,
but they are manufactured, tremendous
— if you are into this —
tremendous fumes.
Gases are
spewing into the atmosphere.
You know
we have a world
right?

So the world is tiny
compared to the universe.
So tremendous (tremendous!)
amount of fumes and everything.
You talk about
the carbon footprint
— fumes are spewing into the air.
Right? Spewing!
Whether it's in China,
Germany, it's going into the air.
It's our air
their air
everything — right?

You want to see a bird graveyard?
You just go.
Take a look.
A bird graveyard.
Go under a windmill someday,
you'll see
more birds
than you've ever seen
— ever
in your life.

A windmill will kill many bald eagles.
After a certain number
they make you turn the windmill off.
That is true.
— By the way
they make you turn it off.
And yet, if you killed one
they put you in jail.
That is OK.

You see all those windmills
They're all different shades of color.
They're like sort of white, but one is like an
orange-white.
It's my favorite color
— orange.

Stealing and Redacting
Fieldwork among Transnational Thieves in Eastern Romania

Trine Mygind Korsby

Sebastian and I are sitting in the car, looking out on to the windy street in the industrial city of Galați in eastern Romania, where he lives.

I started my ongoing research on sex work, pimping, and human trafficking in Italy and Romania in 2007, and I got to know Sebastian in 2011. The research started out by focusing on young women working in sex work, their process of being officially identified by the Italian state as victims of human trafficking, and the relationships they have with the people who travelled with them to Italy and worked as their pimps — and who in some cases were later convicted of human trafficking.[1] In terms of definitions, a "pimp" is defined as someone who procures, facilitates, manages, or similarly contributes to commercial sex transactions.[2]

My research subsequently moved to focusing on the lives of the pimps[3] and the human traffickers, concentrating on their business models, moral

---

1   Trine Mygind Korsby, "Hemmeligheder, distance og kontrol af viden: Menneskehandel i Italien og Rumænien," in *Familie og Slægtskab – Antropologiske Perspektiver*, eds. Karen Fog Olwig and Hanne Mogensen (Copenhagen: Samfundslitteratur, 2013), 131–46, and Trine Mygind Korsby, "Complex Intimacies: Sex Work, Human Trafficking and Romance between Italy and the Black Sea Coast of Romania," in *A Sea of Transience: Politics, Poetics and Aesthetics along the Black Sea Coast*, eds. Tamta Khalvashi and Martin Demant Frederiksen (New York: Berghahn Books, 2023), 66–79.

2   Amber Horning, Roisin Bermingham, Julie Sriken, and Christopher Thomas, "Pimps' Self-Presentations in the Interview Setting: 'Good Me,' 'Bad Me,' and 'Badass Me'," *Journal of Human Trafficking* (2022): 1–22.

3   Despite the fact that most of my informants also engage in other criminal activities, such as credit-card fraud, scams, and theft, they mainly refer to themselves as having an occupation as *pește* (fish), which is Romanian slang for pimp. Other, more academic terms such as "third-party facilitator" are unfamiliar to this group of people and is not how they define themselves or how they are defined by others, for example by sex workers or business partners. See Trine Mygind Korsby, "Hustlers of Desire: Transnational Pimping and Body Economies in Eastern Romania," PhD diss., University of Copenhagen, 2015; Trine Mygind Korsby, "The Brothel Phone Number: Infrastructures of Transnational Pimping in Eastern Romania," *The Cambridge Journal of Anthro-*

landscapes and social relationships, and how they manage to extend their local pimping businesses in Romania to other EU countries.[4] Doing fieldwork among the pimps showed me that they combine pimping with other criminal activities, such as organized theft, especially carried out abroad, on which I will be shedding light in this chapter.

Practices of Redaction

In this chapter, through the case of Sebastian, I will first show some of the internal conflicts across hierarchies that can arise within a group of men in their twenties and thirties who go abroad to steal. This is done in order to introduce the field of transnational stealing and the complexities and conflicts of this field, in which Sebastian navigates. I will then move to focus on Sebastian's family dynamics and show how his family manages their knowledge about his illegal activities abroad. I will present these ethnographic aspects through an engagement with the overall theme of "redaction" in this volume. Compared with other similar concepts, redaction is interesting to think with, since it instantly makes one think of how powerful systems work to edit and control. However, by analyzing my own practice of "redacting" my field notes during fieldwork, I suggest that the concept of redaction can also be used to illuminate and critically analyze the practices that we as anthropologists engage in during fieldwork — in the name of safety and anonymity — in order to protect our fields, our informants, and ourselves. Simultaneously I suggest that redaction can function as an analytical concept to capture how my informants "redact" by concealing different aspects of their illegal enterprises within their families.

In this chapter, I show how this practice of redaction is preferred in some families in order for their family life to run smoothly, and that a particular kind of silent knowing exists between Sebastian and his parents regarding his illegal transnational activities, without them being articulated. The concealing and avoidance — that is, the redaction — of his illegal activities in their interactions and communications thus result in an "open secret."[5] Just as in my field notes, which are redacted and curated in order to ensure anonymity, the social practices within the family allow some information and some details to stand out and be seen, while other kinds of information are not accentuated or mentioned.

Overall, the chapter sheds light on participation in these different but nonetheless related practices of redaction and their implications.

---

pology 35, no. 2 (Autumn 2017): 111–24; and Trine Mygind Korsby, "Reading Desires: Romanian Pimps Striving for Success in the Transnational Street Economy," *Migration and Society* 6 (2023): 57–69.
4   Korsby, "Hustlers of Desire"; Korsby, "The Brothel Phone Number"; and Korsby, "Reading Desires."
5   Cf. Michael Taussig, *Defacement: Public Secrecy and the Labor of the Negative* (Stanford: Stanford University Press, 1999).

At the Casino

Sebastian is 26 years old, he has extensive experience as a pimp, and he has previously taken his pimping business abroad to Italy and Spain. However, pimping is not the only illegal business endeavor that Sebastian and my other informants engage in. Abroad, they are also involved in large-scale burglaries of private homes, thefts from shops or industrial complexes, organized pickpocketing, and credit card fraud. Locally, some of them are active in the business of lending money to people in need at high interest rates. Often the money is collected — because people simply cannot pay it back in time — through threats and violence. Sebastian and other informants also engage in small-scale scams both abroad and locally in Romania, such as different pyramid schemes promising participants payments or services that never actually materialize. In Sebastian's case, the scams, which he originally carried out locally in Galaţi — such as the sale of items that would never appear after money had been handed over, or the sale of fraudulent insurance solutions — quickly became too complicated for him. This was mainly because people knew who he was, and it was not difficult to track him down when he operated in his own city and neighborhood.

These different paths to moneymaking present themselves to my interlocutors in waves, and for longer periods of time there is nothing to do, and thus no income. At these times, Sebastian and the others will simply sit around and wait for something to happen or some opportunity to present itself to them.[6] Sometimes this opportunity can come in the form of going abroad with others to steal from stores or warehouses.

We are sitting in his dad's car. Sebastian does not have a car himself, but luckily he can charm his way into borrowing his parents'. Sebastian is smoking a Kent cigarette through the open window, scouting the empty street. "Oh, here we go," he says, as a black Mercedes pulls up in front of the local casino. The casino is a gathering point for Sebastian and the other pimps and hustlers in the area. Here they meet to hang out and gamble, to discuss their business, and to engage in collaborative efforts with one another. Most of these men are in their twenties and thirties, and many of them have been friends since childhood.

Three guys get out of the black Mercedes wearing black trainers, hoodies, down vests, and small men's bags, mainly fake Louis Vuittons.

The casino consists of three consecutive red-painted rooms containing a few black leather sofas, several plastic tables with fake marble coverings, and a row of slot machines that takes up an entire wall. Sebastian always shakes his head when explaining to me how much money he has lost on the slot machines in the casino over the years. He loves playing the slot machines for the rush of colorful images rolling in front of his eyes, until they shudder to a halt in unexpected combinations, a luxury that he can spend hour after hour on.

We walk up to the casino, and as we are standing outside in the cold, we start chatting with the three men. They are arguing with Sebastian about

---

6   Korsby "Hustlers of Desire."

recent business endeavors involving the theft of large amounts of clothes in Italy that did not go as planned. Even though only a few words are spoken, and the atmosphere is mainly characterized by smoking cigarettes and kicking small stones on the ground, it is clear that the three men are upset at how Sebastian has handled the situation since returning to Romania. We leave the casino, Sebastian mumbling swearwords through gritted teeth, but otherwise diffident and quiet.

How to Steal: Backpacks and Aluminum Foil

The next day I ask Sebastian about the situation at the casino, and he explains how one of the local *pește mare* (big fish) had set up the situation in Italy. The "big fish" work at the management level of several illegal activities both locally and abroad, such as pimping, cloning credit cards, and organizing burglaries.[7] Sebastian explains: "Yes, ▉, he arranged it. He paid for my ticket to Italy. And you know, ▉ was a sweet place to be. Do you have any idea how many thieves there are there? There's a reason for that: all the tourists. It's sweet. We were five guys there, we worked every day. But some were also cheating ▉. They did not always tell him the truth about how much they got, because he gets a percentage. So now… that is part of the problem."

We are sitting in his parents' living room, which is where I am currently staying. The family couch, which is covered with a big, fluffy, red and orange blanket, has been turned into my bed for a while. It is a humble household. Sebastian's parents both used to work at the local steel factory, but like many others in Galați, they have suffered unemployment. During the socialist period, Galați was a lively industrial city with a large steel factory employing people from all over the region of Moldavia.[8] Many of these were peasants as well as industrial workers, traveling to the factory every day, but simultaneously engaging in small-scale agricultural activities in the countryside.[9] Today the factory employs only about 10% of its former workforce, which has led to massive unemployment among both the rural commuters — who were the first to lose their jobs during the post-socialist de-industrialization phase — and the urban population.[10] Among these people were Sebastian's parents, who also lost their jobs. Living in Moldavia, one of the poorest regions of Romania,[11] and seeing all the strug-

---

7   Korsby, "The Brothel Phone Number," 118.
8   The historical and geographical region of Moldavia used to be an autonomous state, but today its western part is part of Romania, its eastern part is within the Republic of Moldova, and its northern and southeastern parts belong to Ukraine. In Romania, Moldavia is divided into smaller counties, which serve as the area's administrative divisions. See Korsby, "Hustlers of Desire," 19.
9   Remus Gabriel Anghel, *Romanians in Western Europe: Migration, Status Dilemmas, and Transnational Connections* (Lanham: Lexington Books, 2013), 7.
10 Korsby, "Hustlers of Desire," 19.
11 Lucian Pop, Dumitru Sandu, Filofteia Panduru, Amalia Virdol, Vlad Grigoraș, Viorica Duma, and Daniel Virdol, *Harta sărăciei în România. Metodologia utilizata și prezentarea rezultatelor. Raport elaborat la cererea Comisiei Naționale*

gles to find employment of the other young men in their neighborhood, his parents know that the prospects for their son are not as bright or straightforward as they might have hoped. Sebastian's criminal activities are not talked about, but his parents are aware of them, and they quietly tolerate his choices and way of life.

I am asking Sebastian more questions about the conflict from the previous evening, and he gets up from the couch and goes into the kitchen to get some aluminum foil. I can hear his mother asking him if we will be home later for dinner. He comes back to the living room and closes the door behind him. I am puzzled what the foil is for, and even more puzzled when he grabs my backpack. He lowers his voice, so that his mother cannot hear us: "So, let me show you how we actually did the stealing in Italy," he says, and starts pulling out long pieces of foil with which he starts padding the backpack inside in very detailed and specific ways. It is a very long process, and extensive meters of aluminum foil are used: first, before getting it into the backpack, the foil is wrapped around one end of a footstool, to get the right round shape, and thereafter it is taped together with strong tape, so it fits into the bag. Sebastian continues: "Okay so, now I haven't done it perfectly, but this is more or less how to do it. You need to wrap it with aluminum, like ten times or more, inside the bag. And you need to put more tape than this. I normally did not use a bag like this, but a much bigger one. Then you put the clothes, or whatever you are stealing, inside. It is smart because the aluminum sends the alarms back, you know, almost like a mirror. So the alarms will not work. The aluminum just has to cover the alarms. If it does not, they will go off."

Sebastian shows me how the thick, taped aluminum foil-shape fits perfectly into my backpack. He continues: "And when you go inside [the store] you don't have an empty bag of course, I have a lot of paper inside, and other stuff, also more heavy things I can easily take out. [...] But it is not only this, we also use these things from sewing machines. Not the needle itself, but those larger metal things that are in a sewing machine [he shows me approximately five centimeters with his fingers]. So for example in ▮, you know the shop, it is a big chain in Europe, you see it everywhere. Well, when you put the metal thing into the kind of alarm they use on the clothes [he shows a twist with his hand], the alarm can open. Then the alarm does not work anymore, it comes off! [he smiles] I always hold that metal thing in my mouth [he laughs]. The police are always searching us for those metal things. They know we use them. [...] And the police caught me three times, but they never found it in my mouth. One time they took my bag and hit me in the head with it [he shakes his head]."

I ask Sebastian more about the logistics and economics of the arrangement, and he explains that all the clothes — between 60 to 100 kilos of clothes per week — are being sent by maxi taxi (Romanian minibus) to Galați, where ▮ would sell them on. In this way, the stolen items are channeled from Italy and other EU countries to Romania — even to the

---

Anti-Sărăcie și Promovare a Incluziunii Sociale de catre Universitatea București și Institutul Național de Statistică (2003), 11–13.

extent that people in Romania can order specific clothing items from ▮,
who will then make sure that they are provided. A while ago, the police
caught one of the shipments that Sebastian was in charge of, and all the
clothes were confiscated, but miraculously no one got caught, he explains.

At night, after everyone is asleep in the apartment, I look at my field
notes about this version of transnational theft, explained — and demonstrated — to me by Sebastian, only to find that my notes are a mess.
Looking through my notes, I notice that every time a name or a specific
place name is mentioned, I have put an X or Y instead, and I have put a
blank area for factual things, such as ages and addresses. In a few places,
I have crossed over numbers and names with a pen. However, because the
notes were written while interviewing Sebastian and because my attention
was on his demonstration with the aluminum foil, I have not been able to
redact a few names and place names sufficiently. I quickly make sure to
correct that. My growing concern about having written information that
could harm my informants has translated into this practice of redaction,
which always calls for an extra layer of further redaction and oversight
afterwards. Both Sebastian's and all my other informants' names are pseudonyms that I use in my field notes, and at the beginning of my fieldwork,
where I still had not fully memorized which pseudonym each name translated into, I had a meticulous and complicated system for remembering the
correct pseudonyms. Names for those who are not in my closest circle of informants did not have a pseudonym attached to them from the beginning,
which resulted in these clunky, black redaction boxes in my notebook, as
the ones above, made with a thick marker.

Hyper-visible Field Notes, Family Dynamics, and Silent Knowing

When looking at the redaction of my field notes, carried out during fieldwork, I noticed that I started to see the redacted areas and words in my
notes as hyper-visible — as an effect of redaction. I would sometimes look
at a page in my notebook, and all I could see were the anonymized names,
the Xs, the Ys, the crossed-out names, and the blanks. They stood out. In a
certain sense, the "numbed" or "shadowed" words, names, and place names
were the structuring devices for my notes, at least visually — but to what
effect? It did not feel like redaction to me — understood as a "taking-away"
or deletion — when sitting in my informants' living room, being in the process of writing the field notes. It felt as if the redaction I was doing was in
the form of organizing, re-assembling, curating, and concealing in order
to be able to write about this field later on without jeopardizing anyone's
anonymity. In the field, it simply felt as if this practice was helping me
manage a challenging fieldwork situation in a criminal field. However, at
the same time, looking at my notes, all that stood out were these shadows.
What I was doing with this practice was making certain parts of my notes
hyper-visible, hyper-important — without being readable. In this way,
and for better and for worse, I experienced my own practice of redacting
field notes in a criminal field as enlarging — making hyper — rather than
as minimizing or shielding. In a way, my notes were images of my field

itself — volatile, un-ordered, operating in the shadows — but at the same time, because of the redaction, they were neat, well displayed, and in a way already analyzed. They were ready to be shown to someone — such as the authorities or competing gangs — eliciting an "appropriate" reaction, as opposed to a reaction that would place any one of my informants in jeopardy.

Being experienced at operating in this shadow realm, my informants are excellent at navigating in different domains that demand different things of them,[12] such as the ways in which they navigate their family lives, where some elements of their illegal, transnational business sometimes need to be concealed. In these situations, they know very well what to cover and what to accentuate. For example, even though he lowered his voice so that his mother could not hear our conversation, Sebastian did not seem particularly concerned about showing me the use of aluminum foil in shoplifting in his parents' living room. When I asked him about it, he said that he could easily come up with an explanation if they had walked in on us. But he would often disappear abroad for weeks, never offering them an explanation — and they would not ask. This is a different kind of "redaction," carried out by my informants in their everyday lives — in Sebastian's and his parents' case, a redaction that appeared almost as a mutually and silently agreed upon secret.

However, how much my informants' families were openly involved in their illegal businesses varied greatly. The family of one informant in particular, Bogdan, was always closely involved in his illegal business plans of traveling abroad, and in the family's small, dusty courtyard, his wife and mother would often participate in planning and negotiating his business operations abroad.[13] In other families, such as Sebastian's, a well-curated navigation of avoiding direct conversations on the topic was practiced. There was a silent knowing in Sebastian's family. As Sebastian put it himself: "I just... don't say anything about what I do in Italy and Spain. They know I go abroad, they're not stupid, but... that's all."

This orchestration of their interactions — one that eliminates a particular set of questions — ensures that their family life in their small two-bedroom apartment runs smoothly, and that no information that could jeopardize Sebastian's position in the family gets in the way. His parents would often say that Sebastian was responsible and a good son, but that they would prefer that he did not spend time with "disgraceful people," as his mother put it — and the conversation would end there.

Just as in my field notes, the practice of managing their social interactions in this manner lets some information and some details stand out and be seen, while other kinds of information are not emphasized or mentioned. Just as the redactions in my field notes, which appear as hypervisible structuring devices, this open secret was a framing and defining feature of Sebastian's family dynamics.

---

12 Korsby, "The Brothel Phone Number," 114–16.
13 Ibid., 119.

Acknowledgments

This chapter is funded by the European Union under Grant Agreement no. 101068833, TRAFFICKER, as well as by the European Research Council (ERC) under the European Union's Horizon 2020 research and innovation program (grant agreement #725194, CRIMTANG). Views and opinions expressed are, however, those of the author only and do not necessarily reflect those of the European Union or the European Research Executive Agency (REA). Neither the European Union nor REA can be held responsible for them. Furthermore, the research for this chapter is supported by funding from Independent Research Fund Denmark (FKK) that funded the project "Fortune Chasers: Transnational Hustling and the Everyday Livelihoods of Organised Theft and Scamming in Europe" (no. 5050-00161B).

Jill Magid

My Sensitivity

"I bring things that are far away in closer to my body.

Drawing over things is a way to get inside them.

I like secrets, not necessary in their exposure but in their very existence.

To enter a system, I locate the loophole.

If my subject is made of clay, I will work in clay.

If my subject is text, I may write.

If my subject is too big, I will grow.

If my subject is out of reach, I'll steal it in a mirror.

Repeating something helps me to perceive it. So does cutting it out.

When in love, I separate a someone from the everyone.

Isolating details is like making bubbles.

An extra becomes the protagonist, after the film is made.

The protagonist disappears; the fact creates a void to be filled by other facts.

Without gravity we end up hovering.

What is considered banal or cliché might be hiding something.

Permission is a material and changes the work's consistency."

— Jill Magid, *Statements*, http://www.jillmagid.com/info/statements.

Jill Magid, *My Sensitivity*, 2007. Four-color silkscreen on Rives BFK paper, 27¼ × 44" (69.9 × 111.8 cm). From the series "The Kosinski Quotes," 2007. Courtesy of the artist and LABOR, Mexico City.

ings. One woman, terrified by my corpse, called a friend for advice, without even realizing that she was admitting she'd been sleeping with another man.

My sensitivity to the slightest change in my environment, and my craving for unusual psychological pressure have made me aware how little other people are aware of their surroundings, how little they know of themselves and how little they notice me.

Once, I attended a party given by a wealthy businessman who had rented paintings from a small, private museum to impress his guests. When the guests arrived, they were greeted with an array of works by major artists, which

Research through Passing in _____ and _____

Emily T. Yeh and A____ Marie Ranjbar

Where are you from?

<u>Fieldnotes, _____, 1996</u>
I was sitting in the Yak Restaurant, a small, dimly lit truck stop in _____ late one summer night when a _____ man sitting at the table next to mine struck up a conversation. He asked me where I am from. I asked him to guess. Kham? Linzhi? Shigatse? Amdo? Chamdo?...
I shook my head "no" at each one. Finally he gave up,

<u>Fieldnotes, _____, 2013</u>
We are driving from _____ to _____. We stop at the midway point and park in the center of a small town. We spot a juice bar and order saffron ice cream topped with carrot juice. We sit giggling on the stairs in front of the café when two female ▆▆▆▆ officers approach us. They point to me and a female colleague and gesture for us to adjust our hijab. One disapprovingly examines my brightly colored turquoise shawl. She demands to know where I'm traveling from and, as I begin to answer, she crossly inquires,

"Where are you from?"

I told him that I am from _____. He was not satisfied with the answer. "Yes, but you're really _____. Where is your family from?" I told him that I am not _____, but _____. He became more and more agitated and angry. Finally, I realized that he thinks I am _____, too proud to admit _____ even after my arrival in the homeland.

<u>Fieldnotes, _____ 2001</u>
At ▆▆▆'s house, ▆▆▆ introduced the two of us as being from the _____ work unit. He said that he is from _____. They asked where I am from and I decide to let him answer on my behalf. He said, "She's from _____. She's a *gyamo* (Chinese woman). Now she's working at our work unit." ~~I was suddenly angry to~~

▆▆▆ cuts me off and explains that I have a strong _____accent, and apologizes for our transgressions. I tighten my shawl as we walk quickly back to the car. When we're a safe distance away, I quietly ask which part of my clothing was offensive. Was it because my scarf had fallen back and exposed my hair? Was it the style of my veil or its bright colors? ▆▆▆ tersely replied that we are no longer in _____ and that I should switch out my shawl for the more formal *maghnaeh* (a type of hijab required in schools and universities).

As part of my doctoral research, I am working with an NGO and _____ is a potential research site. We arrive to _____ and, at a colleague's house, I change into a long shirt and a *rousari* (a loose fitting hijab). ▆▆

~~be from _____ and to have to play this ruse yet again.~~ I thought: "I'm here legitimately ███ working for ____'s project, why do I have to pretend yet again that I'm someone I'm not? Why can't I just be_____?" _____ looked at me. "She's not a *gyamo*! I thought she was a _____ [woman from _____]." I said, "yes, I'm a _____." "No, you're not! You look like a ____!..."

glances at my outfit. She removes her black robes and *maghnaeh* and dresses me with her outer garments. I glance at the mirror and remark that I look like _____. It's an inside joke. ███ knows that I have been writing my field notes in Harry Potter books _____. I am mortified that I still do not know how to dress for formal meetings. On the walk to the government office, I'm told by ███ to keep my voice down or, better yet, not to speak. The ███ comes to my defense and says that I am a member of this NGO team. Exasperated, ███ replies that I look _____ but, if someone hears me speak, they will know I'm an _____ citizen and the NGO's work will be in jeopardy. I do not speak a word during the entire meeting.

* * *

Who am I?

Passing is not necessarily a deliberate act, but rather a relationship between a person and others who do or do not confirm that person's "real" identity. The failure of any single set of criteria to unfailingly guarantee recognition means that, as Paul Gilroy puts it, "the desire to fix identity in the body is inevitably frustrated by the body's refusal to disclose the required signs of absolute incompatibility people imagined to be located there."[1] Passing may produce a disjuncture between what is felt "inside" and what is recognized from the outside.

Deliberate or not, passing is a form of self-redaction. As a technique of the state to erase and obscure, to withhold needed information behind the veil of security, redaction produces uncertainty, ambiguity, and ignorance, and thus enhances state power. Redaction of the self, particularly in contexts of state redaction, is, by contrast, double-edged. It can be a protective response to state surveillance, an agentive erasure that slips through the cracks of silence and immobilization, allowing movement through a form of invisibility. Simultaneously, it can be a form of complicity, a reinforcement of state authority. It begs questions about what constitutes ethical being and relating, and about how we experience selfhood.

If the body itself is not an unambiguous sign, neither are its stylizations, mannerisms, and performances. Clothing can be chosen and languages can be learned, but other elements of what Pierre Bourdieu calls *hexis* — bodily dispositions such as accent, comportment, and posture—are much harder to perform differently.[2] Even putting on certain clothing can feel like a deliberate repudiation or betrayal of one's self, even if as poststructurally informed theorists we accept intellectually that our subjectivities are shaped by discourses and our identities are not in fact inherent, unalterable essences.

---

1 Paul Gilroy, *Against Race: Imagining Political Culture Beyond the Color Line* (Cambridge: Harvard University Press, 2000), 104.
2 Pierre Bourdieu, *Outline of a Theory of Practice*, trans. Richard Nice (Cambridge: Cambridge University Press, 1977).

Ethics, responsibility, citizenship

<u>Fieldnotes_____November 2000</u>
I had told my research sponsor ▮▮ that I needed an official introduction letter in case anyone asked me any questions, but in the letter _____ carefully left out the fact that I am ____, using only my _____ name.... After dinner ▮▮ took me to see his junior high classmate, ▮▮ in ▮▮ former teacher, government official, and Party member....
He in turn introduced me as a relative, from _____, saying I had gone to _____ to study when I was very young, but could speak some _____....

<u>Fieldnotes_____January 2015</u>
Weeks after arriving to ____, I am finally able to set up an interview with an environmental scientist at the University of ____. Dr. ▮▮ is the professor of my research assistant, ▮▮, and has agreed to meet with me based on her recommendation. Over the phone, ▮▮ gives Dr. ▮▮ my name and university affiliation. While this is part of my ____, it is also strategic because, on paper, I appear to be an ____ student studying in ____. On the surface, this seems transparent, however,

I know it is unlikely that ▮▮ would agree to an interview with an _____.

He told me that he would introduce me to ▮▮ as well as ▮▮, that he would explain my situation to them and then they would help me out. ▮▮ told me several times that I should just be sure to tell families that I am not a ____ or a _____.

~~I felt very uncomfortable with this and told ▮▮ so.~~ This is not what my ____ said. What would I say if they asked me why I was taking notes in English?! What if they asked me why my parents went from ____ to ____? What if someone finds out who I really am?

I told ▮▮ that I really did not want to ____ about my identity.... Look, he said, "First of all, if you tell them you are from ____ no one is going to tell you anything real! You won't be able to learn anything at all! And if you just tell them ____ then **they are not responsible**. If someone asks them, they can just say they have no idea who you are, all they know is that you are from ▮▮. But if you tell them you are from ___ **then they are responsible**."

The point, then, is almost to help officials—to make it so that they do not have to be responsible for me.... ~~I am so confused....~~ ___ says one thing, but everybody who has

The _____ government surveils university faculty, ~~and the possibility that I might unintentionally cause harm to a research participant weighs heavily on me...~~

Dr. ▮▮ greets ▮▮ warmly but looks at me quizzically when I greet him in ____. We both know that Dr. ▮▮ is reacting to my accent and that he now knows I am ____. ▮▮ is sensitive to people turning down interviews with me but, given that this is her professor, she says nothing. She constantly corrects people who refer to me as an ____, insisting that I am an ____ citizen with strong ____ in the country....

Dr. ▮▮ escorts us to another room, and we are followed by an unidentified man. Following a carefully crafted introduction to my project, I ask, "What are the causes of ▮▮▮▮▮?..." As our conversation continues, the unidentified man begins to fade from my consciousness. I ~~forget myself and~~ ask, "Has the government done enough to save ▮▮▮?"

Dr. ▮▮ subtly reacts by rephrasing the question: **"Has the government done too much to save ▮▮▮ given that the farmers have ▮▮▮▮?"** I ~~am somehow oblivious~~

helped me out, from ▮▮ to ▮▮ to ▮▮, everyone except ▮▮ (all friends with ▮▮ in ____) have refused to help me out unless I say I am ____ or ____ ....

to the significance of the restated question and respond, "No, has the government...." Dr. ▮▮ cuts me off, glancing at the unidentified man who has now looked up from his tea. "Excuse me," he says with a smile, "Your ____ is fine. I did understand your question about ____ correctly. I'm happy to _____." Dr. ▮▮ excuses himself and, before leaving, he gives me the name of ____ academic working in the region. "International research collaborations are important to this Center. You may contact Professor ▮▮ if you are interested in an affiliation with this Center." The implication is clear. As an ____ student at a ____, I can only work with this Center under the auspices of a ____ university.

* * *

What constitutes ethical research? There are many situations in which the assumptions of Institutional Review Boards do not hold.[3] Consider, for example, that scholars at universities in Australia, Singapore, and beyond have recently been forced by their ethics offices to demonstrate that they have permission for their research from the government of Myanmar. As Magnus Fiskesjö argues, "research should be ethical, but unethical governments should not be given a veto to kill the research."[4] Would a genocidal state give permission to study oppression? Is it necessary, nonetheless, to study?

If our interlocutors want to assist with our research, but insist that we present ourselves as being of a different citizenship or ethnicity, is that ethical? A literal reading of standard institutionalized IRBs would say no. But what if the pressing need of one's potential interlocutors is first and foremost to not have the knowledge of who you really are, or where you are really from? What if their ignorance—say, the redaction—of that part of your identity is what can offer a veneer of protection in an authoritarian state?

And to complicate things, what if your interlocutors are wrong? Is it ethical to follow their lead, to assume their knowledge and ability to weigh the contextual risks is more informed than yours? What if we find ourselves in the paradox that, "to have behaved ethically was to have behaved unethically."[5]

* * * * *

---

3   Deborah G. Martin and Joshua Inwood, "Subjectivity, Power, and the IRB," *The Professional Geographer* 64, no. 1 (2012): 7–15.
4   Magnus Fiskesjö, "Research Ethics, Violated," *Allegra Lab*, May, 2020, https://allegralaboratory.net/research-ethics-violated/.
5   Richa Dhanju and Kathleen O'Reilly, "Human Subjects Research and the Ethics of Intervention: Life, Death, and Radical Geography in Practice," *Antipode* 45, no. 3 (2013): 513–16.

RESEARCH THROUGH PASSING IN _____ AND _____

Who is being watched?

<u>Fieldnotes, ____ 2018</u>

███ has set up a meeting for me with ███. We've met before, when _____ came to ███ and even before that, back in 2012, in ____. ███ and ███ work together often, so it shouldn't be a problem. Everything is set. I take a long subway ride and meet ███ at the exit; we take a taxi, go to the fancy gated apartment building that ███'s student has purchased for him. ███ can't remember the exact apartment number, though, and has to call. But ███'s face changes. It's not convenient today. ███ goes in by herself. I wait outside, sitting on the curb, trying to look inconspicuous, before heading to a coffee shop down the street as it becomes clear I'll be there for a while. Later I learn that ███ has been warned not to meet with any foreigners today. But how did they know? I have not communicated with ███ directly.

<u>Fieldnotes, ____ 2012</u>

Every Wednesday, I take a taxi from my ____'s house in ███ to the local university campus. When I arrive to the campus's main gates, I walk around the US and Israeli flags painted on the ground and nod at the security guards as I pass by. I have a weekly _____ literature lesson with a friendly professor in the ____ Department. After a few sessions together, she begins to coyly ask questions framed through the poetry of Robert Frost to ascertain my ____.... Eventually, we move our lessons to her apartment. She makes me take the battery out of my phone and leaves them in the kitchen. I discover that Professor ███ had previously served as a ____....

I begin to notice a car with unmarked plates parked outside of my ____'s house each afternoon. We never see who has parked the car. My ____ asks me daily whether or not I am using a VPN and reminds me to never disclose anything ____ over the phone. He warns me not to trust anyone outside of our immediate family, and tells me that I can no longer go to Professor ███'s apartment.

Which one of us is being monitored?

* * * * *

Is it safe for me to ask if you're okay?

____ 2018

It's been a full decade since I've seen ███. <s>I've been too terrified to try contact over social media, even though</s> I still have ███'s ███ address and also managed to procure his ███ account. Now that I am here in person, I want desperately to do so, but <s>I am very nervous and indeed,</s> I have been warned against it by friends. Foreigners are dangerous. I don't want to bring further scrutiny, or harm. But I feel I must do it; <s>it feels too much like losing a part of myself otherwise. I want to ask,</s>

_____, _____, November 2019

Protests have erupted throughout _____. On November 16, 2019, I wake up to a screenshot of a Google Map that my friend sent me on Telegram, a day before the messaging app is blocked. The map is marked with road closures throughout the capital, indicating where Iranians have used their cars to block major roads in protest of a substantial increase of gas prices.... I want to call ███ and ask,

"Are you okay?"

As it is, I have lost touch with almost everyone from my dissertation research, as well as subsequent projects. I walk with my kids past the entranceway a few times. Are there ▇▇▇ watching? We come back the next day. We enter the courtyard, bang on the door. Fortunately, one of ▇'s sons comes to let us in before we're out there for too long. ▇▇▇ has changed. I shouldn't be surprised but I am; my memories are frozen in time because of ▇▇. His hair is now white and his eyes have gone bad, so he squints in the dark room. ▇▇▇ chain smokes now, lighting up one cigarette after another, and another, and another. He tells me about how when he was ▇▇▇, they tell him it was because ▇▇▇. Are you sure it's okay for ____ here? I ask. It's fine, he says, they know who ____ and out, but it's okay, he reassures me.

Whenever I am in ____, I am always two steps behind on the latest encrypted apps needed to circumvent _____ and ____. During my fieldwork in 2013, ____ was the only means of having an open conservation, but this was soon blocked, leading ____ to become the preferred choice. After this was blocked during the 2017–18 protests, my _____ friends switched to ____....

I now try to call ▇ and ▇ but no one answers. For the first time in several years, I call landlines. My conversations with ▇ and ▇ are generic and our tones are lighthearted. I can only hint at my question: Are you okay?

* * *

Cutting off ties — whether to family members or close friends — is another sort of redaction, one we are pressured to perform ourselves: an excising of some parts of ourselves to secrecy, silence, to fragments that live on only in memory.

* * *

Research through passing in Tibet and Iran

My dilemmas of self were multiple, and concerned whether I was — or tried to be, or wanted to be — read as (ethnically) Chinese or Tibetan, and additionally, as an American (citizen) or not. The unwelcoming atmosphere and hard constraints on foreign social scientists doing research in Tibet made my being from the US a potentially dangerous fact for my interlocutors. Being read as a Tibetan from the US would make me that much more subject to state surveillance and suspicion. Some Tibetans I encountered, though, insisted that that is what I must be, or assumed that to be the case, and decided to trust me more — rather than less — as a result.

Being Chinese posed problems too. While reasonably fluent, my Chinese is by no means

While I generally frame my fieldwork through the insider–outsider literature, within Iran, I feel less like an insider than someone who is passing as Iranian. My father left Iran a year before the 1979 Revolution and, given the intense anti-Iranian sentiment during the hostage crisis, I was raised without an Iranian consciousness. When I was 21, I visited Iran for the first time, alone, and finally met my relatives.

My "passing" in Iran is dependent on not speaking. I look like my father and have unconsciously adopted many of his mannerisms. Most people do not know that I am a foreigner until my accent and grammatical mistakes betray my American identity.

During fieldwork, I try to embody certain "feminine attributes" that are surveilled in

that of a native speaker; I am incapable of writing meaningful field notes in Chinese characters. Within the broader context of the Sino-Tibetan "problem," too, I often felt unwilling or at least, deeply unhappy, to be recognized as Chinese. In the Yak Restaurant, in response to the man's questioning, the words, "I'm Chinese–American" refused to leave my mouth. I did not want him to identify me with the condescending attitudes I had witnessed many Chinese hold of Tibetans. But this was lost on my interlocutor. Instead, the way that I passed but refused to admit to either passing or not passing, together with my refusal to be hailed as a Tibetan, or Tibetan-American, grounded in part in an attempt to tell an ethical "truth" about myself, was experienced by my interlocutor as a denial of his vision of an imagined community of Tibetans.

post-revolutionary Iran. I am attentive to my outward appearance, especially how different veiling practices are required to traverse certain spaces. On several occasions when I've been stopped in the street by morality police, I enact mannerisms that convey modesty, such as averting my gaze, and wordlessly handing over my ID cards that identify me as an Iranian citizen. While passing can imply some degree of deceit, when conducting research in an authoritarian setting, passing feels like an ethical imperative to protect my family and colleagues.

* * *

In authoritarian regimes of hypervisibility which control in part through the disciplining of bodies in space, the self-redaction that is passing is complicit with state redaction as censorship, surveillance, and bureaucracy. It is simultaneously necessary and enabling, because it constitutes a condition of unlocatability that allows for the possibility of passage through space, which is a precondition for what we call fieldwork.

* * *

NO.	NAME IN FULL	SEX	DATE OF BIRTH	PROFESSION OR OCCUPATION	NATIONALITY	PASSPORT NO.
	██████████	M		SERVICES	AMERICAN	
	██████████	M		SERVICE	AMERICAN	
	██████████	M		SERVICE	AMERICAN	
	██████████	M		SERVICE	AMERICAN	
	YEH EMILY TING	F	17.12.1971	HOUSEWIFE	AMERICAN	
	██████████	M		SERVICE	AMERICAN	

Fig 28.1. "Occupation: housewife." Passing as a housewife was necessary for Yeh to cross the border from Nepal into Tibet one year, as determined by a tour operator for a group of US-based researchers.

Fig. 28.2. An identification card for ██████████ with which Ranjbar passes as a citizen of Iran.

Trevor Paglen

White Sands Missile Range; Alamogordo, New Mexico; Distance ~35 miles

"His art proffers a visibility that can only be partial, because it is organized around the requirements of secrecy, on the one hand, and generated from information too terrifying to assimilate, on the other."

— Pamela M. Lee on Trevor Paglen in "Open Secret: The Work of Art between Disclosure and Redaction," *Artforum* 49, no. 9 (May 2011), https://www.artforum.com/print/201105/open-secret-the-work-of-art-between-disclosure-and-redaction-28060.

White Sands Missile Range; Alamogordo, New Mexico; Distance ~35 miles, 2012, C-print, 60 × 48 in, 152.4 × 121.92 cm. © Trevor Paglen, Courtesy of the Artist; Altman Siegel, San Francisco; and Pace Gallery

From Behind Black Bars
Productive Redactions and Mass Incarceration in Xinjiang Uyghur Autonomous Region, 2017–2022

Alessandro Rippa and Rune Steenberg

> *Quiet is the new loud.*
> —Kings of Convenience, 2001[1]

As she finally opens the boxes of files documenting torture in Guantanamo, where her client has been held for years without trial, Nancy Hollander — protagonist defense lawyer in the *The Mauritanian* (2021), played by Jodie Foster — exclaims in disbelief: "But it is all redacted!"

The camera shows the sheets: indeed, only single words are legible between rows of blackened bars.

The message is clear: the government is hiding something terrible. The black bars conceal. At the same time they spur on the imagination. What is hidden beneath them in the dark? It must surely be monstrous. Why else would it be redacted? What is being suggested by the redaction feels almost more real and scary than if it were actually visible. In this gloomy silence of the black, the few legible words scattered on small white islands in a sea of in-transparency — now freed from all the other words to drown in — achieve a much more forceful significance. The narrative is controlled by the black bars of redaction. The film uses their suggestive power as an effect to drag the viewer's imagination through them and into the story. It's a trick, a craft older than Alfred Hitchcock and Orson Welles. Older than film itself, in fact, and used well beyond this medium.

The black bars of redaction not only hide, they also highlight. They suggest significance and draw in our imagination. Without the redaction, in an overflowing stream of information some things may be much better hidden. Furthermore, the black bars of redaction can also suggest things that may not actually be the case. They can be used to advance narratives that could otherwise be challenged by unredacted information and fully visible complexities.

Inspired by Hollywood films and Cold War novels, our usual associations with redaction are brutal secret police and corrupt politicians trying

---

[1] Kings of Convenience, *Quiet is the New Loud* (Astralwerks, 2001).

to hide their wrong-doings. Yet, once we see redaction as a tool to control narratives and not just to hide atrocities, we realize that it can be used productively not only by repressive regimes but also by many others. These may even include NGOs, newspapers, and scholars who view themselves as fighting repressive regimes. Redaction can help protect informants, comply with laws and ethics regulations, be sensitive to trauma, or ignite emotions. It can also be used to hide existing evidence that could complicate a specific narrative which one wishes to push. The imagined truth behind the black bars of redaction can be much clearer, stronger, and more compelling than the often messier and more inconclusive actual evidence hidden behind them. Redaction evokes the lure and power of the half-revealed, which may be used to exaggerate as well as to play down or hide.

In this chapter we show how redaction can be seen as a performative action aimed primarily at shaping a narrative in one's own interest. We show how this is employed by both state and non-state actors, pursuing conflicting agendas in discussions around state violence and mass incarceration in the Xinjiang Uyghur Autonomous Region (XUAR) in the 2010s. As the camp system in XUAR was arguably the first of its kind on such a massive scale to be built during the digital age, much information has been available early on. This includes satellite imagery of the camps, recorded witness accounts, and public tenders for its construction and hiring of security personnel, but also leaked documents circulated privately. Yet, while information on what was happening in the camps has been available, both Chinese state authorities and actors opposing the People's Republic of China's (PRC) policies in Xinjiang apply redactive approaches to limit this availability. These practices of redaction are a means not just of obliteration[2] but also of controlling what is forefronted; a magnifying lens that, in drawing attention to particular black spaces, directs, disrupts, and shapes the space of narrative possibilities and probabilities.

Controlling the Narrative of the Xinjiang Camps

Efforts by all sides to control the narrative have been at the very heart of reporting on the securitisation, mass surveillance, and mass incarcerations in Xinjiang since 2017.

Early work by scholars, journalists, and activists was aimed at shining a light on the factuality and scale of the abuses, then still obscured by lack of information. The Chinese government initially denied the existence of internment camps and reeducation centres for minoritized Muslim peoples in the XUAR, and Western companies and governments, too, were reluctant to confront the mounting evidence. It felt much like the classical story portrayed in movies like *Erin Brockovich*, *Outbreak*, or *The Mauritanian*, of a powerful state or corporation and its economically dependent collaborators seeking to mute the courageous attempts of activists, lawyers, doctors,

---

2 Solmaz Sharif, "The Near Transitive Properties of the Political and Poetical: Erasure," *Evening Will Come: A Monthly Journal of Poetics* 28 (2013): https://www.thevolta-org.zulaufdesign.com/ewc28-ssharif-p1.html.

and journalists to break the silence and reveal abuses for the world to see and judge.

By late 2018, in large part thanks to such efforts, the suffering of Uyghurs and other minoritized people in Xinjiang had been widely reported. Large human rights organisations like Amnesty International and Human Rights Watch were taking up the topic, while governments and international bodies such as the UN and EU expressed grave concern. Scholars and journalists became increasingly outspoken in their condemnation of the Chinese government's actions. They began to work more closely with the Uyghur diaspora and brought more funding for both documentation and advocacy. In 2019, a number of well researched reports, testimonies, and other evidence such as leaked government documents; tenders for camp construction, buying security equipment, and hiring guards; satellite images; and secretly filmed footage had eliminated all reasonable doubts about the truthfulness of the camps and the violence and indoctrination taking place in them.

Now, instead, reports of abuses in Xinjiang were increasingly being picked up by prominent China-hawkish politicians in the US, UK, Turkey, and Europe to promote their own political and geo-strategic efforts. This changed the tone and purpose of much of the reporting. More politicians took up the debate and the reporting on Xinjiang in Western media changed towards a less explorative and more sensationalist tone. It became increasingly unnuanced and politically charged. Voices and evidence that complicated the narratives presented were seemingly left out or systematically redacted while other factors were selectively promoted and repeatedly quoted.[3] Particularly, reporting on the drop in Uyghur birth rates, forced sterilization, sexual violence in the camps, and forced labor schemes, while rightfully calling out horrendous crimes committed by the Chinese Party-State and its functionaries, often lacked context, nuance and methodological precision. This lack seemed to betray a political bias rather than general incompetence as the parts left out were generally the ones complicating or questioning the most condemning conclusions. The Erin Brockovich moment seemed to have finally passed when US authorities made a point out of calling the atrocities in Xinjiang "genocide" while continuing to trade with China on a massive scale and retaining diplomatic ties.

The Chinese government, too, changed its strategy to control the narrative. It abandoned its early position denying the camps' existence. Instead, they were presented as vocational training centers and de-extremification facilities for people who had been infected with "ideological diseases."[4]

---

3   Rune Steenberg, "Suppression of the Uyghurs: Let's Stick to the Facts," *Geneva Solutions*, July 26, 2021, https://genevasolutions.news/peace-humanitarian/suppression-of-the-uyghurs-let-s-stick-to-the-facts.

4   Speech by Chinese Communist Youth League Xinjiang Branch, March 2017, quoted in Human Rights Watch, *"Eradicating Ideological Viruses": China's Campaign of Repression Against Xinjiang's Muslims*, September 2018, 1. https://www.hrw.org/sites/default/files/report_pdf/china0918_web2.pdf.

Understanding that the black bars of denial may indeed spur on people's imagination, they chose to selectively reveal. Groups of international journalists and some diplomats, as well as scholars, were invited on guided tours through chosen camps. The footage and testimonies gained from such Potemkin visits confirmed the existence of the camps as part of a massive system of internment for people who had not committed crimes. But, for many observers the visits also countered imaginaries of the camps as being akin to the Nazi-style death-camps of World War II. Such comparisons had been drawn by activists and analysts, particularly before any images of the inside of the camps were available. The visits proved massive abuses of the rights of the local population, but they also supported assumptions that there was a wide variety of different types of camps, and hinted at improvements in the conditions of some of them after 2018, and thereby they countered the worst fears of many observers. For some China-friendly journalists, influencers, and politicians, these visits even succeeded in painting a positive picture of the camps as being benevolent measures of counter-terrorism and poverty alleviation.

To a degree the Chinese government's choice to reveal selected strategic parts of their system succeeded in shaping the narrative. They added to the available information and thus complicated or even slightly watered down the existing narratives that were dominated by the powerful and condemning testimonies given by camp survivors.

Redacted Visits

Most diplomats invited to join such guided tours to the XUAR camps organized by the Chinese government declined the invitation. Members of the Danish, EU, and UN diplomatic missions explained to us that this was because the access they were offered was selective and restrictive, dictated by the Chinese government. There would be no free choice of place, interview partners, or format of conversation. In other words, the visits would only show the aspects that the government wanted to be seen. They would be offered a controlled narrative of a redacted reality. In spring 2022 UN special rapporteur for Human Rights, Michelle Bachelet, decided to go on a trip to China during which she also visited Xinjiang; she received much criticism for accepting such selective and redacted access, while she presented it as a quest to create a dialogue and build trust.[5]

In 2019, while many declined invitations to visit Xinjiang's camps, some went, drawn by curiosity and the hunt for a good story. For some of them, the real-time redaction seems to have worked. Journalists, especially from countries highly dependent on Chinese economic or political support, including Pakistan and Sudan, were generally supportive of Chinese policies

---

5   Michelle Bachelet, "Dialoguer ne signifie pas tolérer ou fermer les yeux," *Le Temps*, July 14, 2022, https://www.letemps.ch/opinions/michelle-bachelet-dialoguer-ne-signifie-tolerer-fermer-yeux.

Fig. 30.1. Screenshot from one of Olsi Jazexhi's videos taken at a Reeducation Center in Kashgar, summer 2019.

in Xinjiang.[6] Others, while critical, chose to report at face value what they had seen without any explicit reflection on what their curated visits may be hiding. They recounted seemingly acceptable conditions in the camps. The redacted access provided a canvas for different narratives but it also revealed basic facts about the mass incarceration program.

Albanian historian Olsi Jazexhi applied to go on such a guided tour in 2019 because he was highly sceptical of Western news reports about the camps in Xinjiang and wanted to debunk what he then saw as "ridiculous rumors." He was shocked at what he found.[7] Young Uyghur men and women were living for months in secluded, high-security facilities in the desert far from their families, jobs, and normal social contexts. While they did not seem to be starved or physically mistreated, they were being taught to denounce central aspects of their own religion and culture. When asked why they were in the facility, they explained that they were being cured from the virus of extremism and cited as proof of their extremism and wrongdoings practices like praying at home, veiling, or sporting beards.

Footage of Uyghur inmate-students singing "if you're happy and you know it clap your hands!" as well as interviews with inmate-students and administration at the camps aired by the BBC drew widespread condemnation and ridicule for being too-obviously engineered and staged with an uncanny degree of cynicism. The realities of the camps were being drowned out by a wall of acting, but similar to blacked-out redaction, its exaggerat-

---

6 Frederik Kelter, "China Targets Friendly Media, Diplomats to 'Tell Story of Xinjiang,'" *Al Jazeera,* January 2, 2024, https://www.aljazeera.com/news/2024/1/2/china-targets-friendly-media-diplomats-to-tell-story-of-xinjiang.

7 Olsi Jazexhi, "The Situation in Xinjiang: Report on My Latest Visit to China [Part 1]," *YouTube,* August 25, 2019, https://www.youtube.com/watch?v=VC1THdpRCPI.

edly colorful stagedness was uncannily hinting at something hidden for at least some of the visitors.

Rob Schmitz, a reporter at NPR, likewise joined a visit. On the walls of the dormitory he discovered the traces of a less redacted reality. "Bear with me, my heart,"[8] someone had scribbled onto the wall in a clear expression of suffering very much in contrast to the praises inmate-students presented to him in the monitored classrooms and supervised interviews.

Besides graffiti and the occasional slip-of-the-tongue, Jazexhi was allowed to record video footage. This provided some insight into the injustice and abuse taking place in these camps by showing students self-criticizing and documenting the lengths of their incarcerations, but the scale of systematic violence could not be accounted for. The redaction taking place here was not that of black bars, but rather that of colourful make-believe, and for many it seemed to hide reality better than the complete denial of access or black-bar-style redaction. The selective disclosure of some camps may indeed have been motivated by an understanding on the side of the Chinese of what gloomy imaginations a complete blocking of information or access to Xinjiang could cause across the world.

While the camps seen by foreign journalists were certainly hand-picked, sanitized, and prepared for the visits, there is no reason to believe that they were entirely fabricated. From camp survivors' testimonies and interviews, we know that conditions were much worse in some other camps. Insufficient space and food, physical violence, intimidation, and rape have been reported by former inmates. Yet, other camp survivors, who have been given less media attention, have also attested to camps with conditions closer to those presented to the journalists. Such testimonies, being less spectacular and complicating the picture drawn in many Western reports have even drawn accusations of complicity with the Chinese government. For these reasons they have rarely been expressed publicly, but Rune Steenberg has recorded and archived a significant number of these.[9] The Potemkin visits to the camps might thus be equated with the "tours" that Chinese leaders undertake to visit "model" factories and villages in various parts of the country. These are not an honest depiction of such facilities and places, but rather represent the ideal or "model" to which all should aspire. In this sense, this form of redaction is not solely intended for a foreign audience: it also targets the PRC's domestic public and higher Party officers themselves. The Party functionaries thus become both authors and audience of skewing and substitutive — as opposed to the purely concealing "black-bar" — redactive practices.

Several camp survivors have reported partaking in such redaction within the system. The inmates were instructed on what to tell inspectors from "above" arriving to inquire about the working conditions in factories. These

---

8   Rob Schmitz, "Reporter's Notebook: Uighurs Held for 'Extremist Thoughts' They Didn't Know They Had," *NPR*, May 7, 2019, https://www.npr.org/2019/05/07/720608802/reporters-notebook-uighurs-held-for-extremist-thoughts-they-didnt-know-they-had.

9   See also *Xinjiang Victims' Database*, https://shahit.biz/eng.

included higher officials inquiring about sexual violence and forced labour in the camps. The inmates were instructed to lie about being content and treated well. In all these cases, the system was censoring itself. Parts of the system were redacting information from other parts. Again, this was done not simply by restricting access — not by black bars — but by filling in the potential void with crafted stories. Classical redaction in itself — the silence, the black bars, the blocked access — draws too much attention and triggers too much imagination about the hidden. Filling the void with other narratives or overflowing the silence with propaganda are ways to mitigate this danger.

Redacted Leaks

In autumn 2019, supporting evidence of the systematic and premeditated nature of the mass internments surfaced in the form of leaked Chinese government documents. The first batch of eleven documents spanning 403 pages provided material for a story published on October 24, 2019 by *The New York Times*. The documents detailed the Chinese government's knowledge and organization of mass incarceration and political indoctrination of local Muslims in XUAR, particularly Uyghurs, Kazakhs, and Kyrgyz. The story included the original and translated versions of eleven original pages out of a total of 403. Another twenty-three pages were published by the International Consortium for Investigative Journalism. Individual names and ID numbers, as well as some place names and organisations, were blackened out, often including the publishing institution. For more than two years, less than fifty redacted pages of the 403 were shared with the public or indeed with human rights organisations and international monitoring groups working on the topic.

In the fall of 2021, the same documents that had been given to *The New York Times* were re-leaked to the Uyghur Tribunal, an unofficial "people's tribunal" on the atrocities committed by the Chinese state in XUAR initiated by Uyghur diaspora organizations (especially the partly US funded World Uyghur Congress and its associated organization, Den Norske Uigurkomitteen) and conservative British politicians and legal practitioners. A selected transcript of three of the eleven documents was published on the Uyghur Tribunal home page with a lengthy introduction by Adrian Zenz from the Victims of Communism Memorial Foundation, a conservative think tank, based in Washington DC. The publications entailed a written stipulation that they should not be republished or used anywhere else without this introduction and interpretation.. This restriction of use sparked a critical response among Xinjiang scholars, voiced on a non-public email listserve. Here the general issue of sharing versus withholding and controlling information was likewise discussed, which resulted in the eventual publication of all eleven documents. The re-leaks were initially presented as new leaks, but when it became widely understood that they were identical to *The New York Times*' Xinjiang Papers, serious concerns were voiced as to why they had not been shared earlier. Conservative politician Marco Rubio accused the NYT of deliberately hiding evidence of Xi Jinping's direct involvement in genocide but was rebutted by James Millward and other experts for instrumentalizing the Uyghur issue for his personal political gains.[10]

Contrary to Marco Rubio's suggestions, it turned out that leaving the documents unpublished and the leaks heavily redacted had allowed for more condemning and spectacular narratives of the abuses in XUAR than a closer reading of the actual documents suggested. Before the documents had been shared with the public or with relevant researchers, quotes from them had already been used to argue for calling the Chinese government's violence against the Uyghurs a genocide. In a report from March 2021, the Newlines Institute had isolated quotes from the NYT article about the leaks, including "wipe them out completely," and "destroy them root and branch," which it attributed to Xi Jinping and the first party secretary of Yarkent, Wang Yongzhi.[11] The report used the quotes to argue that they constituted evidence of an "intent to destroy" the Uyghurs as a people and thus of genocide. The report claimed that Xi and Wang had been referring to Uyghurs generally, while the original *New York Times* article it referenced presented them as talking more narrowly about "terrorists" as a constructed threat in order to legitimize the state violence and mass incarcerations in XUAR.

After two years these statements could finally be viewed in their context. The context proved more in line with the NYT's initial interpretation than the reading of the Newlines Institute. Having finally gained access to the leaks more than two years after their first appearance in the Western media landscape, Adrian Zenz formulated the shift in perspective that the two-year delay in publication of the leaks had produced in his and some of his colleagues' thinking about Chinese government violence in Xinjiang:

> Xinjiang scholars (including this author) have so far tended to frame state discourses of counterterrorism as a propagandistic façade concealing ulterior motives. However, after careful review of the material, the author is now inclined to think that the XUAR leadership appears to have quite thoroughly internalised official state discourses on terrorism, extremism, and related framings of the alleged threat that they pose to the state. Arguments that the state is simply using counterterrorism as a cover for achieving other political goals such as ethnocultural assimilation are at least partially valid. In light of the new evidence, they are, however, incomplete.[12]

---

10 "Rubio to New York Times: Why Did You Cover Up Xi Jinping Role in Genocide," *Marco Rubio* press release, November 30, 2021, https://www.rubio.senate.gov/public/index.cfm/2021/11/rubio-to-new-york-times-why-did-you-cover-up-xi-jinping-role-in-genocide.

11 *The Uyghur Genocide: An Examination of China's Breaches of the 1948 Genocide Convention* (Washington, DC: Newlines Institute for Strategy and Policy, 2021).

12 Adrian Zenz, "The Xinjiang Police Files: Re-Education Camp Security and Political Paranoia in the Xinjiang Uyghur Autonomous Region," *Journal of the European Association for Chinese Studies* 3 (2022): 298.

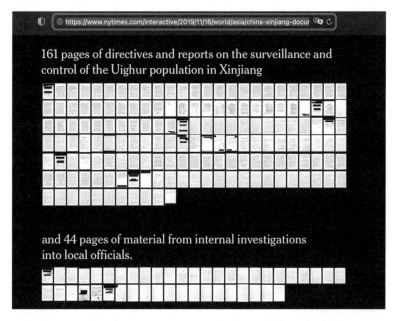

Fig. 30.2. A screenshot from Austin Ramzy and Chris Buckley, "'Absolutely No Mercy': Leaked Files Expost How China Organized Mass Detentions of Muslims," *The New York Times*, November 16, 2019, https://www.nytimes.com/interactive/2019/11/16/world/asia/china-xinjiang-documents.html. Most of the documents visible here were not released or shared with researchers. Only two years later they were re-leaked and then released in transcript upon pressure by international scholars.

In other words, while the reality of abuse that the leaks revealed is horrific and condemnable, the imagination triggered by their redaction and non-publication had produced even more demonizing perspectives.

Some months after the initial leak of the Xinjiang Papers was presented in the NYT, another leak appeared. In February 2020, a 137-page list containing the names of 311 camp detainees from Qaraqash in southern Xinjiang was shared by Asiye Abdulahad, an Uyghur activist based in the Netherlands. The so-called Qaraqash List contains the names of detainees in Qaraqash with relatives living abroad. The names were arranged in rows providing information for each name in columns. It includes the individual's ID number, address, employment, age, religious practice, names of relatives, social circles, and detention status. When published in the conservative *Journal of Political Risk* and subsequently in several news media, all last names and the personal part of the identity numbers of those listed were redacted but their addresses, first names, and the first names of their children were left legible. This practice of redaction is clever, because it allows relatives and friends of these individuals who know them from their home towns to identify them by their addresses, children's names, and spouses' names while still keeping a degree of privacy. Someone who does not know them could not easily identify them. But it also means that the redacted list does not allow for a systematic documentation of the people on the list as victims in the way pursued by international human rights organisations and important documenting observer platforms like the Xinjiang Victims Database, Shahit.biz. In other words, it makes documenting and counting victims more difficult. The exact identification of individuals is made all but impossible and thus verifications or double mentions from other sources cannot be accounted for. Such an uncertainty can be used by the Chinese to deny any significant number of victims, but it can also be used by those aiming to exaggerate the numbers. Uncertainty permits extrapolations and projections to become established as quasi facts.

Up until spring 2022, all attempts at estimating the total number of detainees who have moved through the camp system between 2017–2020 or who have been held at any given moment rely heavily on imprecise extrapolations and guesses.[13] That needn't have been the case. An unredacted use of the Qaraqash List and several similar lists covering southern XUAR townships could have provided much more precision in these numbers. These lists were held by private researchers and only recently, upon much pressure from international scholars and human rights organizations, were they shared with the wider community. At the time these were shared, they had been held for more than two years. With the publication and sharing of a new set of leaks in May 2022, dubbed the Xinjiang Police Files and including 5000 images of Uyghurs in police custody as well as data on more than 300,000 people, more precision has been achieved. Some extrapolations and speculations had previously set the number of detainees at a given point in time at up to three million. Even the number of eight million had been flaunted by activists. Since the release of the lists, estimates have now generally settled around one to one-and-a-half million having been detained in camp or imprisoned at some point in time between 2017–2020, not all at the same time.[14]

On January 26, 2021, *The Intercept* published an investigation based on another leak, this time of surveillance data from Ürümchi.[15] They too redacted the very few documents that they chose to show in the story. All names and identity numbers were fully blacked out, as well as the security level in some cases. They had worked on the data for almost two years, during which they had only shared it with a few researchers who had helped them with the authenticity assessment and analysis of the data. The Intercept had not shared it broadly with experts or human rights organizations

---

13 Jessica Batke, "Where Did the One Million Figure for Detentions in Xinjiang's Camps Come From?," *ChinaFile*, January 8, 2019, https://www.chinafile.com/reporting-opinion/features/where-did-one-million-figure-detentions-xinjiangs-camps-come.

14 Zenz, "The Xinjiang Police Files," and Adrian Zenz, "Public Security Minister's Speech Describes Xi Jinping's Direction of Mass Detentions in Xinjiang," *ChinaFile*, May 24, 2022, https://www.chinafile.com/reporting-opinion/features/public-security-ministers-speech-describes-xi-jinpings-direction-of-mass.

15 Yael Grauer, "Revealed: Massive Chinese Police Database. Millions of Leaked Police Files Detail Suffocating Surveillance of China's Uyghur Minority," *The Intercept*, January 29, 2021, https://theintercept.com/2021/01/29/china-uyghur-muslim-surveillance-police/.

before publication of their article. After publication, faced with repeated requests by scholars and fierce debate with the editors of *The Intercept*, the journalist holding the leaked documents, Yael Grauer, left the platform and chose to share it with select groups and researchers afterwards.[16] This, much like the other leaks, happened more than two years after they had received the data.

Significant amounts of material held by media outlets and researchers in the West were not shared for more than two years. This includes thousands of lists and other files held by private researchers, more than 400 pages of leaks claimed by the NYT and ICIJ, the Qaraqash-list of 137 pages, and the hundreds of pages upon which *The Intercept* based their investigations. The effect has been to slow down the analysis and development of a clearer understanding of the atrocities in XUAR, to the detriment of the suffering of minoritized people in the region. Why have they only been shared so late?

Professional ambition, corporate media considerations, national data protection laws, and a genuine concern about personal data protection certainly play a role. Yet the systematic bias in what is redacted and what is not also suggests more political and ideological motives behind the choices not to share or to redact certain information. In a few cases where the unredacted or unpublished originals are known to us, the data that was redacted would have provided a more differentiated and nuanced picture of the atrocities in Xinjiang than that presented by the institutions and individuals who did the redaction. In other words, here too, the redaction seems to both hide and highlight in order to control the narrative.

Behind Black Bars: What Redaction Says

There is no doubt that the main redactor and withholder of information regarding the mass incarceration and state violence in the XUAR is the Chinese government. Its motivation to do this is clear. Since the beginning of the mass incarceration, there has been a concerted effort to limit and control Uyghurs' contacts with relatives abroad and to block the work of journalists and researchers in the region. This has at times taken the form of brute force and direct intimidation. In other cases, such as in the arranged visits to "reeducation" facilities illustrated above, or in the case of massive Chinese social-media propaganda campaigns concerning Xinjiang,[17] au-

---

16 Vicky Xiuzhong Xu, James Leibold, and Daria Impiombato, "Exposing the Chinese Government's Oppression of Xinjiang's Uyghurs," *The Strategist*, October 19, 2021, https://www.aspistrategist.org.au/exposing-the-chinese-governments-oppression-of-xinjiangs-uyghurs/.

17 Emily Upson, *"The Government Never Oppresses Us": China's Proof-of-Life Videos as Intimidation and a Violation of Uyghur Family Unity* (Washington, DC: Uyghur Human Rights Project, 2021), and Rune Steenberg and Seher, "In What Purport to be Lifestyle Videos, Uyghur Influencers Promote Beijing's Narrative on Their Homeland," *ChinaFile*, August 4, 2022, https://www.chinafile.com/reporting-opinion/features/what-purport-be-lifestyle-videos-uyghur-influencers-promote-beijings.

thorities have taken a proactive approach, flooding the potentially explosive silence with selected, curated, and sometimes invented (mis)information. The Chinese government restricts information in order to downplay reports of human rights violations in Xinjiang and seeks to gloss over its redaction by filling the void with a flood of propaganda.

However, contrary to the narrative of an oppressive state limiting information while human rights activists, journalists, and academics were joining forces to dig out the evidence, as seemed suitable to the initial phase of reporting in the atrocities in Xinjiang, redaction of material and the withholding of information has not been done solely by the Chinese state apparatus, but also by those seeking to hold it accountable for its violence and abuses. If released earlier, the large amounts of information withheld and redacted by private researchers and media outlets could have added important details and nuance to our understanding of the atrocities, allowing for a more precise estimation of their scale and dynamics. Also this information could have benefitted individual Uyghurs in the diaspora, eased their pain, and helped them make informed decisions about their own activism by giving clarity about individual destinies and developments of the system. While the motivation behind the redaction by journalists, researchers, and think-tanks is less clear than in case of the Chinese government, and while the involved actors are more heterogeneous, the redactions often seem to support the arguments and interpretations that they seek to advance. Many of them tend to downplay the degree of complicity of Western companies and governments in creating a global system that allows for and supports state violence, securitization, land grabs, and the high-tech surveillance and labor exploitation of racialized populations. Such omissions help to amplify global Islamophobia and to cast "Wars on Terror" as legitimate reasons to violate international law and human rights.[18]

Information that could challenge the narrow and binary media and policy narratives on Xinjiang seems to have been systematically restricted. This has allowed for readings that would not have been supported by the evidence if all available information had been accessible and properly considered. These selective redactions divert the reader's attention away from complexity and nuance towards more simplistic guided imaginations that are better compatible with certain political agendas pushing for geo-political polarization and a self-acquitting binary of good (though not perfect) against evil.

Conclusions

The two examples presented here — Chinese state-organized Potemkin visits and the redaction of leaked documents by media and researchers — cannot be equated. In addressing them together we do not aim to compare

---

18 Darren Byler, *Terror Capitalism: Uyghur Dispossession and Masculinity in a Chinese City* (Durham: Duke University Press, 2021), and Sean R. Roberts, *The War on the Uyghurs: China's Internal Campaign against a Muslim Minority* (Princeton: Princeton University Press, 2020).

them morally but rather to point to one of the most powerful aspects of the practice of redaction. Redaction, besides hiding, also has the ability to highlight and amplify aspects of contexts and events. Rather than merely a mode of concealment, it is better understood as a tool to control and shape narratives. In obscuring some content but leaving selected information legible, redaction ignites the imagination. Black bars highlight a narrative that is not explicitly formulated in full. This makes them as powerful as any written word. The intended message needs not be explicitly stated. It arises in the interplay between the black bars, the words left un-redacted, and the imagination of the reader or viewer.

Redaction as a way to steer attention and spur imagination is not monopolized by large oppressive state apparatuses; journalists, researchers, activists, and liberal politicians, too, indulge in this practice.

The Chinese government chose to allow some camps to be seen — surely choosing the most sanitized ones and initiating staged performances in them — in order for these pictures to influence the global imagination surrounding the Xinjiang camps. They tried to take control of the narrative by allowing some visibility to counter the much louder "black bars" of their direct silencing. The redactions done by journalists, researchers, and activists confronting China's crimes in XUAR are rooted in complex reasons, including the protection of victims and whistleblowers, the adherence to data protection laws, and organizational and personal ambitions. Yet, much evidence also points to attempts by some of them to control the narrative in order to advance particular political and ideological interests by letting the black bars speak with deafening silence. By withholding certain information, they compromise clarity and transparency to hide aspects that could complicate their preferred narratives.

We have in this chapter focused on the concept and practice of redaction. We defined it rather widely as the selective disclosure of some information and the conscious and marked hiding of other information, whether this be typically through blacking out text in documents, by allowing access to detention facilities while controlling which parts of them are visible, or by not sharing documents. We see redaction as one special technique amongst many to manipulate and control a narrative through selective presentation of information. What makes redaction special within these techniques are the traces that it leaves to signal to a reader that omission has taken place. When these traces take the classical form of (metaphorical or literal) black bars, the obviousness of the omission invokes powerful imaginations. The act of redaction can be highlighted or made less visible depending on the wished-for effect.

Acknowledgments

This work was supported by OP JAK Project "MSCA Fellowships at Palacký University I," CZ.02.01.01/00/22_010/0002593 and by Horizon Europe coordination and support action 101079460-REMOTEXUAR-HORIZON-WIDERA-2021-ACCESS-03.

Both authors would like to thank the editors of the volume, as well as Darren Byler, M███████, A███, and N███ for their comments on earlier versions of this manuscript.

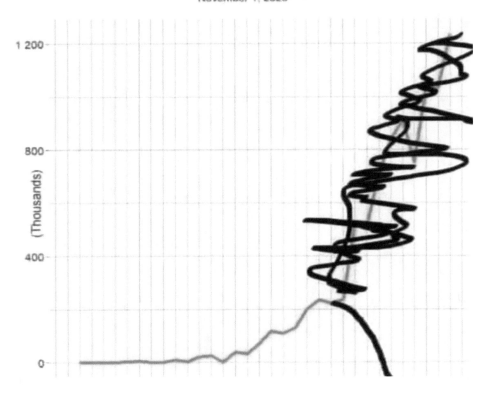

Things Not Revealed:
A Redacted Ethnography of the CIA

Carole McGranahan

"There was so much snow. Blue sky. No clouds. It was cold but pleasant. We were happy there. Oh were we happy."

Adam told me this. Adam was not his real name, but a code name. The man I knew as Baba Lekshey others knew as Adam. All the Tibetan soldiers who trained at Camp Hale, a secret Central Intelligence Agency (CIA) camp high in the Rocky Mountains, were given "American" code names. Baba Lekshey was someone with whom I visited frequently, mostly in Kalimpong, but sometimes in Kathmandu. We would talk about Kham and politics and fighting the Chinese. We would talk about the past as if it were not a foreign country, but was instead a place in which he wished he were still living. Baba Lekshey taught me many things. One day as we sat talking, he thought of something he wanted to share with me.

"I have an *Inji* name," he said.

"What?," I responded, surprised that he had an English name. "Really? What is it?"

"Let me find it," he said, "I forget what it is."

Baba Lekshey was a monk. As a young man in Tibet, he had been a trader and had a family. Then the Chinese communist army invaded. The world was turned upside down. Lekshey joined other civilians in a newly formed citizens' army devoted to defending Tibet, Buddhism, and the Dalai Lama, the country's political and religious leader. He and his fellow soldiers fought against the People's Liberation Army, safely escorted the Dalai Lama on his 1959 escape to exile in India, and then continued their armed struggle against the Chinese through 1974. The soldiers laid down their arms only after a personal plea from the Dalai Lama. In order to atone for the violent acts they committed on the battlefield, some soldiers took monks' vows later in life. Baba Lekshey was one of them.

He reached into his robe and pulled out a wallet. He rustled through it until he found what he was looking for. It was a piece of paper folded into a small square. Slowly he unfolded it, then squinted at the word written on the paper.

"Adam," he said, triumphant. "My name was Adam."

Names and Stories

CIA officers gave American names to all the Tibetan soldiers who trained at Camp Hale. Mark. Tim. Pete. Noel. Lee. Adam. The American "teachers" knew the Tibetans mostly by these names. The Tibetans, in turn, knew the CIA officers as Mr. Zeke and Mr. Tom and Mr. Ray and the like. Ray Starke was a "commo," or communications guy who taught radio skills at Camp Hale. As Ray tells it, he spent most of his two years there "joined at the hip, five and a half days a week" with his Tibetan partner Tashi Chutter. Ray and Tashi Chutter and most everyone else I spoke with about their time at the camp had story after story of what had happened there.

"I rigged up a transmitter," Ray told me. "Tashi and the other guys would do broadcasts around camp, the news and stories in Tibetan." He shook his head, reflecting back on it. "I was never quite sure how far the range was. It was a very low power transmitter, but you never know how far the range might've been. Imagine if people in neighboring towns had been able to pick up these broadcasts in Tibetan! If headquarters ever found out that we were doing that, they would've had a fit."

Headquarters was in Langley, Virginia, just outside of Washington, DC. Men in the field had a fair amount of disdain for those back at headquarters. "Sometimes," Ray said, "head honcho-types from headquarters would come out to the camp. They would go on and on about how lucky we were to be stationed there, about how beautiful it was and so on. We would beg to differ. It was no picnic. We were living in army conditions. The toilets were all in one row with no divider between each. The HQ guys did not like this. There was one guy from HQ who would try to wait until there was no one else in the toilet so that he could go in to do his business. I would keep my eye on him. One day I came out of class and saw this man go into the toilet. So I went in and sat down on a toilet right next to him and struck up a conversation, 'Isn't it great here? Beautiful. Wonderful. Wouldn't trade it for anything. How is your time here going?' He laughed. "Joking is how we passed a lot of the time. For those guys from headquarters, to say that they had been out to the camp was a notch on their belt."

This disjuncture between the headquarters and the camp mattered. The men at the camp knew the Tibetans personally and made efforts to learn about Tibet. "Agency people," on the other hand, "were not always too smart," as Ray put it. One thing they got wrong was language. Men back at headquarters had put together the Tibetan telecode book. He shook his head.

"You can tell they didn't know anything about Tibetan. They based the code on Chinese. But Tibetan is an alphabet language rather than a character language."

Ray developed a separate alphabet code for Tibetan, but the Agency wouldn't change it. "The character code made no sense. It also meant the Tibetans had to carry around a huge book of coded sentences. Using this code took much longer than it would've with the alphabet code." He repeated, "The people at the Agency didn't even know Tibetan wasn't a character language."

Four decades and multiple other operations later, the Tibet mission mattered most to Ray. He was indignant about some aspects and grateful for others. Yet, that day as we sat at his home in Florida talking, Colorado seemed very far away. And then it was time for lunch.

Personal Archives

Ethnography involves sitting down together to share food and drink. This is true even when it is with CIA officers. After speaking many times on the phone, I met Ken in person at his home in Maryland. We sat and had cold drinks and snacks before turning to business. Ethnography, of course, is never only about the business at hand. Coming to know another person, situating them in their world, in the world, is a commitment to building a relationship. It was easy to like Ken. On the phone he had been welcoming and eager to talk. In person he was the same. Like every retired CIA officer with whom I met, he positioned me as a kindred spirit. When we first met, I was a PhD student doing research with Tibetan veterans of the Chushi Gangdrug army, with men such as Baba Lekshey. Chushi Gangdrug was a volunteer army formed in the 1950s by citizens to defend their leaders, their families, their religion, and their country from the People's Liberation Army. This Tibetan fight against the communist People's Republic of China caught the attention of the US. The CIA partially funded and trained the Tibetan soldiers. That is why I was at Ken's house drinking lemonade on a hot summer day.

I hadn't expected to find kinship with CIA agents. Ken was not the first. Before he and I met, I had already spoken with other retired agents around the country. Some I spoke with on the phone, some I met in person, and I would go on to meet many more. They were all white men, but they were not homogenous. Their class backgrounds, their personalities, and their positions with the CIA varied. Despite these differences, they were clearly a brotherhood bound together by experience and commitment. The experience was working together in a hidden camp in Colorado. The commitment was to the other group of men with whom they lived and worked there and to their cause: Tibet.[1] My scholarly work to learn and tell the Tibetan side of the story was seen, to my surprise, as a similar commitment. Even my critiques of the CIA were welcome; these men had their own critiques, some of which were deeply and personally felt. Ken was one of those who was committed to acting on his critiques.

Ken was also the consummate host. For years he had been the CIA's Officer-in-Residence at Harvard's John F. Kennedy School of Government. He was as proper as he was affable, and thus after a proper amount of time had passed, he said, "Shall we go upstairs?" Upstairs was his collection of materials from his time working on the Tibet operation. I sat down and he pulled out file after file of documents dating back to the 1950s and to

---

1 Carole McGranahan, "Love and Empire: Tibet, the CIA, and Covert Humanitarianism," in *Ethnographies of U.S. Empire*, eds. Carole McGranahan and John F. Collins (Durham: Duke University Press, 2018), 333–49.

the Colorado camp. These were things I had never seen before, never read about before. Each had a story attached to it. I could've sat for hours listening to his stories; I did sit for hours listening, learning, and taking pages and pages of notes.

This visit, my first to Ken's home, was right after his book *Orphans of the Cold War: America and the Tibetan Struggle for Survival* came out.[2] He would later write a second book about Tibet, *Beyond Shangri-la: America and Tibet's Move into the Twenty-First Century*.[3] That first day, as we sat together and looked through his personal archives, I felt like a child in a candy store, excited at the materials arrayed before me. Yet I also wondered why these materials were in someone's home rather than in a museum or the archives of a Tibetan organization such as Chushi Gangdrug. This was not the first time during my research that I wondered this.

Then, Ken pulled out a box that gave me chills. "These," he said, "are my own files." He started taking papers out of the box to show me.

"When I started working on the book, I had to request my files from the Agency." He laughed. "I had to do this the same as any other researcher."

He opened up a file and took out some papers. "These are my own reports. I wrote these. Every single report here is one I wrote." He handed them to me. Each page was heavily redacted. His own reports came back to him with the details obscured; someone had redacted the very words Ken himself had written.

Invitation

To redact is to mask information. Redaction renders information invisible but its obscuration visible. In other words, you are made aware that something is being withheld. This visual aspect of redaction matters. It conveys purpose in a different way than simply deleting information or withholding it entirely. Redaction is part refusal, part tease.

CIA histories of Tibet involve layers of unknowing. Redaction is only part of it. There are things that were not known, but should've been known, such as basics about the Tibetan language. But there were other things too: from Colorado, the CIA sent men back to India and Nepal with hand-picked leaders, "the best and brightest" of the trainees. American understandings of leadership qualities did not match family and place-based Tibetan leadership structures. To lead was a hereditary position, not an achieved one. CIA lack of awareness of Tibetan social-political organization had repercussions: men died, disputes flared up, resentment lingered.

Not knowing is not neutral. This is especially so for an "intelligence" agency. Intelligence is about certain types of knowing and certain types of knowledge. The Tibet operation deviated from CIA norms in meaningful

---

2   John Kenneth Knaus, *Orphans of the Cold War: America and the Tibetan Struggle for Survival* (New York: PublicAffairs, 1999).
3   John Kenneth Knaus, *Beyond Shangri-La: America and Tibet's Move into the Twenty-First Century* (Durham: Duke University Press, 2012).

ways, but it was still an American operation acting in American imperial interests.

Public secrets were another component of the unknowing. A public secret is a secret that is publicly known, but not acknowledged by those involved. The CIA-Tibet connection was a public secret for a very long time, a tantalizing story for journalists and CIA watchers. In the Tibetan community, it was not so much a public secret as an arrested history, on hold until the time came to tell it. And then in 2010, the CIA proclaimed this operation no longer secret.

On August 26, 2010, I received an email from a staff member of US Senator Mark Udall (Democrat, Colorado). I had known it was coming, but it was still thrilling to see it in my inbox. The email read:

> You are cordially invited to a ceremony commemorating the role of Camp Hale, Colorado, in connection with the training of Tibetan Freedom Fighters.
>
> WHAT: Unveiling a plaque commemorating the role of Camp Hale, Colorado, in connection with training of Tibetan Freedom Fighters.
>
> WHEN: Friday, September 10, 2010
>
> WHERE: Camp Hale, Colorado

The invitation went on to explain that years earlier, Senator Udall had met Ken Knaus, who told him about training Tibetan soldiers at Camp Hale. Ken and the other officers had long wanted to honor the commitments they had made to the Tibetan community. Specifically, he wanted to publicly acknowledge the CIA-Tibet operation and to do so at Camp Hale itself with an historic plaque. Senator Udall proved to be the perfect partner to make that goal a reality.

Ceremony

Ken Knaus and Ray Starke were at the Camp Hale ceremony. So many people were there. Tibetan veterans. Their families. Retired CIA officers. Their families. Years had passed. Some of the men had not seen each other for over four decades. Flags were raised, incense was offered, and then Senator Udall gave opening remarks. Prayers were said. Speeches were made. Tears were shed.

At one point after the main ceremony had concluded and the plaque was unveiled, I stood with Ken and Ray. We talked about the ceremony and caught up on life and families, and they teased me about the fact that my book *Arrested Histories: Tibet, the CIA, and Memories of a Forgotten War* had finally come out.[4] It was in fact published the day of the Camp Hale

---

4 Carole McGranahan, *Arrested Histories: Tibet, the CIA, and Memories of a Forgotten War* (Durham: Duke University Press, 2010).

ceremony. In the book, I wrote about how the CIA had never publicly acknowledged the Tibet operation and how at Camp Hale there was no sign at all that the Tibetan soldiers had trained there. The book was thus out of date on the very day it was published. But that day, it didn't matter at all. The ceremony was one of dignity and joy, even if parts of the history were bittersweet.

To each other, Ken and Ray were "Jim." These were not code names, but a reference to Kingsley Amis's book *Lucky Jim*, of which the two were both fans. On one of my visits to his home, Ray shared stories with me about walking with Ken among the Colorado wildflowers, talking about philosophy, laughing and calling each other Jim. Back at camp, others had similar pastimes—playing practical jokes, creating art, reading, and writing. They also made maps of Camp Hale. Ray showed me one at his home. Ken had several in his home office. They each told me of their desire to go back to try and find the campsite. When the operation closed down, they had to destroy the camp. At the time, the goal was to make the area appear as if the camp had never been there at all. Now, almost fifty years later, here they were again at Camp Hale.

The plaque commemorating the Tibetan-CIA camp is located in a very public, easily accessible location. The camp is not. With a twinkle in his eye, Ray said to me, "We brought the map. We're going to go see if we can find the spot."

As the Tibetan veterans gathered after the plaque dedication for a second ceremony, this time of religious prayer and offerings, the CIA veterans climbed into their rental cars and drove up into the mountains in search of the campsite. When they returned, they told me they had been unable to find the site. They could no longer locate the site where they had lived, where over a five-year period several hundred men had lived together.

The training camp site is still there, but not visible. The plaque now tells the story. Nothing, it appears, is redacted. This is instead a story of disclosure and acknowledgment, of a request for redemption. This is the human part of the story: one group of men saying to another group, "We respected you. We tried. We failed. We remain committed."

To Know, To Matter

There are things we don't know. There are things we choose not to learn. And, there are things we hide. Redaction, however, is not necessarily performed by an individual subject (or agent as this particular case may be). In the case of the CIA, redaction is institutional. It is in the name of the state and is in service to the state. What is redacted is not always what matters to the stories we need to tell. It might matter to other stories and to other times. It might matter elsewhere or otherwise. It might not matter at all.

Fathers and Daughters

When she was a girl, Doma Norbu did not know why her father spoke English with an American accent. That was unusual in India, where it was more common to have a British accent. She thought it was from watching Hollywood movies. It was years later that she learned that he was connected to the CIA. Her father, Athar Norbu, was one of the first Tibetan soldiers trained by the CIA. He was a telegraph operator who accompanied the Dalai Lama and his resistance entourage on their escape to India in 1959.

On the other side of the world, another little girl was similarly unaware of aspects of her father's work. It wasn't until 2005 when as an adult Lisa Cathey noticed a "Free Tibet" sticker on her father Clay's golf cart. This was not the expected bumper sticker one might see in his retirement community, so she asked him about it. To her surprise, he told her he had worked with the Tibetan army as part of his CIA career. He told her that Tibetans believed in their cause, in the independence of their country, and that helping them was a good thing. The Tibet operation had been a good one. He told her that he realized its importance more now than he had at the time.

Both Doma and Lisa were at the 2010 Camp Hale ceremony. Other sons and daughters were there too, representing their fathers and families. One was Sonam Yangzom, daughter of Ratu Ngawang, a resistance army commander. At the ceremony, she read a letter from her father. In it, he thanked Ken Knaus for US support for Tibet and for making the installation of the plaque possible. He asked everyone at the Camp Hale ceremony to remember those Tibetans who gave their lives for Tibet, and especially for remembrance of Tibetan soldiers who had trained at Camp Hale and died on missions into Tibet. He named six of them: Andrugtsang Ngawang Phulchung, Andrugtsang Yeshi, Ratutsang Lobsang Gelek, Shalotsang Atso, Dolma Golok, and Dholutsang Phulchung.

These are their Tibetan names. These are their names. I do not know their American names. Any master list of what American names were given to which Tibetan soldiers is long gone, either discarded or buried deep in the archives. It was not one of the documents in Ken's collection, redacted or not. In both names, though, they are remembered. We remember them in speeches and ceremonies, in family lore, in writing, and sometimes in small pieces of paper we keep folded close to our hearts. To his daughters back in Tibet, Baba Lekshey's name was Pala. *Father.*

Where Are ~~Ohlone~~ Place Names?

Kären Wigen

In 2013, a white Stanford freshman tried to see her campus through the eyes of its Indigenous inhabitants. For her contribution to a class counter-atlas (defined as any collection of maps that the administration would not or could not make), she decided to show the university lands as they might have looked in Ohlone days. Her starting point was a basic research question: where had Native inhabitants lived? Where were their hamlets, their hunting grounds, their borders, and their burial sites? How did they occupy their homeland, and what did they call it? Since no Indigenous maps of the area survived, and since early European maps of California made only crude gestures toward Native peoples' presence, Jen West sought out the university archaeologist to request guidance. While the interview was granted, the detailed information she sought was withheld. In the interest of protecting Native remains from desecration, the university had decided not to share their locations. West would have to deduce where the Ohlone had lived by learning what they valued.

Initially, that effort proceeded at an encouraging pace. It was amply attested that Ohlone lifeways had revolved around fresh water, hunting grounds, obsidian quarries, and vistas of Mount Diablo (the cosmic axis of the Ohlone world) — sites whose locations could be readily inferred from a topographical map (fig. 33.1). But while rivers and ritual sites might be deduced, place-names turned out to be stubbornly elusive. Given the density of Native settlement in the Bay Area, the landscape must have bristled with Ohlone names. Yet pre-conquest toponyms had almost completely disappeared. More than in most of the West, Native polities in California had been swept off the landscape, overwritten by Spanish or American names.

Figure 33.1 shows how West handled this disturbing lacuna. Unable to supply indigenous placenames, she underlined their erasure. Heavy black lines stood in where toponyms should have been. Likewise, with no way to reconstruct Ohlone territory, she simply cut her base-map at the jagged property-lines of the university's 8,180-acre parcel (while letting woodlands and rivers spill out to the paper's edge). The resulting canvas had a deeply defamiliarizing effect. Its heavily blacked-out labels, in particu-

▶ Fig. 33.1. ~~Ohlone~~ *Stanford Lands*, by Jen Ward West. Final project for History 95N, *Maps and the Modern Imagination*, Fall 2013; included in the 2013 Stanford Counter-Atlas, edited by Kären Wigen. Reproduction courtesy of Jen West.

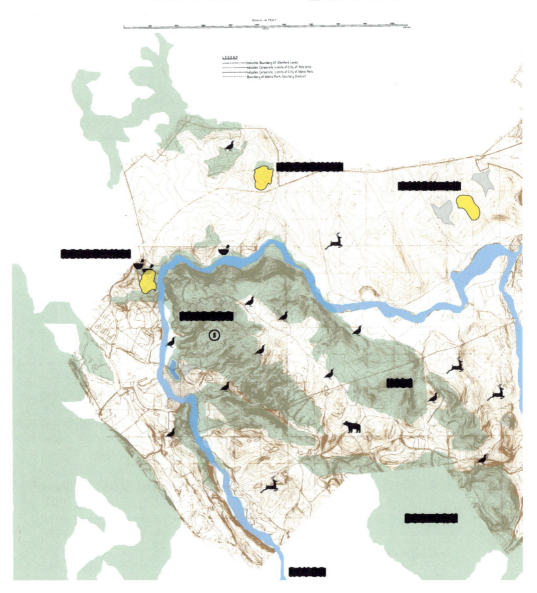

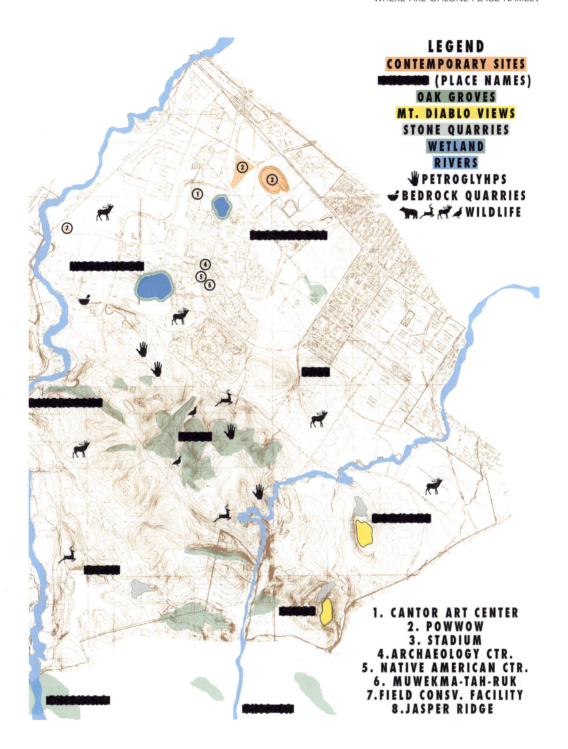

lar — incongruous among the bright polygons and leaping stags — stirred a sense of disquiet that lingered in the mind.

In its title as in its design, "~~Ohlone~~ Stanford Lands" anticipated the project of this volume. Running up against the limitations of conventional cartography, West chose not to dodge them but to reveal them. Using the universal visual codes of censorship, her map bears silent witness to the razing of Native North America.

▇ in the Field
Lies, Silences, Half-Truths

Franck Billé

Hohhot, China. October 2005.

Met Liyuan again today. At first, when she approached in the canteen of the Neimenggu Daxue (University of Inner Mongolia) where I had begun studying Chinese in August, I wasn't too sure about her. She was extremely driven and clearly eager to practice her English. But I didn't have many friends and I missed speaking to someone without struggling with the language. So I had agreed to meet. And to meet again. This is now our fourth meeting and I feel we have somehow become a little closer. We have both relaxed. She has opened up about herself, her family, and her plans for the future, in ways that seem less tactical. I have also relaxed, and concluded that if this is going to be some sort of friendship, I also have to tell her about my life back in London. She also needs to know I am unavailable, I thought, just in case she is indeed being tactical and sees me as more than just language practice, as her ticket out of China. So I tell her about ▇ and about our life together back home. She seems totally unfazed. She asks a few questions but nothing intrusive. She is respectful and open-minded. Nothing has changed, and we will meet again soon.

My later text messages go unanswered.

Hohhot, China. April 2006.

Over the past few months I have been meeting a group of people about once a week. ▇ ▇, a Han girl from Baotou; Maggie, an Inner Mongolian also from Baotou; Tanaka, a Japanese exchange student who is fascinated by Mongolian culture and is learning the horsehead fiddle; and Jimmy, an American from Michigan. Even though most of them could easily switch to English, Chinese is the language we use for communication. Initially I think they took pity on me. Barely able to string a sentence together and needing everything to be explained to me several times, I was not exactly the wittiest of interlocutors. But as weeks passed a genuine friendship has developed, especially with Jimmy and ▇ ▇. We often meet independently of the group, for lunch or dinner.

I am especially relaxed with Jimmy, whom I told very early on I'm ▇. It's often easier to assess people you share a culture with. Values generally come together in clusters. Someone like him, who is young, has left home to do a Master's degree in Chinese history, in Chinese, in a somewhat remote

part of China, and who is often critical of his own culture and of himself, was not likely to turn out to be narrow-minded. ▓▓ out to him was a non-issue.

With ▓▓ openness is more difficult. She is young and intelligent, but she has not traveled much beyond Inner Mongolia. Will she react like Liyuan a few months ago — politely, but cutting all ties without a second thought? When I tell her, her reaction is somewhat subdued, and I leave the restaurant feeling unsure and nervous as to what she really thinks. But why had I expected a different outcome? After all, separated by gender, status, and backgrounds, and with a big age gap between us (15 years), there was little space — nor the cultural expectation — for ▓▓ to provide a different kind of response.

We continue to meet regularly, and after I return home we stay in touch on Facebook.

Tokyo, Japan. August 2015.
A conference has brought me to Tokyo for a few days, and ▓▓ and I are meeting for lunch at a small restaurant downtown. She's been living in Japan for several years now and I'm amazed at how linguistically and culturally fluent she has become, switching adeptly back and forth between Chinese and Japanese languages and personas. Our exchange has become more fluid. She tells me about her job and about cultural differences. I tell her about my new life in California. She's seen some of the pictures I posted on Facebook. She may actually move to California as well, she tells me. Her boyfriend has been offered a job in LA.

Oakland, California. September 2019.
Scrolling on FB, I see the meme of a white guy wearing a t-shirt with the text:

1. 美国
2. 二十九岁
3. 工作
4. 四年了
5. 没有

Smiling, I save it to my photo stream. The five statements (in English: America; 29; work; 4 years; I'm not) are immediately recognizable to anyone who has spent any significant time in China. The questions I had been asked during my fieldwork in China had invariably followed the same pattern, and in the same order: 1. Where are you from? 2. How old are you? 3. Are you a student or do you work? 4. How long have you been in China? 5. Are you married?

My first contact with ▓▓ had not been any different.

This volley of questions can feel intrusive to an outsider. Age is not generally the second question asked of strangers in Europe or the US. But over time, I came to see this initial exchange as nothing more than a way to break the ice, a way for people to categorize me, to make sense of my presence in their country. For an ██ anthropologist, these questions were not particularly problematic. They did not pry into my private life and they allowed me to interact with people, at least initially, without having to provide supplemental texture to the relationships I was building with my interlocutors.

But this perpetual elusiveness also troubled me. Constant auto-redactions created gaps, distance. They turned me into a guarded, distant, aloof alter ego I didn't recognize and didn't particularly like. Without an organic back-and-forth, I worried my questions to my interlocutors felt business-like and inquisitive. The relationships I would form in the course of my fieldwork in China (and later in Mongolia and in Russia) were built on lies, silences, and half-truths. I constantly wondered — were they genuine friendships?

It would take several more months, until close to the time I would be leaving, for me to offer a corrective addendum (to a few select people) to my initial responses.

Blagoveshchensk, Russia. September 2011.
A new research project has taken me to the Russian Far East, where I'll be carrying out fieldwork in the Russian city of Blagoveshchensk, on the edge of the country, a stone's throw from the Chinese city of Heihe, across the Amur River. In some ways doing research there is easier for me. My Russian is far better than my Chinese and, more importantly, I can blend into the background. I do not look Russian, and my accent ultimately gives me away, but in a place without much tourism, anyone who's not Asian is by default Russian — *rossiyanin* if not *russkiy*.[1]

Today I'm meeting Igor, an acquaintance of an acquaintance of my friend ██. She doesn't know him in person but thinks he will be an interesting person to talk to. Igor is a fluent Chinese speaker who moved a year ago to Heihe, where he has established a number of relationships with Chinese traders. In this unusually bipolar border region where the river traces a fault line between two countries with very little cultural overlap, individuals living and working on both sides are rare. Conversations with him are thus certain to be illuminating with regard to the cultural, political, and ethnic dynamics I'm interested in.

If Igor indeed turns out to be a source of endless ethnographic detail, this is not a relationship I'm going to relish. Igor has one particular preoccupation: ██████████. Specifically the need to defend Russia from the malignant influence of the West. Over the next few weeks, every time we meet he unfailingly returns to his obsession. And every time, I ignore, I deflect, I redirect.

---

[1] Russian distinguishes between Rossiyanin (a Russian citizen) and Russkiy (an ethnic Russian). I have frequently been mistaken for someone from the former Soviet Union.

Heihe, China. October 2011.

Tonight I'm meeting Igor together with his wife, Irina. In her early 30s, Irina is a few years older than him. With Asian features and striking blue eyes, she embodies the intimate entanglement of two populations long separated by a heavily surveilled border and subject to relentless, decades-long propaganda. As we sit down to have dinner at a local restaurant, it doesn't take long for the topic of ▮▮▮▮▮▮▮ to come up again. Irina smiles. "Yes, that's a big topic for Igor. He hates **GAYS**. You're not **GAY**, right?"

In China, elusiveness in my responses to personal questions from interlocutors had helped me carve out spaces of ambiguity. In Russia, these strategies are no longer available to me. ▮▮▮▮▮▮▮ is heavily politicized, commonly equated with pedophilia, and tied to liberal Western values perceived to be incompatible with Russia's. On my mind are also the recent cases of Russian ▮▮ men getting beaten up after being lured through dating apps. A more likely outcome in tonight's scenario is the immediate loss of access to interlocutors in this small provincial town.

Seething with an anger I try my best to conceal, I reply. "No."

I'm not sure they believe me.

Our later meetings and exchanges are laced with diatribes against ▮▮ and incongruous invitations. Igor suggests we go to the country together. We can go hunting, drink beer, and stay together in a tent. I'm suddenly getting a strong Brokeback Mountain vibe.

Back home, I gradually space out my email responses to him. By the time I return to Blagoveshchensk, in 2014, we're no longer in touch.

Blagoveshchensk, Russia. April 2014.

When I return to the field, Russia has just annexed Crimea and is subject to economic sanctions. Attitudes toward the West have shifted and hardened, although my French passport continues to buy me quite a lot of good will. Since my last visit, anti-▮▮ legislation (the federal law "for the Purpose of Protecting Children from Information Advocating for a Denial of Traditional Family Values") has been passed. Foreigners now risk being arrested, fined, and detained for up to 15 days, then deported. This requires even more explicit forms of denial and excision of my family at home, especially in the context of the interviews I am planning to do with college and university students.

Another development is the more widespread use of social media, notably Facebook and its less liberal Russian counterpart, V Kontakte. To keep my life at home insulated from the field, I've created a separate friend category, "Acquaintances," who essentially cannot see any of my posts. And, in an abundance of caution, I tell most interlocutors I'm not on social media.

Blagoveshchensk, Russia. May 2014.

▮▮, a new interlocutor, is a young woman in her early twenties. She strikes me as smart, openminded, shy, and a little nerdy. I think we're going to get on well. We've already met a couple of times and the conversation flows easily. With limited experience outside of Russia, she's full of questions about life in London.

But as we talk one day over coffee I realize that she is very much pro-Putin and politically conservative. Out of the blue, she tells me that Americans cannot adopt Russian kids. I know that Russian Federal law 272-FZ ("On Sanctions for Individuals Violating Fundamental Human Rights and Freedoms of the Citizens of the Russian Federation") defines sanctions against US citizens involved in "violations of the human rights and freedoms of Russian citizens" and also prohibits US citizens from adopting Russian children.[2]

This decision was taken following the death of a Russian infant adopted by American parents who was forgotten in a car and died of a heatstroke — though it was also a political decision, taken in retaliation for US sanctions. But ▓▓'s explanations are different. She tells me adoptions are no longer allowed because Americans torture, rape, and kill adopted children. This statement leads to a lively discussion during which I emphasize that American parents are just as loving as Russian parents, and while abuse does occur — everywhere in the world! — rape and torture are just as horrifying in the US as well.

I feel my words make sense to her but they clearly land on top of sedimented layers of urban myths, rumors, media stories, and political narratives.

In the evening we exchange Facebook messages. She wants to chat about kids and crimes again. She tells me that adoptions by Americans are not allowed because of same-sex marriages which are illegal in Russia. I steel myself for what I know is coming next.

Instead, she tells me about this fifteen-year-old Russian kid who came out as ▓▓ and who had a hard time at school, picked on by the other students and by the teachers. She says that it's weird that men get turned on by the idea of two women together but they are horrified to think of two men together. She thinks it makes no sense.

She asks me if girls in the West have tattoos and piercings. Yes, they're quite common. I tell her I used to have a couple of piercings myself. She giggles and asks where. Then she tells me she has two: bellybutton and tongue. The girl is full of surprises.

This exchange also has me rethink my earlier assumption that values come in clusters. I had found George Lakoff's argument in his book *Think of an Elephant* persuasive, specifically how US Republican and Democratic values form coherent sets that articulate around a core model.[3] My interac-

---

2   The law also suspends the activity of politically active non-profit organizations that receive funding from American citizens or organizations.

3   These can be summarized succinctly as the "strict father" model versus the "nurturant parent" model. See George Lakoff, *Don't Think of an Elephant! Know Your Values and Frame the Debate* (White River Junction: Chelsea Green Publishing, 2004). Lakoff's argument is developed from his earlier analysis of language's metaphoric undercarriage, where he contends that metaphors are not found in random assemblages but that they come organized within larger metaphoric constellations. In his later work Lakoff is careful to point out that these are radial categories, that is, clusters of contiguous conceptual metaphors that have central models as well as variations on those models.

tions with ▬ and later with other Russian interlocutors problematized that neat model and demonstrated that, in practice, conflicting beliefs and opinions frequently cohabit within the same individuals. Later still, with the US entering the "age of post-truth," I would have plenty of opportunities to hear virtually identical myths and disbeliefs voiced by people located very differently on the political spectrum. So much for neat dichotomies and classifications.

London, UK. August 2015.
A Russian colleague based at the University of ▬ in the Russian Far East tells me about a potential opening that might interest me. They have a new department eager to establish itself as a world class research center, and having a scholar associated with Cambridge and Berkeley would help raise their profile. Would I have to go there a lot? No. They'd be happy with a couple of short visits a year, remote mentoring, and two or three articles a year listing them as my affiliation. Sounds like a great deal. The money won't be great but I am currently unemployed. Let's go for it.

I fill out an application form, send a copy of my passport, and submit various other documents. The administrator is currently away but will get in touch with me soon. A couple of months later, it looks like they might need a couple more publications from me, and it would be great if I could organize a workshop. They'll send a new application form for me to sign. Weeks later, a new form arrives but the details of the deal are wrong and the time to be spent onsite has been cut. I'm told a new administrator is working at the university now and that we'll need to renegotiate. But the person is currently unavailable so I'll have to be patient. After a few more weeks I finally get the final deal. I no longer have to travel to ▬ at all any more, it can all be remote. But the low salary is now contingent on publishing twelve peer reviewed articles per year. A lesser number will be reflected, pro rata, on the remuneration.

I email them back, calling them unprofessional, and pull the plug.

Oakland, California. April 2016.
I've grown tired of stressing over Facebook, of having this two-speed account and constantly worrying about potential leaks in my careful curations. I decide to remove the "acquaintances" tag and to merge everybody into the same category. And whatever happens, happens.

As it turns out, nothing happens.

My Facebook friends in Blagoveshchensk see my previously concealed posts and tick "Like." ▬'s mom even sends me a friend request and starts engaging with my posts by liking and commenting on photos and stories of our dog Max and, later, of our son ▬.

Was I trying to conceal something everyone already knew?

How transparent was that closet door, anyway?

Online. June 2017.
My newfound digital freedom does not last long. Doubts reemerge, this time about the changing political landscape at home. I'm probably over-

thinking this, but what if the country continues descending into authoritarianism? What if Trump gets reelected? Will this spell a further slipping away of democratic practices? Will reposting memes critical of the Trump administration jeopardize a future application for US citizenship? I find myself scrubbing my Facebook account, just in case, and thinking twice before I post anything.

Oakland, California. February 2021.
As I discuss this project on redaction with my colleague at the University of ▮▮▮▮▮▮, I find out that the primary reason I didn't get the job is because the university's administration found out I was ▮▮. So the endless delays, which I had attributed to ineptitude, were politically motivated. Anxious about my presence at the university, and especially about a lecture content that could put them at odds with the current legislation, they increasingly cut down contact time. Ultimately this was still no guarantee, so they offered a deal they knew would be unacceptable.

In a book on the "dark geography of the Pentagon's secret world," Trevor Paglen writes:

> Secrets…often inevitably announce their own existence. For example, when the government takes satellite photos out of public archives, it practically broadcasts the locations of classified facilities. Blank spots on maps outline the things they seek to conceal. To truly keep something secret, then, those outlines also have to be made secret. And then those outlines, and so on.[4]

Ultimately my careful elisions, excisions, blurrings, carvings, and curations… served no purpose. On the contrary, like the practice of redaction itself, all cohered to highlight a silence that echoed throughout my fieldwork. A silence readily decoded by my interlocutors. An alternative form of coming out.

Online. March 2013.
Igor tries to add me on Facebook.
    I ignore the request.

---

4 Trevor Paglen, *Blank Spots on the Map: The Dark Geography of the Pentagon's Secret World* (New York: New American Library, 2010).

Jenny Holzer
Palm, Fingers and Fingertips (Left Hand) 000395

Jenny Holzer, *Palm, Fingers and Fingertips (Left Hand) 000395* (2007). War Paintings, Palm Painting Project. Oil on linen, 58 × 44 in. (147.3 × 111.8 cm). Text: US government document. © 2007 Jenny Holzer, member Artists Rights Society (ARS), NY.

NAME: (Last, First, MI)		CASE#	
SSN:		TAKEN BY: SA	
SIGNATURE:	b(7)(C)-2	DATE: 19 Nov 04	b(7)(C)-1

PALM, FINGERS & FINGERTIPS (LEFT HAND)

FOR OFFICIAL USE ONLY
LAW ENFORCEMENT SENSITIVE

022963
(EXHIBIT_____)

000395

DOD-044688

Jenny Holzer
Right Hand, DOD-044403

Jenny Holzer, *Right Hand, DOD-044403* (2007). War Paintings, Palm Painting Project. 58 × 44 in. (147.3 × 111.8 cm). Text: US government document. © 2007 Jenny Holzer, member Artists Rights Society (ARS), NY.

Case#: 0114-04-CID083-66

Date: 22 Jun 04

(b)(6) 2 - (7)(C) -2

022678
U00207

DOD-044403

Bibliography

Aho, Brett, and Roberta Duffield. "Beyond Surveillance Capitalism: Privacy, Regulation and Big Data in Europe and China." *Economy and Society* 49, no. 2 (2020): 187–212. DOI: 10.1080/03085147.2019.1690275.

Aizenman, Hannah. "Daniel Borzutzky's Poems Channel Cacophony in an Age of Calamity." *The New Yorker,* March 31, 2021. https://www.newyorker.com/books/page-turner/daniel-borzutzkys-poems-channel-cacophony-in-an-age-of-calamity.

Albrecht, Jan Philipp. "How the GDPR Will Change the World." *European Data Protection Law Review* 2, no. 3 (2016): 287–89. DOI: 10.21552/EDPL/2016/3/4.

Anghel, Remus Gabriel. *Romanians in Western Europe: Migration, Status Dilemmas, and Transnational Connections.* Lanham: Lexington Books, 2013.

Applebaum, Anne. "Autocracy Inc." 19th Annual Seymour Martin Lipset Lecture, *National Endowment for Democracy,* December 1, 2022. https://www.ned.org/events/nineteenth-lipset-lecture-anne-applebaum-autocracy-inc/..

Bachelet, Michelle. "Dialoguer ne signifie pas tolérer ou fermer les yeux." *Le Temps,* July 14, 2022. https://www.letemps.ch/opinions/michelle-bachelet-dialoguer-ne-signifie-tolerer-fermer-yeux.

Banaji, Shakuntala. "*Vigilante Publics:* Orientalism, Modernity and Hindutva Fascism in India." *Javnost: The Public* 25, no. 4 (2018): 333–50. DOI: 10.1080/13183222.2018.1463349.

Batke, Jessica. "Where Did the One Million Figure for Detentions in Xinjiang's Camps Come From?" *ChinaFile,* January 8, 2019. https://www.chinafile.com/reporting-opinion/features/where-did-one-million-figure-detentions-xinjiangs-camps-come.

Blanchot, Maurice. "The Essential Solitude." In *The Space of Literature,* translated by Ann Smock, 21–34. Lincoln: University of Nebraska Press, 1982.

Bourdieu, Pierre. *Outline of a Theory of Practice.* Translated by Richard Nice. Cambridge: Cambridge University Press, 1977.

Brown, Tony C. *Statelessness: On Almost Not Existing.* Minneapolis: University of Minnesota Press, 2022.

Buck-Morss, Susan. *Dreamworld and Catastrophe: The Passing of Mass Utopia in East and West.* Cambridge: MIT Press, 2002.

Buffetrille, Katia. "The Evolution of a Tibetan Pilgrimage: The Pilgrimage to A myes rMa chen Mountain in the 21st Century." In *21st Century*

Tibet: Symposium on Contemporary Tibetan Studies, 1-28. Taipei: publisher unknown, 2003. https://case.edu/artsci/tibet/sites/default/files/2022-05/The%20Evolution%20of%20Tibetan%20Pilgrimage-%20The%20Pilgrimage%20to%20A%20myes%20rMa%20chen%20Mountain%20in%20the%2021st%20Century.pdf.

Burgess, Matt. "What Is GDPR? The Summary Guide to GDPR Compliance in the UK." *Wired*, March 24, 2020. https://www.wired.co.uk/article/what-is-gdpr-uk-eu-legislation-compliance-summary-fines-2018.

Byler, Darren. *Terror Capitalism:. Uyghur Dispossession and Masculinity in a Chinese City*. Durham: Duke University Press, 2021.

Byrd, Jodi. "Silence Will Fall: The Cultural Politics of Colonial Agnosia." Unpublished manuscript, n.d.

Cage, John. *A Year from Monday: New Lectures and Writings*. Middletown: Wesleyan University Press, 1967.

Chandler, David. "A World without Causation: Big Data and the Coming of Age of Posthumanism." *Millennium: Journal of International Studies* 43, no. 3 (2015): 833–51. DOI: 10.1177/0305829815576817.

Chang, Jung, and Jon Halliday. *Mao: The Unknown Story*. London: Jonathan Cape, 2005.

Cole, David. *Torture Memos: Rationalizing the Unthinkable*. New York: New Press, 2009.

Constitution of the People's Republic of China. 1982.

Craze, Joshua. "Excerpt from a Grammar of Redaction." In *Dissonant Archives: Contemporary Visual Culture and Contested Narratives in the Middle East*, edited by Anthony Downey, 385–400. London: I.B. Tauris, 2015.

———. "In the Dead Letter Office." In *Jenny Holzer: War Paintings*, edited by Thomas Kellein. Cologne: Walther König, 2015.

———. *The Grammar of Redaction*. Exhibited in New York at the New Museum, 2014.

———. "The Secret's Signature." In Jenny Holzer, *Belligerent*. 2018. Box with seven 60 × 79 cm posters. Madrid: Ivory Press, 2017.

Critchley, Simon. *Infinitely Demanding: Ethics of Commitment, Politics of Resistance*. London: Verso Books, 2007.

Cushing, Tim. "New York Times Suffers Redaction Failure, Exposes Name of NSA Agent and Targeted Network in Uploaded PDF." *Techdirt*, January 28, 2014. https://www.techdirt.com/2014/01/28/new-york-times-suffers-redaction-failure-exposes-name-nsa-agent-targeted-network-uploaded-pdf/.

De León, Jason. *The Land of Open Graves: Living and Dying on the Migrant Trail*. Berkeley: University of California Press, 2015.

Derrida, Jacques. *Archive Fever: A Freudian Impression*. Translated by Eric Prenowitz. Chicago: University of Chicago Press, 1996.

Dhanju, Richa, and Kathleen O'Reilly. "Human Subjects Research and the Ethics of Intervention: Life, Death, and Radical Geography in Practice." *Antipode* 45, no. 3 (2013): 513–16. DOI: 10.1111/j.1467-8330.2012.01048.x.

Diamond, Sigmund. *Compromised Campus: The Collaboration of Universities with the Intelligence Community, 1945–1955.* New York: Oxford University Press, 1992.

Dixon Jr., Herbert B. "Embarrassing Redaction Failures." *American Bar Association,* May 1, 2019. https://www.americanbar.org/groups/judicial/publications/judges_journal/2019/spring/embarrassing-redaction-failures/.

Douglas-Jones, Rachel, Marie Blønd, and Luuk Blum, eds. *Common Erasures: Speaking Back to GDPR.* Copenhagen: ETHOS Lab, 2020.

Douglas-Jones, Rachel, and Marisa Leavitt Cohn. *GDPR Deletion Poems.* Copenhagen: ETHOS Lab, 2018.

Dündar, Fuat. *İttihat Ve Terakki'nin Müslümanları İskan Politikası, 1913–1918.* Istanbul: İletişim Yayınları, 2001.

———. *Modern Türkiye'nin Şifresi: İttihat Ve Terakki'nin Etnisite Mühendisliği, 1913–1918.* Istanbul: İletişim Yayınları, 2008

Dzenovska, Dace, and Larisa Kurtović. "Introduction: Lessons for Liberalism from the 'Illiberal East.'" *Society for Cultural Anthropology,* April 25, 2018. https://culanth.org/fieldsights/introduction-lessons-for-liberalism-from-the-illiberal-east.

"'Eradicating Ideological Viruses': China's Campaign of Repression Against Xinjiang's Muslims." *Human Rights Watch,* September 2018. https://www.hrw.org/sites/default/files/report_pdf/china0918_web.pdf.

Fiskesjö, Magnus. 2020. "Research Ethics, Violated." *Allegra Lab,* May, 2020. https://allegralaboratory.net/research-ethics-violated/.

Gibson, Mel, dir. *Braveheart.* Paramount Pictures, 1995.

Gilroy, Paul. *Against Race: Imagining Political Culture Beyond the Color Line.* Cambridge: Harvard University Press, 2000.

Gordillo, Gastón R. *Rubble: The Afterlife of Destruction.* Durham: Duke University Press, 2014. DOI: 10.1215/9780822376903.

Grauer, Yael. "Revealed: Massive Chinese Police Database. Millions of Leaked Police Files Detail Suffocating Surveillance of China's Uyghur Minority." *The Intercept,* January 29, 2021. https://theintercept.com/2021/01/29/china-uyghur-muslim-surveillance-police/.

Grenacher, Manuel. "GDPR, The Checklist for Compliance." *Forbes,* June 4, 2018. https://www.forbes.com/sites/forbestechcouncil/2018/06/04/gdpr-the-checklist-for-compliance.

Groom, Amelia. "There's Nothing to See Here: Erasing the Monochrome." *e-flux* 37 (September 2012). https://www.e-flux.com/journal/37/61233/there-s-nothing-to-see-here-erasing-the-monochrome/.

Gudonis, Marius, and Benjamin T. Jones, eds. *History in a Post-Truth World: Theory and Praxis.* New York: Routledge, 2021.

Han, Byung-Chul. *The Transparency Society.* Translated by Erik Butler. Stanford: Stanford University Press, 2015.

Hartman, Saidiya V. "Venus in Two Acts." *Small Axe: A Caribbean Journal of Criticism* 12, no. 2 (2008): 1–14. DOI: 10.1215/-12-2-1.

Hartman, Saidiya V., and Frank B. Wilderson, III. "The Position of the Unthought." *Qui Parle: Critical Humanities and Social Sciences* 13, no. 2 (2003): 183–201. DOI: 10.1215/quiparle.13.2.183.

Heller, Joseph. *Catch-22: A Novel.* New York: The Modern Library, 1961.

Heller-Roazen, Daniel. *No One's Name: An Essay on Infinite Naming.* New York: Zone Books, 2017.

Holmes, Douglas R., and George E. Marcus. "Collaboration Today and the Re-Imagination of the Classic Scene of Fieldwork Encounter." *Collaborative Anthropologies* 1 (2008): 81–101. DOI: 10.1353/cla.0.0003.

"Hong Kong Media Tycoon Jimmy Lai Ordered Back to Jail." *BBC News*, December 31, 2020. https://www.bbc.com/news/world-asia-china-55496039.

Horning, Amber, Roisin Bermingham, Julie Sriken, and Christopher Thomas. "'Pimps' Self-Presentations in the Interview Setting: 'Good Me,' 'Bad Me,' and 'Badass Me'." *Journal of Human Trafficking* (2022): 1–22. DOI: 10.1080/23322705.2022.2078592.

Hoshur, Memtimin. *The Classmates.* Translated by M. and Darren Byler. Forthcoming.

Hovannisian, Richard G., ed. *Armenian Tigranakert/Diarbekir and Edessa/Urfa.* Costa Mesa: Mazda Publishers, 2006.

Howe, Sarah. "A Note about 'Two Systems.'" *Law Text Culture* 18, no. 1 (2014): 249–57. http://ro.uow.edu.au/ltc/vol18/iss1/14.

———. "Sarah Howe | Two Systems || Radcliffe Institute." *YouTube*, November 6, 2015. https://www.youtube.com/watch?v=dDHa4OEqaeo.

Human Rights Watch. *"Eradicating Ideological Viruses": China's Campaign of Repression Against Xinjiang's Muslims.* September 2018. https://www.hrw.org/sites/default/files/report_pdf/china0918_web2.pdf.

Jaffrelot, Christophe. *Modi's India: Hindu Nationalism and the Rise of Ethnic Democracy.* Translated by Cynthia Schoch. Princeton: Princeton University Press, 2021.

Jaffrelot, Christophe, and Gilles Verniers. "A New Party System or a New Political System?" *Contemporary South Asia* 28, no. 2 (2020): 141–54. DOI: 10.1080/09584935.2020.1765990.

Jazexhi, Olsi. "The Situation in Xinjiang: Report on My Latest Visit to China [Part 1]." *YouTube*, August 25, 2019. https://www.youtube.com/watch?v=VC1THdpRCPI.

Jeffrey, Craig. "'A Fist is Stronger than Five Fingers': Caste and Dominance in Rural North India." *Transactions of the Institute of British Geographers* 26, no. 2 (2001): 217–36. DOI: 10.1111/1475-5661.00016.

Jongerden, Joost. *The Settlement Issue in Turkey and the Kurds: An Analysis of Spatical Policies, Modernity and War.* Leiden: Brill, 2007. DOI: 10.1163/ej.9789004155572.i-355.

Jongerden, Joost, and Jelle Verheij, eds. *Social Relations in Ottoman Diyarbekir, 1870–1915.* Leiden: Brill, 2012. DOI: 10.1163/9789004232273.

Kelter, Frederik. "China Targets Friendly Media, Diplomats to 'Tell Story of Xinjiang.'" *Al Jazeera*, January 2, 2024. https://www.aljazeera.com/news/2024/1/2/china-targets-friendly-media-diplomats-to-tell-story-of-xinjiang.

Kévorkian, Raymond H. *Le génocide des Arméniens.* Paris: Odile Jacob, 2006.

Kévorkian, Raymond H., and Paul B. Paboudjian. *1915 Öncesinde Osmanlı İmparatorluğu'nda Ermeniler.* Translated by Mayda Saris. Istanbul: Aras Yayıncılık, 2012.

Khalili, Laleh. *Time in the Shadows: Confinement in Counterinsurgencies.* Stanford: Stanford University Press, 2012.

King, Andrew David. "The Weight of What's Left [Out]: Six Contemporary Erasurists on Their Craft." *The Kenyon Review,* November 6, 2012. https://kenyonreview.org/2012/11/erasure-collaborative-interview.

Kirchheimer, Otto. *Political Justice: The Use of Legal Procedure for Political Ends.* Princeton: Princeton University Press, 1961.

Knaus, John Kenneth. *Beyond Shangri-La: America and Tibet's Move into the Twenty-First Century.* Durham: Duke University Press, 2012.

———. *Orphans of the Cold War: America and the Tibetan Struggle for Survival.* New York: PublicAffairs, 1999.

Koch, Natalie. "'On the Cult of Personality and Its Consequences': American Nationalism and the Trump Cult." In *Spatializing Authoritarianism,* edited by Natalie Koch, 194–221. Syracuse: Syracuse University Press, 2022.

Korsby, Trine Mygind. "Complex Intimacies: Sex Work, Human Trafficking and Romance between Italy and the Black Sea Coast of Romania." In *A Sea of Transience: Politics, Poetics and Aesthetics along the Black Sea Coast,* eds. Tamta Khalvashi and Martin Demant Frederiksen, 66–79. New York: Berghahn Books, 2023.

———. "Hemmeligheder, distance og kontrol af viden: Menneskehandel i Italien og Rumænien." In *Familie og Slægtskab — Antropologiske Perspektiver,* eds. Karen Fog Olwig and Hanne Mogensen, 131–46. Copenhagen: Samfundslitteratur, 2013.

———. "Hustlers of Desire: Transnational Pimping and Body Economies in Eastern Romania." PhD Diss., University of Copenhagen, 2015.

———. "Reading Desires: Romanian Pimps Striving for Success in the Transnational Street Economy." *Migration & Society* 6, no. 1 (2023): 57–69. DOI: 10.3167/arms.2023.060106.

———. "The Brothel Phone Number: Infrastructures of Transnational Pimping in Eastern Romania." *Cambridge Journal of Anthropology* 35, no. 2 (2017): 111–24. DOI: 10.3167/cja.2017.350209.

Lakoff, George. *Don't Think of an Elephant! Know Your Values and Frame the Debate.* White River Junction: Chelsea Green Publishing, 2004.

Lee, Pamela M. "Open Secret: The Work of Art Between Disclosure and Redaction." *Artforum,* May 2011. https://www.artforum.com/print/201105/open-secret-the-work-of-art-between-disclosure-and-redaction-28060.

Leong, Michael. "'Remembering / might also be hijacked': Travis Macdonald's *The O Mission Repo* (Fact-Simile Editions, 2008)." *Michael Leong's Poetry Blog,* May 12, 2009. https://michaelleong.wordpress.com/2009/05/12/"remembering-might-also-be-hijacked"-travis-macdonald's-the-o-mission-repo-fact-simile-editions-2008/.

Lewis, Robin Coste. "The Race within Erasure." Lecture for Portland Arts & Lectures, Literary Arts, February 25, 2016. https://literary-arts.org/archive/robin-coste-lewis-2/.

Li, Zhisui. *The Private Life of Chairman Mao: The Memoirs of Mao's Personal Physician.* Edited by Anne F. Thurston. Translated by Hongchao Dai. New York: Random House, 1994.

Liu, Ming, and Ling Lin. "'One Country, Two Systems': A Corpus-assisted Discourse Analysis of the Politics of Recontextualization in British, American and Chinese Newspapers." *Critical Arts* 35, no. 3 (2021): 17–34. DOI: 10.1080/02560046.2021.1985156.

Lorde, Audre. *The Selected Works of Audre Lorde.* Edited by Roxane Gay. New York: W.W. Norton & Company, 2020.

Luman, Douglas. "Book Review: The O Mission Repo." *Found Poetry Review*, 2014.

Macdonald, Travis. "A Brief History of Erasure Poetics." *Jacket 2* (2009). http://jacketmagazine.com/38/macdonald-erasure.shtml.

———. *The O Mission Repro: A Repro of the O Mission Error Attacks on Unit.* Santa Fe: Fact-Similie Editions, 2008.

Magid, Jill. *Statements.* http://www.jillmagid.com/info/statements.

Makley, Charlene E. *The Battle for Fortune: State-Led Development, Personhood, and Power among Tibetans in China.* Ithaca: Cornell University Press, 2018.

Manor, James. "A New, Fundamentally Different Political Order: The Emergence and Future Prospects of 'Competitive Authoritarianism' in India." *Economic and Political Weekly* 56, no. 10 (March 2021). https://www.epw.in/engage/article/new-fundamentally-different-political-order.

Marcus, George E. "The Para-Site in Ethnographic Research Projects." In *Experimenting with Ethnography: A Companion to Analysis,* edited by Andrea Ballestero and Brit Ross Winthereik, 41–52. Durham: Duke University Press, 2021.

Marks, John. "How To Spot A Spook." In *Dirty Work: The CIA in Western Europe,* edited by Philip Agee and Louis Wolf, 29–39. New York: Dorset Press, 1978.

Martin, Deborah G., and Joshua Inwood. "Subjectivity, Power, and the IRB." *The Professional Geographer* 64, no. 1 (2012): 7–15. DOI: 10.1080/00330124.2011.596781.

Masco, Joseph. "Mutant Ecologies: Radioactive Life in Post–Cold War New Mexico." *Cultural Anthropology* 19, no. 4 (2004): 517–50. DOI: 10.1525/can.2004.19.4.517.

Mayer, Jane. *The Dark Side: The Inside Story of How the War on Terror Turned into a War on American Ideals.* New York: Anchor, 2009.

McGranahan, Carole. *Arrested Histories: Tibet, the CIA, and Memories of a Forgotten War.* Durham: Duke University Press, 2010.

———. "Love and Empire: Tibet, the CIA, and Covert Humanitarianism." In *Ethnographies of U.S. Empire,* edited by Carole McGranahan and John F. Collins, 333–49. Durham: Duke University Press, 2018.

McIntyre, Lee. *Post-Truth.* Cambridge: MIT Press, 2018.

Miller, E. Ce. "Blackout Poetry Is A Fascinating Art You Can Try At Home Right Now." *Bustle*, August 28, 2017. https://www.bustle.com/p/what-is-blackout-poetry-these-fascinating-poems-are-created-from-existing-art-78781.

Min, Lisa. "North Korea So Far: Distance and Intimacy, Seen and Unseen." PhD diss., University of California, Berkeley, 2020.

———. "Redacted Letters to the Other Korea." *Interactions* 27, no. 2 (April 2020): 90–91. DOI: 10.1145/3378569.

Min, Lisa, Hoon Song, and John Lie, eds. *North Korea Seen and Unseen*. Berkeley: University of California Press, forthcoming.

Mirzoeff, Nicholas. "All The Monuments Must Fall #Charlottesville." August 14, 2017. http://www.nicholasmirzoeff.com/bio/all-the-monuments-must-fall-charlottesville.

Mong, Derek. "Ten New Ways to Read Ronald Johnson's 'Radi Os.'" *The Kenyon Review* 37, no. 4 (2015): 78–96. https://www.jstor.org/stable/24781146.

Nichanian, Marc. *The Historiographic Perversion*. Translated by Gil Anidjar. New York: Columbia University Press, 2009. DOI: 10.7312/nich14908.

Nietzsche, Friedrich. *Thus Spoke Zarathustra: A Book for All and None*. Translated by Walter Kaufmann. New York: Viking Press, 1954.

Öktem, Kerem. "Incorporating the Time and Space of the Ethnic 'Other': Nationalism and Space in Southeast Turkey in the Nineteenth and Twentieth Centuries." *Nations and Nationalism* 10, no. 4 (2004): 559–78. DOI: 10.1111/j.1354-5078.2004.00182.x.

———. "The Nation's Imprint: Demographic Engineering and the Change of Toponymes in Republican Turkey." *European Journal of Turkish Studies: Social Sciences on Contemporary Turkey* 7 (2008). DOI: 10.4000/ejts.2243.

Owens, Patricia. *Economy of Force: Counterinsurgency and the Historical Rise of the Social*. Cambridge: Cambridge University Press, 2015.

Paglen, Trevor. *Blank Spots on the Map: The Dark Geography of the Pentagon's Secret World*. New York: New American Library, 2010.

Parks, Stephen. "Doris Cross: The Painted Word. Interview with Doris Cross." *ARTlines*, February 1981. http://artlinesarchive.blogspot.com/2012/03/doris-cross-painted-word.html.

Philip, M. NourbeSe. *Zong! As Told to the Author by Setaey Adamu Boateng*. Middletown: Wesleyan University Press, 2008.

Pollari, Niina. "Form N-400 Erasures." *tyrant books*, February 23, 2017. https://magazine.nytyrant.com/form-n-400-erasures/.

Pop, Lucian, Dumitru Sandu, Filufteia Panduru, Amalia Virdol, Vlad Grigoras, Viorica Duma, and Daniel Virdol. *Harta sărăciei în România. Metodologia utilizata și prezentarea rezultatelor. Raport elaborat la cererea Comisiei Naționale Anti-Sărăcie și Promovare a Incluziunii Sociale de catre Universitatea București și Institutul Național de Statistică*. 2003.

Povinelli, Elizabeth A. "Disturbing Sexuality." *South Atlantic Quarterly* 106, no. 3 (2007): 565–76. DOI: 10.1215/00382876-2007-015.

Price, David H. *Anthropological Intelligence: The Deployment and Neglect of American Anthropology in the Second World War.* Durham: Duke University Press, 2008.

———. *Cold War Anthropology: The CIA, the Pentagon, and the Growth of Dual Use Anthropology.* Durham: Duke University Press, 2016.

———. *The American Surveillance State: How the U.S. Spies on Dissent.* London: Pluto Press, 2022.

———. *Threatening Anthropology: McCarthyism and the FBI's Surveillance of Activist Anthropologists.* Durham: Duke University Press, 2004.

Ramzy, Austin, and Chris Buckley, "'Absolutely No Mercy': Leaked Files Expost How China Organized Mass Detentions of Muslims." *The New York Times,* November 16, 2019. https://www.nytimes.com/interactive/2019/11/16/world/asia/china-xinjiang-documents.html.

Rancière, Jacques. "Ten Theses on Politics." Translated by Davide Panagia and Rachel Bowlby. *Theory & Event* 5, no. 3 (2001). DOI: 10.1353/tae.2001.0028.

Reeves, Madeleine. "#Trumpistan: On the Cunning Familiarity of the Authoritarian Absurd." *Cultural Anthropology,* April 25, 2018. https://culanth.org/fieldsights/trumpistan-on-the-cunning-familiarity-of-the-authoritarian-absurd.

"Regulation (EU) 2016/679 of the European Parliament and of the Council of 27 April 2016 on the Protection of Natural Persons with Regard to the Processing of Personal Data and on the Free Movement of Such Data, and Repealing Directive 95/46/EC (General Data Protection Regulation)." *Official Journal of the European Union* L 119 (May 4, 2016): 1–88. http://data.europa.eu/eli/reg/2016/679/oj.

Riles, Annelise, ed. *Documents: Artifacts of Modern Knowledge.* Ann Arbor: University of Michigan Press, 2006.

Risen, James. *State of War: The Secret History of the CIA and the Bush Administration.* New York: Free Press, 2006.

Roberts, Sean R. *The War on the Uyghurs: China's Internal Campaign against a Muslim Minority.* Princeton: Princeton University Press, 2020.

Robins, Natalie S. *Alien Ink: The FBI's War on Freedom of Expression.* New York: William Morrow, 1992.

Rouvroy, Antoinette. "The End(s) of Critique : Data-Behaviourism versus Due-Process." In *Privacy, Due Process and the Computational Turn: The Philosophy of Law Meets the Philosophy of Technology,* edited by Mireille Hildebrandt and Katja de Vries 143–67. New York: Routledge, 2013. DOI: 10.4324/9780203427644-9.

Rubinstein, Raphael. "Missing: ~~Erasure~~ | Must Include: Erasure." *Under ~~Erasure~~.* https://www.under-erasure.com/essay-by-raphael-rubinstein/.

"Rubio to New York Times: Why Did You Cover Up Xi Jinping Role in Genocide." *Marco Rubio,* press release, November 30, 2021. https://www.rubio.senate.gov/public/index.cfm/2021/11/rubio-to-new-york-times-why-did-you-cover-up-xi-jinping-role-in-genocide.

Ryz, Lawrence, and Lauren Grest. "A New Era in Data Protection." *Computer Fraud & Security* 2016, no. 3 (2016): 18–20. DOI: 10.1016/S1361-3723(16)30028-8.

Sands, Philippe. *Torture Team: Rumsfeld's Memo and the Betrayal of American Values.* London: St Martin's Press, 2008.

Schmitz, Rob. "Reporter's Notebook: Uighurs Held for 'Extremist Thoughts' They Didn't Know They Had." *NPR*, May 7, 2019. https://www.npr.org/2019/05/07/720608802/reporters-notebook-uighurs-held-for-extremist-thoughts-they-didnt-know-they-had.

Selinger, Eric. "'I Composed the Holes': Reading Ronald Johnson's 'Radi Os.'" *Contemporary Literature* 33, no. 1 (1992): 46–73. DOI: 10.2307/1208373.

Sethi, Aman, "As Kashmir is Erased, Indian Democracy Dies in Silence." *Huffington Post*, August 5, 2019. https://www.huffpost.com/archive/in/entry/kashmir-erased-article-370-scrapped-indian-democracy-in-darkness_in_5d47e49be4b0acb57fcf1b4d.

Shapland, Jenn. Review of *Doris Cross: Selected Works*, at Marfa Book Co., Marfa, TX. *Southwest Contemporary,* September 1, 2017. https://southwestcontemporary.com/doris-cross-selected-works/.

Sharif, Solmaz. "The Near Transitive Properties of the Political and Poetical: Erasure." *Evening Will Come: A Monthly Journal of Poetics* 28 (2013). https://www.thevolta-org.zulaufdesign.com/ewc28-ssharif-p1.html.

Sharpe, Christina. *In the Wake: On Blackness and Being.* Durham: Duke University Press, 2016. DOI: 10.1215/9780822373452.

Shoshan, Nitzan. *The Management of Hate: Nation, Affect, and the Governance of Right-Wing Extremism in Germany.* Princeton: Princeton University Press, 2016.

Smart, Alan. "Hong Kong's Twenty-First Century Seen From 1997." *City and Society* 9, no. 1 (1997): 97–115. DOI: 10.1525/ciso.1997.9.1.97.

Song, Hoon. "Two Is Infinite, Gender Is Post-Social in Papua New Guinea." *Angelaki* 17, no. 2 (2012): 123–44. DOI: 10.1080/0969725X.2012.701053.

Sorace, Christian, and Nicholas Loubere. "Biopolitical Binaries (or How Not to Read the Chinese Protests)." *Made in China Journal,* December 2, 2022. https://madeinchinajournal.com/2022/12/02/biopolitical-binaries-or-how-not-to-read-the-chinese-protests/.

Spivak, Gayatri Chakravorty. "Translator's Preface," In Jacques Derrida, *Of Grammatology*, ix–lxxxvii. Translated by Gayatri Chakravorty Spivak. London: John Hopkins Press, 1976.

Springer, Simon. *The Anarchist Roots of Geography: Toward Spatial Emancipation.* Minneapolis: University of Minnesota Press, 2016. DOI: 10.5749/minnesota/9780816697724.001.0001.

Stalcup, Meg, and Joshua Craze. "How We Train Our Cops to Fear Islam." *Washington Monthly*, March 9, 2011. https://washingtonmonthly.com/2011/03/09/how-we-train-our-cops-to-fear-islam/.

Steenberg, Rune. "Suppression of the Uyghurs: Let's Stick to the Facts." *Geneva Solutions*, July 26, 2021. https://genevasolutions.news/peace-humanitarian/suppression-of-the-uyghurs-let-s-stick-to-the-facts.

Steenberg, Rune, and Seher. "In What Purport to be Lifestyle Videos, Uyghur Influencers Promote Beijing's Narrative on Their Homeland." *ChinaFile*, August 4, 2022. https://www.chinafile.com/reporting-opinion/features/what-purport-be-lifestyle-videos-uyghur-influencers-promote-beijings.

Stewart, Kathleen. "Atmospheric Attunements." *Environment and Planning D: Society and Space* 29, no. 3 (2011): 445–53. DOI: 10.1068/d9109.

———. *Ordinary Affects*. Durham: Duke University Press, 2007.

Steyerl, Hito, and Laura Poitras. "Techniques of the Observer: Hito Steyerl and Laura Poitras in Conversation." *Artforum,* May 2015. https://www.artforum.com/print/201505/techniques-of-the-observer-hito-steyerl-and-laura-poitras-in-conversation-51563.

Stoetzer, Bettina. "Ruderal Ecologies: Rethinking Nature, Migration, and the Urban Landscape in Berlin." *Cultural Anthropology* 33, no. 2 (2018): 295–323. DOI: 10.14506/ca33.2.09.

Stone, Rachel. "The Trump-Era Boom in Erasure Poetry." *The New Republic,* October 23, 2017. https://newrepublic.com/article/145396/trump-era-boom-erasure-poetry.

Strom, Dao, and Neil Aitken. "On Erasure: Quotes from Robin Coste Lewis's Lecture 'The Race Within Erasure.'" *de-canon,* May 9, 2017. https://www.de-canon.com/blog/2017/5/9/on-erasure-from-robin-coste-lewiss-lecture-literary-arts.

Strathern, Marilyn. *The Gender of the Gift: Problems with Women and Problems with Society in Melanesia.* Berkeley: University of California Press, 1988.

Tachjian, Vahé. *Daily Life in the Abyss: Genocide Diaries, 1915–1918.* Translated by G.M. Goshgarian. Oxford: Berghahn Books, 2017. DOI: 10.2307/j.ctvw04f4m.

Taşğin, Ahmet, and Marcello Mollica. "Disappearing Old Christian Professions in the Middle East: The Case of Diyarbakır Pushee-Makers." *Middle Eastern Studies* 51, no. 6 (2015): 922–31. DOI: 10.1080/00263206.2015.1044525.

Taussig, Michael T. *Defacement: Public Secrecy and the Labor of the Negative.* Stanford: Stanford University Press, 1999.

The Uyghur Genocide: An Examination of China's Breaches of the 1948 Genocide Convention. Washington, DC: Newlines Institute for Strategy and Policy, March 2021. https://newlinesinstitute.org/wp-content/uploads/Chinas-Breaches-of-the-GC3-2.pdf.

Tolkien, J.R.R. *The Lord of the Rings.* 3 vols. London: George Allen & Unwin, 1954–1955.

Tsing, Anna Lowenhaupt. *The Mushroom at the End of the World: On the Possibility of Life in Capitalist Ruins.* Princeton: Princeton University Press, 2015. DOI: 10.1515/9781400873548.

Tyrrell-Morin, Clare. "Prize-Winning Hong Kong-Born Poet Sarah Howe Makes Verse of City's Basic Law." *South China Morning Post Magazine,* July 7, 2016. https://www.scmp.com/magazines/post-magazine/arts-music/article/1986620/prize-winning-hong-kong-born-poet-sarah-howe.

Üngör, Uğur Ümit. *The Making of Modern Turkey: Nation and State in Eastern Anatolia, 1913–1950.* Oxford: Oxford University Press, 2011.

Üngör, Uğur Ümit, and Mehmet Polatel. *Confiscation and Destruction: The Young Turk Seizure of Armenian Property.* London: Bloomsbury, 2011.

Upson, Emily. *"The Government Never Oppresses Us": China's Proof-of-Life Videos as Intimidation and a Violation of Uyghur Family Unity.* Washington, DC: Uyghur Human Rights Project, 2021. https://docs.uhrp.org/pdf/POLVReportFinal_2021-01-29.pdf.

Vartanyan Dilaver, Aylin. "From Longing to Belong to Shaping the Longing: Dwelling with Armenian Women in Istanbul." PhD diss., European Graduate School, forthcoming.

Vega, Facundo. "On Bad Weather: Heidegger, Arendt, and Political Beginnings." In *Weathering: Ecologies of Exposure,* edited by Christoph F.E. Holzhey and Arnd Wedemeyer, 227–43. Berlin: ICI Berlin Press, 2020.

Verdery, Katherine. *My Life as a Spy: Investigations in a Secret Police File.* Durham: Duke University Press, 2018.

Weiss, Erica, and Carole McGranahan. "Rethinking Pseudonyms in Ethnography: An Introduction." *American Ethnological Society,* December 13, 2021. https://americanethnologist.org/online-content/collections/rethinking-pseudonyms-in-ethnography/rethinking-pseudonyms-in-ethnography-an-introduction/.

Wu, Cheng'en. *Journey to the West.* Translated by Anthony C. Yu. Chicago: University of Chicago Press, 1977.

Xu, Lynn. "Who Is Doris Cross?" *Poetry Foundation,* April 25, 2014. https://www.poetryfoundation.org/harriet-books/2014/04/who-is-doris-cross.

Xu, Vicky Xiuzhong, James Leibold, and Daria Impiombato. "Exposing the Chinese Government's Oppression of Xinjiang's Uyghurs." *The Strategist,* October 19, 2021. https://www.aspistrategist.org.au/exposing-the-chinese-governments-oppression-of-xinjiangs-uyghurs/.

Yadırgı, Veli. *The Political Economy of the Kurds of Turkey: From the Ottoman Empire to the Turkish Republic.* Cambridge: Cambridge University Press, 2017. DOI: 10.1017/9781316848579.

Yıldırım, Umut. "Mulberry Affects: Ecology, Memory, and Aesthetics on the Shores of the Tigris River in the Wake of Genocide." In *War-Torn Ecologies, An-archic Fragments: Reflections from the Middle East,* edited by Umut Yıldırım, 27–66. Berlin: ICI Berlin Press, 2023. DOI: 10.37050/ci-27_2.

———. "'Resistant Breathing': Ruined and Decolonial Ecologies in a Middle Eastern Heritage Site." *Current Anthropology* 65, no. 1 (2024): 123–49. DOI: 10.1086/728897.

———. "Space, Loss and Resistance: A Haunted Pool-Map in South-Eastern Turkey." *Anthropological Theory* 19, no. 4 (2019): 440–69. DOI: 10.1177/1463499618783130.

Yurchak, Alexei. *Everything Was Forever, Until It Was No More: The Last Soviet Generation.* Princeton: Princeton University Press, 2006.

———. "Fake, Unreal, and Absurd." In *Fake: Anthropological Keywords,* edited by Jacob Copeman and Giovanni da Col, 91–108. Chicago: HAU Books, 2018. https://haubooks.org/fake/.

Zenz, Adrian. "Public Security Minister's Speech Describes Xi Jinping's Direction of Mass Detentions in Xinjiang." *ChinaFile,* May 24, 2022.

https://www.chinafile.com/reporting-opinion/features/public-security-ministers-speech-describes-xi-jinpings-direction-of-mass.

———. "The Xinjiang Police Files: Re-Education Camp Security and Political Paranoia in the Xinjiang Uyghur Autonomous Region." *Journal of the European Association for Chinese Studies* 3 (2022): 263–311. DOI: 10.25365/jeacs.2022.3.zenz.

Contributors

A███ is an anthropologist of India.

Franck Billé is a cultural anthropologist and geographer based at the University of California, Berkeley, where he is program director for the Tang Center for Silk Road Studies. His core research focus is on borders, space, sovereignty, and materiality. He is the editor of *Voluminous States* (Duke 2020), and author of *Somatic States* (Duke, Forthcoming). More information about his current research is available at www.franckbille.com.

Darren Byler is an anthropologist in the School for International Studies at Simon Fraser University in Vancouver, British Columbia. He is the author of an ethnography titled *Terror Capitalism: Uyghur Dispossession and Masculinity in a Chinese City* (Duke University Press 2022) and a book titled *In the Camps: China's High-Tech Penal Colony* (Columbia Global Reports 2021). His current research interests are focused on policing, carceral theory, and global China.

Shane Carter is a former high school history-social science teacher and currently the program coordinator for Office of Resources for International and Areas Studies (ORIAS) at UC Berkeley. ORIAS offers professional learning programs for educators, focused on helping teachers better understand World History and other international topics across disciplines. Shane is also the author of two podcast series: *Points In Between*, about the experiences of newcomer students in US schools, and *Future Imperfect*, about the anticipated effects of climate change in California.

████ is a lecturer ████████████████ University. They completed their PhD in Language & Rhetoric ██ University ██████. They grew up in the Uyghur homeland in northwest China and founded a ████████████, teaching ████ hundreds of Uyghur students. In the US, they taught ████████████ University ██████████ College. Their primary teaching and research interests include ████████████, language education, ████████, and translation.

ChatGPT was launched by OpenAI in November 2022. It is built on top of OpenAI's GPT-3 family of large language models, and is fine-tuned with both supervised and reinforcement learning techniques. ChatGPT was launched as a prototype on November 30, 2022, and quickly garnered attention for its detailed responses and articulate answers across many domains of knowledge.

Joshua Craze is a writer currently completing a book for Fitzcarraldo Editions about war, silence, and bureaucracy in South Sudan. His fictions, essays, and reportage have been published by *n+1, The Guardian, Foreign Policy,* and *The Baffler,* among many other venues. He exhibited his "Grammar of Redaction" at the New Museum in New York in 2014; he was a UNESCO Artist Laureate in Creative Writing in the same year. He has collaborated with Jenny Holzer on two projects about redaction: a book-box *(Belligerent,* Ivory Press, 2017) and the catalogue essay he wrote for *Jenny Holzer: War Paintings* (Walther König, 2015). His other writings on redaction have been published in *ASAP/Journal, Media-N,* and in *Archival Dissonance: Knowledge Production and Contemporary Art* (I.B. Tauris/Ibraaz, 2015). He has been writing a novel entitled *Redacted Mind* for a decade now, much excerpted, never finished, and one day, he tells himself, he will send it off to the printers.

Donyol Dondrup is a researcher and his scholarship is partly a product of self-censorship. His research explores ▮▮▮▮▮▮▮▮ the politics of fear ▮▮▮▮▮ hope ▮▮▮▮ creativity.

Rachel Douglas-Jones is an Associate Professor of Anthropological Approaches to Data and Infrastructure at the IT University of Copenhagen. She is the head of the Technologies in Practice research group, and PI of the Moving Data, Moving People project (2020–2026). Recent publications include participation in the editorial collective of *The Handbook of the Anthropology of Technology* (Palgrave, 2022), and *Towards an Anthropology of Data* (with Antonia Walford and Nick Seaver, JRAI, 2021).

Trine Mygind Korsby is an Assistant Professor at the Department of Anthropology, University of Copenhagen. She has researched the themes of sex work, sex work facilitation, human trafficking, transnational crime, and criminal livelihoods in Romania and Italy since 2007. Her recent publications include "Complex Intimacies: Sex Work, Human Trafficking and Romance between Italy and the Black Sea Coast of Romania" (in *A Sea of Transience,* Berghahn Books, 2023) and participation in the editorial collective of *Transnational Street Business: Migrants in the Informal Urban Economy* (with Camilla Ravnbøl and Anja Simonsen, Migration and Society, 2023).

Charlene Makley is Professor of Anthropology at Reed College in Portland, Oregon. Her work has explored the history and cultural politics of ▮▮▮▮-building, ▮▮▮▮-led development and Buddhist revival among Tibetans in China's ▮▮▮▮ ▮▮▮▮▮▮ ▮▮ since 1992. Her second book, *The Battle for Fortune:* ▮▮▮▮*-Led Development, Personhood and* ▮▮▮▮ *among Tibetans in China,* published in 2018 by Cornell University Press and the Weatherhead East Asia Institute at Columbia University, is an ethnography of state-local relations in the historically ▮▮▮▮▮ region of ▮▮▮▮▮ (▮▮ ▮▮▮▮▮ ▮▮▮▮▮▮)

in the wake of China's Great Open the West campaign and during the ██ ████ ██████ on ██████ █████.

Annie Malcolm, PhD, is a writer, researcher, and educator. Her doctoral dissertation in anthropology is an ethnography of an art village in South China. She has published her writing in *Quartz, SFMOMA, Yishu: Journal of Contemporary Chinese Art,* and *Expose Art Magazine.* She has taught anthropology at UC Berkeley and curated an exhibition at Minnesota Street Project in San Francisco. She currently writes for visual artists in the Bay Area and conducts research on community healing, journalism, and wellbeing.

Carole McGranahan is an anthropologist and historian who teaches at the University of Colorado Boulder. Her research involves ethnographic and historical research on the CIA, Tibet, and the Cold War, as well as questions of citizenship and political asylum in the Tibetan diaspora. Her publications include *Arrested Histories: Tibet, the CIA, and Memories of a Forgotten War* (2010), *Imperial Formations* (2007, with Ann Stoler and Peter Perdue), *Ethnographies of US Empire* (2018, with John Collins), and *Writing Anthropology: Essays on Craft and Commitment* (2020).

Lisa Min is an anthropologist based in Seoul, teaching courses on politics and visuality at Yonsei University. She is currently working on two book projects that begin with north Korea, that open up the "place called north Korea" as a question and provocation for doing and writing anthropology.

N████ is an anthropologist of Kashmir.

Anjali Nath is Assistant Professor at the Institute of Communication, Culture, Information, and Technology at the University of Toronto Mississauga. Her work focuses on the visual culture of US militarism, with a focus on document redaction, transparency, and the archives of state violence. Her book, *A Thousand Paper Cuts: US Empire and the Bureaucratic Life of War,* is a critical reckoning with the racial and imperial work of paper as mobilized in the service of American militarism.

David H. Price is a Professor of Anthropology at Saint Martin's University in Lacey, Washington. He wrote a three-volume series for Duke University Press using FOIA documents and archival sources examining American anthropologists' interactions with intelligence agencies: *Threatening Anthropology* (2004) examined McCarthyism's impacts on anthropology; *Anthropological Intelligence* (2008) documented anthropological contributions to World War II, and his *Cold War Anthropology* (2016) explored Cold War interactions between anthropologists, the CIA, and Pentagon. His latest book, *Cold War Deceptions: The Asia Foundation and the CIA* (2024), draws on declassified CIA documents and a massive archival collection to establish how the CIA used the Asia Foundation in the 1950s and '60s for covert political ends. He is a founding member of the Network of Concerned Anthropologists.

A____ **Marie Ranjbar** is a feminist political geographer with the Department of Women & Gender Studies at the University of Colorado Boulder. Since 2012, she has conducted research in Iran that examines the political conditions that make it challenging for Iranian citizens to speak openly about human rights and how activists strategically frame rights narratives as a means of political mobilization, both locally and transnationally. Dr. Ranjbar's work is published in *Antipode*; *Annals of American Association of Geographers*; *ACME: An International Journal for Critical Geographies*; *Environment and Planning E*; *Gender, Place & Culture*; *Hypatia*; and *Political Geography*, and her research has been supported by the American Association of University Women, the National Endowment for the Humanities, the ZEIT-Stiftung Foundation, and the Social Science Research Council.

Alessandro Rippa is Associate Professor at the Department of Social Anthropology, University of Oslo, and project director at the Rachel Carson Center for Environment and Society, LMU Munich. He is the author of *Borderland Infrastructures: Trade, Development, and Control in Western China* (Amsterdam University Press, 2020) and a co-editor of the *Routledge Handbook of Asian Borderlands* (2018).

Rune Steenberg is an anthropologist working on Xinjiang Uyghur Autonomous Region and the Uyghurs. He has conducted extensive fieldwork in XUAR, Central Asia, China, and Indonesia and published widely on topics ranging from kinship to cross border trade, informality, corruption, narratives, and mass incarceration. He received his PhD from Freie Universität Berlin in 2014 and is currently a researcher at Palacký University Olomouc. Since 2018 he has also been working as an Uyghur interpreter for asylum seekers, activists, journalists, and human rights organizations and has participated in several documentary films on the tragedies in XUAR.

Kären Wigen is Professor in the Department of History at Stanford University. She received her PhD in Geography from the University of California at Berkeley. Her research interests include world history, the history of maps, and Japanese history. Her current project is an edited volume on Territorial Imaginaries.

Emily T. Yeh is a professor of geography at the University of Colorado Boulder. She conducts research on development and nature-society relations, mostly in Tibetan parts of the PRC, including the political ecology of pastoralism, conflicts over access to natural resources, vulnerability to and knowledge of climate change, the cultural and ontological politics of nature conservation, and the conjunctural production of environmental subjectivities. Her book *Taming Tibet: Landscape Transformation and the Gift of Chinese Development* explored the intersection of the political economy and cultural politics of development as a project of state territorialization. She is also editor or co-editor of *Mapping Shangrila: Contested Landscapes in the Sino-Tibetan Borderlands*, *Rural Politics in Contemporary China*, and *The Geoeconomics and Geopolitics of Chinese Development and Investment in Asia*.

Umut Yıldırım is an Assistant Professor of Anthropology at the Graduate Institute Geneva, Switzerland. Her research is available in platforms such as *Current Anthropology* (2021, 2024) and *Anthropological Theory* (2019). She also edited the book volume, *War-torn Ecologies, An-Archic Fragments: Reflections from the Middle East* (ICI Berlin Press, 2023). Previously, she held research fellowships in various academic institutions in the US and Germany; worked as an independent researcher in Palermo, Sicily; and taught political anthropology at various universities in Istanbul, Turkey. When she's not tending to her academic duties, she's busy ███████████████████████.

Index

accidental redactions, 28, 172–73
affiliation, 211–12, 256

agnosia, 153

annotations, 154
anonymity, 122, 127, 134; anonymization, 54–67; anonymous subjects 19, 30 32–33, 40, 198
archaeology, 88–91, 168, 245
archives, 152–56, 170, 173, 226, 239–40, 243; destruction, 153; public, 28, 257
army:
authenticity, 17, 230; authentic self, 249–257
authoritarianism, xiii, 18–24, 117, 179–85, 212, 257

battle: 113; battlefield, 237

Black feminism, 154
black: bars, 221–33; sites, 28, 33, 38, 41
blockade, 156–60

breathing, 155
bribery, 71–72
redaction, 111–15

bureaucracy, 33–34, 38, 72, 110, 125–126, 215; bureaucrat, 69, 71, 174, 176; propaganda bureau, 10

camps, 222–

censorship: 18–20, 22, 29–34, 50, 54–67, 92, 117–18, 167–68, 172–73, 215, 227, 248

documents, 27–34; operatives, 38

citizenship, 97, 121, 124, 127, 153, 179, 211–12, 237, 239, 255, 257

code names, 237–38, 242

colonial, 118, 123, 125, 156; occupation, 119, 165; violence, 37; anticolonial, protection, 69, 159; colonialism, 153, 155; settler, 115; postcolonial, states, 185; violence, 37

conspiracy, 20–21

crackdowns, 98–99

denial, 151–58, 215, 223, 226, 253

destruction, 154–55, 157; archival, 153; environmental, 105

discrimination 141; ethnic, 71, 74; sexual, 249–57

eco-redaction, 151–60; *see also* environment

encryption, 214

environment, 108–11, 181, 211; environmental history, 155; political, 20, 22, 256; *see also* eco-redaction

erasure 19–20, 22–23, 31, 88–89, 97–99, 104–5, 110, 113–17, 153, 181, 210, 245; ecological erasures, 151–60; in maps, 245–48; poetry 84–85, 121–35, 162–65

ethics, 18–19, 210, 211–12, 215, 222

ethnicity, 71, 74–75, 212, 214, 252; multi-ethnic relations, 152

ethnography, 122, 124, 134, 185, 191–92, 239, 252; ethnographic experience, 51; ethnographic practice, 19, 156, 180, 185; ethnographic research, 98, 184; ethnographic writing, 118

excision, 126, 214, 253, 257

extrajudicial detention, 97

fake, 22, 199; faking, 71

family, 70, 77, 118–19, 159, 181–84, 198, 200–203, 209, 211–15, 225, 237, 239–43, 249; traditional family values, 253

see

feminist theory, 154

fieldwork, 19–20, 50–51, 113, 151–52, 179–85, 191, 197–203, 214–15, 251–52

see

fossils, 27

gay, *see* LGBT

genocide:
geopolitics, 22
grassroots, 110

hate speech, 141, 253

human trafficking, 197

illegibility, 20, 126
illiberal regimes, *see* authoritarianism
incarceration, 98, 221–33

intelligence, 36, 76–77, 167–70, 182–183, 237, 240; *see also*

interlocutors, 19; 21–23, 50, 104, 154, 180–85, 212–15, 249, 252–57

journalists, 28, 36, 40, 108, 115, 118, 169, 179, 222–27, 230, 232–33, 241

K

land, *see* environment
landscape, 104, 113–16, 158, 160, 245; *see also* environment

LGBT, 189–92, 249–57
livestock, 105–9

maps, 41, 152, 213, 242, 245–48, 257; counter maps, 245–48
213; indigenous maps, 245

media, 37, 115, 229, 231; social media, 21, 119, 181, 231, 253; state, media, 113

nationalism,
neoliberalism,

news,   cable news   newspapers.
NGOs

noumena,

pastoralism.

photographs   redacted,
pika,
pimping, 197–200
playfulness,
poetry,
pogrom,
populism
pornography

propaganda,   bureau   campaign.
protests,

queer, *see* LGBT

reeducation,

same-sex marriages,
satellite imagery,
secret.   black sites,   open,
                     police file   public,
sex work.
sexuality.

surveillance,

temporality, 23, 153, 155
terror, 116–17; counter-terrorism, 224, 228; terrorism, 14, 40, 74, 183, 228;

toponomy, 151–52, 245–48
torture, 28–39, 77, 97–98, 117, 221, 255
transparency, 17–21, 123, 211, 221, 233, 256
▮▮▮▮▮, 17, 21, 22, 126; administration, 21; ▮▮▮▮▮ 24; and architecture, 174; election of, 22, 257; and erasures, 17, 126; and poetry, 194–95

violence, xiii, 14, 20, 23, 38, 88, 90–91, 199; anti-LGBT 253; baptismal, 110, 117–18, 151; police, 75; postcolonial, 37; sexual, 223, 226; state, 20; 38–40, 69, 77, 99, 104, 110, 115–18, 152–53, 158, 179–83, 222–32, 237

war, 116; ▮ War, 20, 22, 221; ▮ wars, 21; ▮ War, 44; ▮ 152, 155–59; war ▮ 28, 31, 32, 36, 38–41, 232; ▮ War II, 224
waterboarding, 32–39

285

Made in the USA
Columbia, SC
03 January 2025